UNDERSTANDING GOVERNANCE IN SOUTH ASIA

Understanding Governance in South Asia

Edited by

ADLURI SUBRAMANYAM RAJU

MANOHAR
2020

First published 2020

ISBN 978-93-90035-04-5

Published by
Ajay Kumar Jain *for*
Manohar Publishers & Distributors
4753/23 Ansari Road, Daryaganj,
New Delhi 110 002

Typeset by
Ravi Shanker
Delhi 110 055

Printed at
Replika Press Pvt. Ltd.

TO

UNESCO Goodwill Ambassador

(Late) Dr. Madanjeet Singh

Philosopher, Diplomat, Philanthropist, Writer, Artist
Founder, South Asia Foundation, New Delhi

Contents

Acknowledgements

I express my gratitude to the South Asia Foundation, New Delhi, for financial support to carryout academic activities at the UNESCO Madanjeet Singh Institute for South Asia Regional Cooperation (UMISARC) and the Centre for South Asian Studies, Pondicherry University. I express my thanks to Prof. Anisa Basheer Khan, former Vice Chancellor (Officiating), for her support in organizing the seminar at the Institute. I am grateful to Prof. Gurmeet Singh, Vice-Chancellor, for his encouragement in carrying out the academic activities at the Institute. I also take this opportunity to thank all the authors sincerely for contributing their valuable chapters to this volume.

ADLURI SUBRAMANYAM RAJU

Contributors

ADLURI SUBRAMANYAM RAJU, Professor and former Head, UNESCO Madanjeet Singh Institute of South Asia Regional Cooperation & Centre for South Asian Studies, Pondicherry University, Puducherry.

I.P. KHOSLA, Former Secretary, Ministry of External Affairs, New Delhi.

PRITHVI RAM MUDIAM, Professor, Department of Political Science, University of Hyderabad, Hyderabad.

RAMESH CHANDRA DAS, Associate Professor, Department of Economics, Katwa College, Katwa, West Bengal.

M.J. VINOD, Professor, Department of Political Science, Bangalore University, Bengaluru.

P. SAHADEVAN, Professor, Centre for South Asian Studies, School of International Studies, Jawaharlal Nehru University, New Delhi.

N. MANOHARAN, Associate Professor, Department of International Studies and History, Christ University, Bengaluru.

UTTARA SAHASRABUDDHE, Professor, Department of Civics & Politics, University of Mumbai, Mumbai.

GAYATRI LELE, Assistant Professor, Department of Political Science, Ramnarain Ruia College, Mumbai.

Gopalji Malviya, Former Dean School of National Security Studies at Central University of Jammu, Jammu.

Rajamanickam Srinivasan, Group Captain (Retd.), Independent Researcher, Coimbatore.

Abhishek M. Chaudhari, Research Analyst, New Delhi.

Shaurabh Anand, School of Natural Sciences and Engineering, National Institute of Advanced Studies, Bengaluru.

Nishant Srinivasaiah, School of Natural Sciences and Engineering, National Institute of Advanced Studies, Bengaluru.

Vaibhavi Palsule, Associate Professor, Department of Political Science, Ramnarain Ruia College of Arts and Science, Mumbai.

Som P. Pudasaini, Executive Member, Nepal Council for World Affairs, Kathmandu.

Biswas Baral, Journalist, *Republica* National Daily, Kathmandu.

Introduction

Adluri Subramanyam Raju

Discourse on governance has been debated since 1985 and it has emerged as a global agenda for development as many countries realized that without addressing the emerging developmental issues and relating them to human beings, states would not be stable and would face social unrest across the globe. Thus the importance of governance has been advocated by the multilateral agencies like the World Bank, the United Nations Development Programme (UNDP), the Development Advisory Committee (DAC) of the Organization for Economic Cooperation and Development and other agencies. To the World Bank, good governance is characterized by 'predictable, open and enlightened policy making; a bureaucracy imbued with professional ethos; an executive arm of government accountable for all its actions and a strong civil society participating in public affairs; and all behaving under the rule of law'.[1] Further, the UNDP defines governance 'as the exercise of political and administrative authority at all levels to manage a country's affairs'. It comprises mechanisms, processes and institutions through which citizens and groups can articulate their interests, exercise their legal rights, meet their obligations, and mediate their differences. This definition clearly identifies three governance arenas: political, economic and administrative. The DAC has defined good governance as 'the rule of law, responsible leadership and effective systems for public management, transparency and accountability'.[2]

Further the UNDP's Human Development Centre (HDC) in its Human Development Report of 1994 defines 'good governance from the standpoint of human development and it reformulated the concept of governance as humane governance encompassing three governance arenas: political, economic and civic'.[3] The second extension of UNDP's view of governance has appeared in the form of a working definition for the World Governance Assessment Project (WGA). Under this project, 'governance refers to the formation and stewardship of the formal and informal rules that regulate the public realm, the arena in which state as well as economic and societal actors interact to make decisions'. [4]

The six indicators used in the latest governance assessment by Worldwide Governance Indicators include: voice and accountability; political stability; government effectiveness; regulatory quality; rule of law, and control of corruption. These six dimensions cover the political, economic and, institutional aspects of governance. These indicators are normative and have a high association with democracy and economic development.

Despite different interpretations of governance and methodological challenges to assess the quality of governance, researchers, policy makers and donors maintain that governance is imperative for development and poverty reduction. Others also allude to this clear link between good governance and the alleviation of poverty.

In a state having effective governance, various problems of socio-economic development are to be addressed. Most developing countries have abundant resources, manpower, institutions, etc., yet they are struggling to achieve economic growth, human development and poverty alleviation. Ineffective public services, leadership crisis, lack of transparency and accountability in administration, ineffective political institutions, etc., are considered to be the main hurdles for governance in the developing countries.

Governance is assessed from a three-dimensional perspective: (a) process by which governments are selected, held accountable, monitored, and replaced; (b) capacity of governments to manage resources efficiently and formulate, implement, and enforce sound policies and regulations; and (c) extent of participation of the citizens in affairs of the state.[5] Lack of service delivery in the areas of health and education, rampant corruption, inaccessibility to justice, lack of regulatory support to the informal and unorganized sectors of the economy where a majority of the poor pursue their livelihoods; and the poor are being threatened due to various forms of insecurity and improper application of power. The primary duty or obligation of a state or a ruler is not only to protect the territory but also to uphold the welfare of the people.

GOVERNANCE IN SOUTH ASIA

Governance in South Asia is something that needs to be reformed to ensure that poverty can be reduced, if not completely eradicated. Due to poor governance and the various means by which governance has fallen short, has led to lack of development and continuance of poverty in South Asian societies.

Governance in this region has remained more or less the same in the last few decades. Some countries were able to start off fine with respect to governance but slowly degraded into a corrupt form of governance. However, the overall performance of governance in the region has definitely improved.

The application of the concept of good governance in South Asia poses a challenge at the implementation level, mainly due to ethnocentricity, regional disparities, division between poor and rich, and rural and urban division among the people. Concepts such as decentralization, citizen engagement, lean public service, privatization, autonomy, public-private partnership may work well in developed countries but may not produce the same results in the region where the majority of poor people expect their government to fulfil their basic needs.

According to the Human Development Report of 1999, nearly half of the population in South Asia suffers from lack of access to adequate food, clean water, sanitation, health facilities, education, and employment. The report reveals that in South Asia one in two people is illiterate, one in five does not have access to clean water, three in five do not have sanitation facilities and one in five children is malnourished, and four out of five suffer from access to financial resources. The poverty profile of South Asia shows that both in terms of income and opportunities, poverty has increased in the region.

In South Asia, special attention has to be given to improve internal security in order to support governance reforms. Governance seeks more coordination, coherence and collaborative networks among the public sector organizations, corporations, private organizations, civil society organizations, and international organizations. Although democracy enhances good governance, the latter is not necessarily equivalent to democracy.

South Asian countries have to learn from each other's experiences and from other parts of the world. For instance, how Bangalore in India has become the second largest software hub the world over or how Grameen Bank in Bangladesh is catering to the micro credit needs of the poor are a few examples from the region. The countries in the region need to develop an indigenous model to find pragmatic solutions to the challenges of good governance. For instance, Bangladesh has introduced reforms in government audit to bring transparency in the audit system whereas India is emphasizing on training of civil servants to enhance their efficiency and effectiveness. Similarly, Sri Lanka and Nepal have adopted various civil society initiatives to promote community collaboration in governance.

South Asian countries can achieve good results through good governance if they develop and adopt an indigenous model rather than simply borrowing models and ideas from the West. The concept of governance, reformulated by the South Asian scholar Mahbub ul Haq seems to be more relevant for the region.

South Asian countries have more or less similar objectives, structures, value systems, cultures, and standards of governance despite different forms of government. The colonial legacy of British administrative system had its impact on centralization. Secrecy, elitism, rigidity, and social isolation is common to all South Asian countries. The post-colonial administrative system is built upon pre-colonial administrative traditions throughout the region. South Asian countries have the lowest human development index and a very low quality of governance.

To address this problem, the UNESCO Madanjeet Singh Institute of South Asia Regional Cooperation (UMISARC) and Centre for South Asian Studies, Pondicherry University, Puducherry, organized this conference on 'Governance in South Asia: Issues and Concerns' during 7-9 February 2017.

STRUCTURE OF THE VOLUME

The present volume consists of four parts containing fifteen chapters.

Part 1: Governance in South Asia: Background

Adluri Subramanyam Raju provides a conceptual analysis of the issue of governance in Chapter 1, 'Governance in South Asia: A Conceptual Analysis'. The chapter throws light on how governance has become very important across the world. It also discusses how poverty can be addressed through implementation of effective governance. The connection between governance and eradication of poverty is highlighted and it argues that if a state delivers effective governance, various problems of socio-economic development would be addressed. South Asian countries are similar in terms of objectives, structure, functions, attitudes, and standards of governing bodies despite having different forms of government. They have to learn from each other's experiences and from other parts of the world in order to maximize the utilities of good governance.

Part 2: Governance and Globalization

I.P. Khosla in Chapter 2, 'Macroeconomics of Governance in South Asia' describes various dimensions of good governance and the issues pertaining to it. Though NGOs, civil society, the private sector, etc., make useful contributions to good governance by way of ideas, manpower, local initiatives and other such efforts, it is the government that has to play the pivotal role and find the bulk of resources. For the proper execution of good governance, South Asia needs political stability, administrative efficiency for timely delivery in the areas of the socio-political spectrum and an active civil society which acts as a watchdog.

Prithvi Ram Mudiam in Chapter 3, 'Governance in Contemporary South Asia: Regional and Global Dimensions' argues that focusing on governance at the national level is no longer feasible or adequate for the countries of South Asia to achieve their national goals. It is imperative that they extend their attention and energies to governance at the regional and global levels as well. The chapter also discusses the kind of regional and global order that is conducive for the countries of South Asia to achieve their national goals in a globalizing world.

Ramesh Chandra Das in the chapter 'Role of Good Governance on Growth of Per Capita Income in South Asia: A Debate on Means and Ends' examines the role of good governance on the growth of per capita income in South Asia under the debate on whether good governance is a means or an end in determining growth of countries. The chapter also argues that improvements in the quality of governance are to be further done in the region to exploit inclusive growth and development of the associated countries.

M.J. Vinod in Chapter 5, 'Changing Global Power Constellation: China's Rise and Its Implications for South Asia' looks into the challenges that the rise of China pose for the institutions of global governance. The impact that the rise of China has on the quasi-unilateral world order in a *de facto* multipolar power constellation needs to be analysed. China's role in global governance mechanisms are broadening and deepening. He argues that the extent to which the rise of China as a non-liberal, non-democratic state, functioning on the basis of a market economy poses challenges to the Western notions of 'legitimacy' of global governance processes needs to be examined. The chapter also analyses the extent to which the future world order could be influenced by the reality of a turbulent multilateralism.

Part 3: Governance and Politics and Violence in South Asia

P. Sahadevan in Chapter 6, 'Governance and Conflict in South Asia', explains the intricate link between governance and conflict, and assesses the role of liberal democratic governance in building peace in conflict-ridden societies like the ones in South Asia. Failure of governance tends to create propitious conditions for conflict, which in turn pose serious challenges to governance itself. He reiterates that there is a need to not only remove governance deficits but also leverage liberal democratic governance to build positive peace by adopting certain progressive policies and institutional mechanisms.

N. Manoharan in Chapter 7, 'Uneasy Partnership: Political Parties and Governance in South Asia' analyses the nature of political parties of South Asia and their importance in taking the governance process forward. The dwindling reputation of political parties in a political system and the impact of the ideological orientation of political parties on the governance of the region are discussed. The assertiveness of civil society and its influence on the accountability of political parties in the region is also discussed in this chapter. The role of internal democracy of parties and its reflection on the larger governance process is also explained.

Uttara Sahasrabuddhe and Gayatri Lele in Chapter 8, titled 'Securitization of Nation-building: Scope and Limits of State Coercion against Insurgent Violence' analyse the case of securitization of nation-building in the context of India through the issue of Naga separatism. Securing territorial integrity is the fundamental part of the governance processes of various countries. Naga identity has emerged as a competing narrative to the dominant narrative of Indian national identity; and Naga separatism has posed an existentialist challenge to the Indian state. The response of the Indian state has been 'securitization' of governance of the threat to security; and the use of coercive power of the state to maintain territorial integrity. The chapter analyses the scope and limits of coercion in the context of Naga separatism.

Part 4: Governance in South Asia: Case Studies

Gopalji Malviya in Chapter 9, 'Statecraft in J&K: Collapse of Governance' analyses the governance in J&K which is characterized by persistent militancy, insurgency, cross-border terrorism and externally fostered internal security threats. A fragile social fabric, rusted state machinery and a crippled bureaucracy are not in a position to take initiatives for delivering the fruits of good governance in J&K. It is clear with present indications that unless the state and the union governments along with the people of J&K change their attitude and mindset, it is difficult to have any hope of improvement in the coming years.

Rajamanickam Srinivasan in Chapter 10, 'Representative Democracy, Identity Politics, and Participatory Governance: The Indian Experiment' examines the foundations of representative democracy, emergence of identity politics as a decisive factor in Indian polity, the effects of identity politics in delivery of social justice and the fissures in the foundation of the Panchayati Raj Institutions. The chapter infers that the seeming incompatibility between representative democracy and participative governance is a myth and that a healthy combination of both can actually be exploited for good governance. The chapter draws the conclusion that the Indian constitutional experiment in balancing representative democracy, identity, and participatory governance can be leveraged to bring about social justice and development closer to the lives of ordinary citizens.

Abhishek M. Chaudhari, in Chapter 11, 'Politics of Performance: A Comparative Study of Governance Models in India', points out that the political discourse in India is generally focused on the ideological side of the parties. Most of the analysts fail to study the performance of the parties through their governance track records. Since the primary objective of any political party is the delivery of governance, it is necessary to study governance records of various parties. This is particularly significant in the case of India, which is a multi-party democracy and a number of political parties across the political spectrum compete and function.

Shaurabh Anand and Nishant Srinivasaiah in Chapter 12, titled 'Wildlife and Governance in India' address the existing governance practices with respect to wildlife conservation and management, their complexities and their impacts on wildlife conservation management in India. Taking two contrasting examples of the Asian elephant and the rhesus macaque, the chapter focuses on wildlife governance in India amidst increasing human-wildlife conflict in the country.

Vaibhavi Palsule in Chapter 13, 'Revisiting Indus Water Treaty' addresses the water issue between India and Pakistan. The chapter discusses how the Indus Water Treaty in 1960 was implemented successfully. However, the author argues that there is an urgent need to revise the treaty. She argues that there should be integrated water governance of Indus water system to be practised by India and Pakistan.

Som P. Pudasaini in Chapter 14 on 'Governance and Geopolitics in South Asia', discusses the myriads of challenges that good governance faces in South Asia in general and Nepal in particular. The countries in South Asia differ significantly in effectiveness of governance and meeting the needs and expectation of the masses. However, factors like education, a young population, rising access to social and other media, increasing efforts to democratize polity, establishment of public and civil society watchdogs, dynamism in many economies, etc., offer opportunities to enhance good governance, eliminate poverty and promote rule of law in the region.

Biswas Baral in Chapter 15, 'The Impact of Political Instability in Governance in Nepal' analyses the political situation in Nepal where in the last seventeen years the government has changed fifteen times. Good governance issues have been put on the backburner particularly after the 2006 People's Revolution, which overthrew the autocratic monarchy. Governance was neglected in the country, which resulted in a marked increase in corruption. The country needs tough constitutional provisions that can guarantee a stable government. Nepal has to quickly settle any remaining constitutional disputes and focus on governance.

NOTES

1. World Bank, *Governance: The World Bank's Experience*, Washington DC: The World Bank, 1994, cited in Abu Elias Sarker and Mohammad Habibur Rahman, 'The Emerging Perspective of Governance and Poverty Alleviation: A Case of Bangladesh', *Public Organize Rev.*, vol. 7, 2007, p. 95.
2. Development Assistance Committee (DAC), 1997, p. 11, cited in Priyanka Bakhshi and Shatabdi Bagchi, 'Role of Government in Poverty Alleviation in India: Expectations and Outcomes', *International Journal of Advanced Research in Management and Social Sciences*, vol. 2, no. 5, March 2013, p. 54.
3. Nasira Jabeen, 'Good or Good Enough Governance in South Asia: Constraints and Possibilities', *Inaugural Address*, Utrecht University, 2 April 2007, p. 7.
4. *Ibid.*, p. 8.

5. D. Kaufmann, A. Kraay and P. Zoido-Lobatón, 'Aggregating Governance Indicators', *World Bank Policy Research Paper*, no. 2195, 2000, cited in Salahuddin M. Aminuzzaman, 'Poverty and Governance: A Quest for Alternative Focus: Bangladesh test Case', *JOAAG*, vol. 2. no. 1, 2007, p. 12.

PART 1

GOVERNANCE IN SOUTH ASIA: BACKGROUND

CHAPTER 1

Governance in South Asia

A Conceptual Analysis

Adluri Subramanyam Raju

INTRODUCTION

The word 'governance' is derived from the Greek verb κυβερνάω [kubernáo] which means to steer and was used for the first time in a metaphorical sense by Plato.[1] From 1985 onwards, the discourse on good governance has been debated and it has emerged as a global agenda for development, as many countries realized the fact that without addressing the emerging issues related to human beings, the state would not be stable and face social unrest across the territory.

The importance of governance has been advocated by multilateral agencies like the World Bank, the United Nations Development Programme (UNDP), the Development Advisory Committee (DAC) of the Organization for Economic Cooperation and Development and other agencies.

Governance can be understood in many ways. We can look at the different definitions according to the different world organizations that provide assistance to bring about good governance reforms in different countries.

This chapter discusses how governance has become important across the world. It also provides a conceptual analysis on the issue of governance and highlights how the South Asian countries can learn from each other's experiences and from other parts of the world in order to maximize the utilities of good governance.

To the World Bank, good governance is characterized by 'predictable, open and enlightened policy making; a bureaucracy imbued with professional ethos; an executive arm of government accountable for all its actions and a strong civil society participating in public affairs; and all behaving under the rule of law'.[2] The DAC has defined good governance as 'the rule of law, responsible leadership and effective systems for public management, transparency and accountability'.[3]

The World Bank defines governance as 'the manner in which power is exercised in the management of a country's economic and social resources for development'.[4] Although the World Bank identified political, administrative and economic aspects of governance, it did not include the political aspects in its policies until recently. The World Bank has its own methodology of assessing the quality of governance, popularly known as Worldwide Governance Indicators (WGI). The six indicators used in the latest governance assessment are: (1) voice and accountability, (2) political stability, (3) government effectiveness, (4) regulatory quality (5) rule of law, and (6) control of corruption. These six dimensions cover the political, economic and, institutional aspects of governance. These indicators are normative and have a high association with democracy and economic development.[5]

Further, the UNDP defines governance 'as the exercise of political and administrative authority at all levels to manage a country's affairs'.[6] It comprises mechanisms, processes and institutions through which citizens and groups articulate their interest, exercise their legal rights, meet their obligations, and mediate their differences. This definition clearly identifies three governance arenas: political, economic and administrative.

In its Human Development Reports, UNDP's Human Development Centre (HDC) defines 'good governance from the standpoint of human development and it reformulated the concept of governance as humane governance encompassing three governance arenas: political, economic and civic'.[7] The second extension of UNDP's view of governance has appeared in the form of a working definition for the World Governance Assessment Project (WGA). Under this project, 'governance refers to the formation and stewardship of the formal and informal rules that regulate the public realm, the arena in which state as well as economic and societal actors interact to make decisions'.[8]

Despite different interpretations of governance and methodological challenges to assess the quality of governance, 'there is a general consensus among researchers, policy makers and donors that governance does matter and indeed good governance is imperative for development and poverty reduction'.[9] 'Governance is a necessity for development and poverty reduction, not a luxury'.[10] Others also allude to this clear link between good governance and the alleviation of poverty.

The World Bank defines governance as: 'The exercise of political authority and the use of institutional resources to manage society's problems and affairs'.[11] 'The way ... power is exercised through a country's economic, political, and social institutions'.[12]

According to March and Oslen, 'Governance presumes a perspective on politics and government, a way of thinking about how things happen in a polity'.[13] Hyden interprets it as 'those measures that involve setting the rules for the exercise of power and settling conflicts over such rules'[14] Landell and Serageldein understand governance as 'means how people are ruled, how the affairs of the state are administered and regulated; it refers to a nation's system of politics and how this functions in relation to public administration and law'.[15]

According to Rhodes, 'Good governance involves the self-organizing and inter-organizational networks characterized by inter-dependence, resource-exchange, rules of the game and significant autonomy from the state'.[16] Bilney defines 'good governance as ... among other things participatory, transparent and accountable. It is also effective and equitable. And it promotes the rule of law.' 'Good governance means the effective management of a country's social and economic resource in a manner that is open, transparent, accountable, equitable'.[17]

If a state is implementing effective governance, then various problems of socio-economic development would be addressed. There are developing countries who in spite of having abundant resources, manpower, institutions, etc., have not been able to achieve economic growth, human development and poverty reduction. Ineffective public services, leadership crisis, lack of transparency and accountability in administration, ineffective political institutions, etc., are considered to be the main hurdles to address the poverty in developing countries. There are several international organizations like the World Bank, UNDP, IMF and NGOs who are focusing on good governance as a precondition to address poverty. The UNDP has put stress on good governance for human development, the IMF on participatory governance and other organizations have focused on enhancing governance.[18]

The World Bank has recognized the following as parameters of good governance:

- Legitimacy of political system which can be best achieved through regular elections and political accountability.
- Freedom of association and participation by various socio-economic, religious, cultural and professional groups in the governance.
- An established legal framework based on the rule of law and independence of judiciary to protect human rights and secure social justice.
- Bureaucratic accountability including transparency in administration.
- Freedom of information and expression.
- A sound administrative system leading to efficiency and effectiveness.
- Cooperation between the government and civil society organizations.[19]

Governance is usually assessed from a three-dimensional perspective: 'a. process by which governments are selected, held accountable, monitored, and replaced; b. capacity of governments to manage resources efficiently and formulate, implement, and enforce sound policies and regulations; and, c. extent of participation of the citizens in affairs of the state.'[20]

The areas of governance that affect poverty are: lack of service-delivery in the areas of health and education, rampant corruption, inaccessibility to justice, lack of regulatory support to the informal and unorganized sectors of the economy where a majority of the poor pursue their livelihoods; and lastly where poor are being threatened due to various forms of insecurity and improper application of power.[21]

GOVERNANCE IN SOUTH ASIA

In principle, the primary duty or obligation of a state or a ruler is not only protecting the territory but also to uphold the welfare of the people. Kautilya, long ago, advised King Chandragupta Maurya how a ruler should be. He said: for a ruler, 'in the happiness of his subjects lies his happiness; in their welfare his welfare. He does not consider as good only that which pleases him but treats as beneficial whatever pleases his subjects.'[22]

Governance in South Asia is something that needs to be reformed to ensure that poverty can be reduced if not completely removed. In his book *Poverty in South Asia*, Navin Mishra discusses the state of governance in South Asia and how that has led to the lack of development. He also discusses how governance is lacking and the various means by which governance has fallen short and has led to the lack of development and the sustenance of poverty in South Asian societies.

POVERTY IN SOUTH ASIA

Poverty is understood in different ways according to the goals and functioning of the organization that defines it. Being poor can be described as follows: 'To be hungry, to lack shelter and clothing, to be sick and not cared for, to be illiterate and not schooled. [...] Poor people are particularly vulnerable to adverse events outside their control. They are often treated badly by institutions of the state and society and excluded from voice and power in those institutions.'[23] Poverty as understood by the UN and World Bank is as follows:

United Nations: 'Fundamentally, poverty is a denial of choices and opportunities, a violation of human dignity. It means lack of basic capacity to participate effectively in society. It means not having enough to feed and clothe a family, not having a school or clinic to go to; not having the land on which to grow one's food or a job to earn one's living, not having access to credit. It means insecurity, powerlessness and exclusion of individuals, households and communities. It means susceptibility to violence, and it often implies living in marginal or fragile environments, without access to clean water or sanitation.[24]

World Bank: 'Poverty is pronounced deprivation in well-being, and comprises many dimensions. It includes low incomes and the inability to acquire the basic goods and services necessary for survival with dignity. Poverty also encompasses low levels of health and education, poor access to clean water and sanitation, inadequate physical security, lack of voice, and insufficient capacity and opportunity to better one's life.[25]

As seen, the UN definition outlines poverty from the standpoint of human insecurity. And that poverty describes a situation where the individual suffers from insecurity and the need to focus on the alleviation of poverty to remove people from insecurity to a state closer to human security.

The World Bank definition brings to light the lack of voice and the insufficient capacity and opportunity to better one's life. These are usually related to the governance of the country or region, where democratic representation and development are understood to be intrinsic to the development and growth of a region. One may say that the World Bank believes in a proportional relation to the link between governance and poverty where with good governance, poverty reduces.

Poverty exists across the world including developed countries. However, poverty in developing countries is more frightening because it has serious consequences such as on health care and increasing crime and violence. Three main commitments were made at the World Summit Social Development held in Copenhagen in March 1995. They were: to estimate overall and extreme income poverty; to set time-bound goals and targets for the substantial reduction of overall poverty and the eradication of extreme poverty; and to implement national anti-poverty plans to reach their targets.[26] Every country is expected to design plans for poverty reduction, identify and allocate funds/resources and involve poor people in the policy making and in the implementation of the various initiatives.

Poverty has multiple dimensions. People not only suffer from having to earn an income but also with deficits in health and education, etc. In the twentieth century, European countries were able to reduce poverty by increasing incomes and providing public facilities such as health care and education. The South Asian states have to facilitate access to basic facilities, which would translate income into a better standard of living. Income of the poor depends on environmental circumstances.

DECENTRALIZATION AND DEMOCRACY

Any high-level commitment to poverty reduction may be undermined without accountability and transparency in implementing policies. Since the poor are not a homogeneous group and they live in different geographic areas and facing different types of challenges, different policies are to be adopted in reducing poverty.[27] For instance, in South Asia, decentralization may be conducive to tackle poverty.

Democracy and decentralization are seen as prerequisite for effective tools to eradicate poverty. Both these processes focus on local needs and aspirations.[28] In other words, this produces systems of governance that are more effective.[29] However, it is unclear how far democracy and decentralization have impact on poverty reduction. So, democratic decentralization uplift the poor is not entirely consistent with the evidence. The World Bank's *World Development Report 2000/1* concluded that 'there was no consistent connection between pro-poorness and democracy. While the very worst performers tend not to be democracies – democracy does provide some kind of safety net – there are non-democracies among the best performers.'[30] Liberal democracy in the west functions with a wide range of rules, norms and customs, an independent judiciary, a free press, systems of transparency, and freedom of association and speech through which people can exercise effective control over public officials.[31] This situation is unlikely to be seen in the developing countries including in South Asian countries.

It is argued that democracy has 'an in-built bias that discriminates against "pro-poor" policies'. There is an allegation that the bureaucracy in a democracy has lack of willingness to introduce legislation that would oppose the interests of dominant groups/ majority in society. Joan Nelson offers four explanations why this would be the case: re-distributive policies (such as land reform and progressive taxation) entail a zero sum character whereby gains for the poor often come at the expense of elite groups in society; 'the poor' constitutes a large group, whose interests and needs are difficult to address; comprehensive poverty programmes may entail extensive institutional change; and truly universal poverty programmes offer few opportunities for patronage.[32]

One of the dangers of decentralization is that it may empower only local elites and there will be no alleviation of poverty and inequality. Thus it is a challenge for democracy in rural areas where large numbers of people are dependent upon a small number of local, powerful elites.[33] However, on the other hand, decentralization or devolution of power can enhance rural livelihoods in a number of ways. First, the establishment and empowerment of local resources and allow access to poor people can obviously improve their livelihood.[34] If local people are empowered by allowing them to take decisions to mitigate poverty, who possess the knowledge, information and encouragement to manage and conserve the resources on which they and their families depend.[35] Empowerment of local administrative bodies can facilitate enhancing participation in decision-making, particularly the groups which have been marginalized by local political processes.[36] Though not necessarily to view that democracy and decentralization are contributing to reduction poverty, but there are evidences across Africa, Asia and Latin America, where introduction of elections, transparency and rights of expression can empower poor people and enhance their ability to participate in local decision-making and encouraging them to hold public officials to account.[37] On the other hand, decentralization can improve effectiveness, quality and accountability of government when elected bodies at local levels have adequate funds and freedom to take decisions. However, unless there is effective and coherent policy in terms of coordination between the higher and local bodies effective measures cannot be implemented to address local problems.

Poverty hounds South Asia like many other social evils. The region has more than one-sixth of the global population, and even a small percentage of people living in poverty is a sizeable number in absolute terms. However, the region has a substantial number of its inhabitants living below the poverty line. In numeric terms, poverty is understood globally as living on less than $1.25/day.

In South Asia, 30 per cent of people live below the poverty line at one dollar a day.

According to the Chronic Report, half of the world's chronically poor live in South Asia and one-third live in India. About one in every eight people in South Asia is seen as chronically poor. One in four poor people belong to the chronically poor category.

Forty-four per cent of Indians live below the $1/day poverty line. In Nepal, Pakistan and Bangladesh people living below poverty line are at 38, 31 and 29 per cent respectively. Data is not available for Bhutan and Afghanistan.[38]

POVERTY GAP

Over the years, there has been a steady decline in the percentage of population living below $1.25 a day. However, poverty is different in the rural and urban settings and the prevalence of poverty is exacerbated by poor state of health and health care systems and lack of access or poor quality of education.

HEALTH SECURITY

Though poverty remains to exist, South Asia has improved life expectancy from 50.3 to 62.9 years from 1970-5 and 2000-5 respectively. South Asia has reduced infant mortality rate from 130 per 1,000 live births in 1970 to 60 in 2005. Adult literacy rate was 47.6 per cent during the period 1985-94 and increased to 59.7 per cent during the period 1995-2005. And so is the case with developing countries, and high, medium and low human development index (HDI) countries.

Though South Asian countries were able to increase their GDP but expenditure on health care declined during the period 1990-2005. India's expenditure on the health sector was 5.2 per cent of its GDP during 1990-8 but declined to 5.1 per cent in 2001 and further reduced to 5 per cent in 2005. Whereas it was opposite in the case of Sri Lanka. Sri Lanka as compared to the rest of South Asia has improved in its expenditure on health care. More number of people in Sri Lanka have access to health care facilities as compared to other parts of South Asia. Though Pakistan maintained the same amount of expenditure on health care during 1990-2001 (3.9 per cent) it drastically reduced to 2.1 per cent in 2005. Similarly, Bangladesh maintained the same expenditure during 1990-2001 but there was reduction in its expenditure on health to 2.8 per cent in 2005. In Nepal expenditure on its health care sector reduced from 5.5 per cent in 1990-8 to 5.2 per cent in 2001 but again increased to 5.8 per cent in 2005. Nepal has spent more than other countries in South Asia in 2005 on health care.

EDUCATION

Education has been seen as instrumental in reducing poverty level. Through education, youth would get an opportunity to get employment as well as know their role in respecting and upholding norms and values in the society. Education is seen as instrumental in reducing illegal activities and promoting peace and stability in the society. India has spent 3 per cent of its GDP in 1980 on education which increased to 3.4 per cent in 1985 and further increased to 3.5 per cent in 1990 and in 1995. However, its expenditure was slightly reduced to 3.3 per cent in 2002-4 and expenditure was increased to 3.8 per cent in 2006. Pakistan has increased its expenditure on education from 2.1 per cent in 1980 to 2.6 per cent in 2006. Bangladesh has increased its expenditure on education from 1.1 per cent of its GDP in 1980 to 2.5 per cent in 2006. Similarly, Nepal increased its expenditure from 1.8 in 1980 to 3.4 per cent in 2006. Sri Lanka has also increased its expenditure, like other countries, on education. The state has to focus on education and empower a larger marginalized group of society and strengthen democratic principles, which can enhance capabilities of the poor and vulnerable groups.[39]

While the percentage of people completing primary education may have increased in the region, the percentage of expenditure on health care in the region is on a steady decline. While one factor is supposed to help in the reduction of poverty by opening doors to people remove themselves from poverty, the inability to ensure a secure healthy life for them, hinders the work done towards removing poverty. Nonetheless, it is heartening to note that poverty levels have reduced in the region. Both poverty and governance play important roles in the human security of individuals and in the HDI. Hence the HDI levels of the region will throw light on the human development of the region.

HDI AND SOUTH ASIA

The HDI comprises three components: (1) life expectancy at birth; (2) educational attainment, comprising adult literacy and a combined primary, secondary, and tertiary enrolment ratio; and (3) a regular income. According to the Human Development Report 2004, the South Asian region falls at the bottom in the group of countries with medium human development. Overall HDI value for South Asia is 0.599 with variations amongst countries ranging from the highest HDI of 0.755 in Sri Lanka to the lowest HDI of 0.527 in Nepal. According to the World Governance Report 2006, the governance percentile of South Asia on governance indicators is low, ranging from 26 to 39.

Political leaders or rulers instead of working for the common people, look for themselves. Democracy has failed to deliver in South Asia and particularly in India, which is the largest democracy of the world. There is a wide gap between the common people and the political elites.[40]

There has been an increased HDI in all major South Asian countries (India, Pakistan, Bangladesh and Nepal), except Sri Lanka during 1995-2005. However, Sri Lanka was doing well compare to other countries in South Asia. Nepal had ranked less in HDI as compared to other countries in South Asia.

GOOD GOVERNANCE IMPLEMENTATION IN SOUTH ASIA

At the international front, the UN has focused on poverty reduction across the world. The Millennium Development Goals (MDG) aimed to free humanity from extreme poverty, hunger, illiteracy and disease by 2015. Together, they form a blueprint for development agreed upon by all the world's countries and the entire world's leading development institutions.

Good governance can mean differently to different countries and can have different implications when it is used for policy and administrative reforms, since each country has a different context of governance and each country may face governance challenges different from other countries. Therefore, it is important that the concept of good governance to be understood 'to find indigenous and pragmatic solutions to its unique problems of governance within the framework of universally accepted values'.[41]

The application of the concept of good governance to developing countries poses a challenge at the implementation level, mainly due to ethnocentricity, regional disparities, division between poor and rich, difference between rural and urban people, and lack of basic needs provided to people. Concepts such as decentralization, citizen engagement, lean public service, privatization, autonomy, public-private partnership may work well in developed countries but may not produce the same results in developing countries where the majority of poor people expect their government to fulfil their basic needs. Even the experiences of one developing country cannot be replicated in another developing country. There are many cases of failure due to mis-governance in South Asia. For instance, the Social Action Program (SAP) in Pakistan could not produce the desired results due to its ineffective implementation.

South Asian countries are similar in terms of objectives, structure, functions, attitudes, and standards of governing bodies despite different forms of government. 'The colonial legacy of an administrative system characterized by centralization, formalism, secrecy, elitism, rigidity, and social isolation is common to all South Asian countries'.[42] This is mainly because the modern system of administration and governance in South Asia had by and large evolved during the British colonial rule. The post-colonial administrative system in all the countries was built upon pre-colonial administrative traditions: fusion of administration and politics, absence of elected governing bodies, etc.[43] South Asian countries are among the lowest group of countries in terms of human development and quality of governance.

Poverty is a major obstacle to good governance in South Asia. According to the Human Development Report of 1999, nearly half of the population in South Asia suffers from poverty, without access to adequate food, clean water, sanitation, health, education, and employment. The report reveals that in South Asia, one in two people is illiterate, one in five does not have access to clean water, three in five do not have sanitation facilities and one in five children is malnourished, and four out of five suffer access to financial resources. The poverty profile of South Asia shows that both in terms of income and opportunities, poverty has increased in the region with the exception for India, where it shows slight progress in terms of poverty reduction.[44]

Any kind of concept or model imported from outside may not succeed but if it is indigenous certainly it will succeed in finding solution to challenges of good governance.

In South Asia including in India, Bangladesh and Nepal, special attention has been given to improve law and order to support governance reforms. Poverty can be defined as '... a state of economic, social and psychological deprivation [which] occurs among people or countries lacking sufficient ownership, control or access to resources to maintain minimum acceptable standards of living.'[45]

Governance seeks more coordination, coherence and collaborative networks among the wide variety of actors such as public sector organizations, corporations, private organizations, civil society organizations, and international organizations. Although democracy enhances good governance, the latter is not necessarily equivalent to democracy.

South Asian countries have to learn from each other's experiences and from other parts of the world. For instance, how Bengaluru in India has become the second largest software market world over and how Grameen Bank in Bangladesh is catering to the micro credit needs of the poor. South Asian countries need to develop an indigenous model to find pragmatic solutions to the challenges of good governance. For instance, Bangladesh has introduced reforms in government audit to bring transparency in the audit system whereas

India is emphasizing on training of civil servants to enhance their efficiency and effectiveness. Similarly Sri Lanka and Nepal have adopted various civil society initiatives to promote community collaboration in governance.

South Asian countries can achieve good governance if they adopt indigenous models rather than simply borrow models and ideas from the West. It is not to say that the Western models are not acceptable or relevant. But we need to concentrate on models on which the countries would easily adapt them to their own institutional contexts. The concept of governance, reformulated by a South Asian scholar Mahbub ul Haq seems to be more relevant for South Asia.

HUMAN DEPRIVATION IN SOUTH ASIA

Sustainable development of a country can be achieved only when we uplift the standard of living of the poor people. There are countries whose growth index does not correspond to the improved living conditions of the majority of the people. The majority of the rural people in the developing countries are facing poverty, inequality and unemployment.

Mahbub ul Haq developed three measures – health deprivation measure, education deprivation measure and income deprivation measure – to assess human development in South Asia. There was considerable less deprivation in health, education and income in India, Pakistan, Nepal and Sri Lanka. Whereas for Bangladesh, it was reported that unlike other countries, health and income deprivation increased and there was decrease in education deprivation.

ROLE OF THE STATE AND NGOs

There has been a debate since 1980 on the role of the state in governance. Due to various factors state is unable to address the new challenges coupled with the traditional ones. International organizations, like the UN have suggested broadening the role of the private sector and civil society organizations. Thus the concept of governance necessitates coordination between the state, the private sector and civil society organizations. However, it is to be noted that without efficient state role, private organizations cannot play an effective role in poverty alleviation. The public sector is no longer defined solely as a planner or service provider. Rather, planning, management and public services can coordinate with each other.[46]

The state has to play a role in creating an economic environment, protecting the vulnerable, improving government efficiency and responsiveness, empowering people, decentralizing the administrative system and reducing gaps between the rich and the poor.[47]

A strong civil society is crucial for good governance and is considered as one of the prerequisites of democracy. Civil society can act as agencies for checks and balances organizations between the state power and the private sector. They contribute to and strengthen both the domains.[48] They also provide a platform to people's participation in economic and social activities. Of the civil society organizations, NGOs' role has become prominent in poverty alleviation over the years.

MDGs AND THE CHRONICALLY POOR: HELPING EACH OTHER

The MDGs are accompanied by targets against which progress can be measured. These MDGs are the following: eradicate extreme poverty and hunger; achieve universal primary education; promote gender equality and empower women; reduce child mortality; improve maternal health; combat HIV/AIDS, malaria and other diseases; ensure environmental sustainability; develop a global partnership for development.

The World Bank has come up with a methodology of using six indicators in assessing the quality of governance known as Worldwide Governance Indicators (WGI). They are: (1) voice and accountability, (2) political stability, (3) government effectiveness, (4) regulatory quality, (5) rule of law, and (6) control of corruption. These six dimensions cover the political, economic and institutional aspects of governance. These indicators are normative and have a high association with democracy and economic development.[49]

CONCLUSION

South Asia ranks poorly on all human development indicators, including low literacy, poor enrolment rates, high dropout rates from primary schools, inadequate facilities and poor quality education. Unlike Sri Lanka, other countries in South Asia are poor with regard to human development indicators. It is clear that ending poverty, ignorance, disease and inequality of opportunity are identified as the major priority for the developing countries. 'Good governance is perhaps the single most important factor in eradicating poverty and promoting development.'[50]

Governance constitutes a major challenge for developing countries. It can have different meanings for different countries and different implications too when it is used for policy and administrative reforms. Since each country has a different context of governance and may be facing governance challenges dissimilar from each other. Similar processes followed by the countries in implementing governance may have different governance outcomes. Similarly, dissimilar processes may give similar outcomes in two different countries. For instance, a country with effective governance may control corruption, whereas in a country with poor governance, the same measures may prove ineffective in addressing corruption.[51] It is not the form of the government that plays a role in governance and poverty reduction but the effectiveness of government and its commitment towards dealing with the issues.

We witnessed that single party dominant political system in China, Malaysia and Singapore have shown remarkable results in convalescing governance outcomes whereas pluralistic party system have also shown positive results in Brazil and India. Similarly, monarchy in UK and Nepal has given different results.

Due to ethnocentricity, regional disparities, division between poor and rich, difference between rural and urban people, lack of basic needs provided to people, developing countries may have problems in strengthening governance. Further, decentralization, citizen engagement, lean public service, privatization, autonomy, public-private partnership may not work well in developing countries. Even the experiences of one developing country may not be replicated to another developing country.

However, South Asian countries are similar in terms of objectives, structure, functions, attitudes, and standards of governing bodies despite different forms of government. This is mainly because the modern system of administration and governance in South Asia had by and large evolved under British colonial rule.

NOTES

1. A.M. Kjaer, *Governance*, Cambridge: Polity Press, 2005, cited in Md. Abu Nayem Miazi and Md. Nahidul Islam, 'Prospect of Good Governance in Bangladesh: A Review', *Prime University Journal*, vol. 6, no. 2, July-December 2012, p. 71.
2. World Bank, *Governance: The World Bank's Experience*, Washington DC: The World Bank, 1994, cited in Abu Elias Sarker and Mohammad Habibur Rahman, 'The Emerging Perspective of Governance and Poverty Alleviation: A Case of Bangladesh', *Public Organize Rev*, vol. 7, 2007, p. 95.
3. Development Assistance Committee (DAC), 1997, p. 11, cited in Priyanka Bakhshi and Shatabdi Bagchi, 'Role of Government in Poverty Alleviation in India: Expectations and Outcomes', *International Journal of Advanced Research in Management and Social Sciences,* vol. 2, no. 5, March 2013, p. 54.
4. Carlos Santiso, 'Good Governance and Aid Effectiveness: The World Bank and Conditionality', *The Georgetown Public Policy Review*, vol. 7, no. 1, Fall 2001, p. 2.
5. Nasira Jabeen, 'Good or Good Enough Governance in South Asia: Constraints and Possibilities', *Inaugural Address*, Utrecht University, 2 April 2007, p. 6
6. UN System Task Team on the Post-2015 UN Development Agenda, *Governance on Development*, May 2012, p. 3, http://www.un.org/millenniumgoals/pdf/Think%20Pieces/7_governance.pdf
7. Jabeen, n. 5, p. 7.
8. *Ibid.*, p. 8.
9. *Ibid.*
10. Bakhshi and Bagchi, n. 3, p. 54
11. World Bank, 1991, cited in Miazi and Islam, n. 1, p. 71.
12. *The World Bank's PRSP Handbook*, http://web.worldbank.org

13. J.G. March, and J.P. Olsen, 'The Concept of Good Governance', Washington D.C., http:unpan1uen.org/intrdoc/groups/public/documents/other/unpan614209, cited in Miazi and Islam, p. 71.
14. G. Hyden, 'Governance and Reconstitution of Political Order', in J. Richard (ed.), *State, Conflict and Democracy in Africa*, Boulder, 1999, cited in Miazi and Islam, n. 1, p. 72.
15. M. Landell and I. Serageldein, *Governance and Development Process, Finance and Development*, Washington D.C., 1991, cited in Miazi and Islam, n.1, p. 72.
16. R.A.W Rhodes, 1997, cited in Miazi and Islam, n. 1, p. 73.
17. Q. Bilney, *Good Governance and Participatory Development in Australia's Aid Program*, Sydney: Development Bulletin, 1994, p. 17.
18. Miazi and Islam, n. 1, pp. 69-70
19. Cited in Miazi and Islam, n. 1, p. 74.
20. D. Kaufmann, A. Kraay and P. Zoido-Lobatón, 'Aggregating Governance Indicators', *World Bank Policy Research Paper*, no. 2195, 2000, cited in Salahuddin M. Aminuzzaman, 'Poverty and Governance: A Quest for Alternative Focus: Bangladesh Test Case', *JOAAG*, vol. 2, no. 1, 2007, p. 12.
21. *Ibid.*, p. 18.
22. L.N. Rangarajan (ed.), *Kautilya: The Arthashastra*, New Delhi: Penguin, 1992; Aasha Kapur Mehta, Andrew Shepherd, Shashanka Bhide, Amita Shah and Anand Kumar, *India Chronic Poverty Report: Towards Solutions and New Compacts in a Dynamic Context*, New Delhi: Indian Institute of Public Administration, 2011, p. 2.
23. International Bank for Reconstruction and Development, *India Country Study on Reducing Poverty, Accelerating Development*, New Delhi: Oxford University Press, 2000.
24. David Gordon, 'Indicators of Poverty and Hunger', 14 December 2005, see http://www.un.org/esa/socdev/unyin/documents/ydiDavidGordon_poverty.pdf
25. World Bank, *Poverty-Poverty and Inequality Analysis,* 5 May 2010, 14 May 2012 http://go.worldbank.org/VFPEGF7FU0
26. United Nations Developmet Programme, *Overcoming Human Poverty: Poverty Report 2000*, New York: UNDP, 2000, p. 18.
27. Hartmut Schneider, 'Participatory Governance for Poverty Reduction', *Journal of International Development*, vol. 11, no. 4, 1999, p. 524.
28. Richard C. Crook and Alan Sturla Sverrisson, 'Decentralization and Poverty Alleviation in Developing Countries: A Comparative Analysis or, Is West Bengal Unique?', *IDS Working Paper* no. 130, Brighton:

Institute of Development Studies at the University of Sussex, 2001; Craig Johnson, 'Local Democracy, Democratic Decentralization and Rural Development: Theories, Challenges and Options for Policy', *Development Policy Review*, vol. 19, no. 4, 2001, p. 521.

29. Johnson, ibid., p. 521.
30. Mick Moore and James Putzel, 'Politics and Poverty', *A Background Paper for the World Development Report 2000/1*, Brighton: Institute of Development Studies, University of Sussex, 1999, p. 8.
31. Anne Marie Goetz Luckham, and Mary Kaldor, 'Democratic Institutions and Politics in Contexts of Inequality, Poverty, and Conflict: A Conceptual Framework', *IDS Working Paper*, no.104, Brighton: Institute of Development Studies, University of Sussex, 2000.
32. Cited in ibid., pp. 33-4.
33. Harry Blair, 'Participation and Accountability at the Periphery: Democratic Local Governance in Six Countries', *World Development*, vol. 28, no.1, 2000, pp. 21-39.
34. Elinor Ostrom, *Governing the Commons: The Evolution of Institutions for Collective Action*, Cambridge: Cambridge University Press, 1990; Johnson, n. 28, p. 526.
35. Arun Agrawal and Clark C. Gibson, 'Enchantment and Disenchantment: The Role of Community in Natural Resource Conservation'. *World Development*, vol. 27, no. 6, 1999, p. 633.
36. For details see Blair, n. 33, pp. 21-39; Crook and Sverrisson, n. 28.
37. For detail see Blair, n. 33, pp. 21-39; Crook and Sverrisson, n. 28.
38. Chronic Poverty Research Centre, 'Understanding Chronic Poverty in South Asia', in *Chronic Poverty Report 2004-05*, Manchester: Institute for Development Policy & Management, University of Manchester, 2005, p. 71, http://www.chronicpoverty.org/uploads/publication_files/CPR1_ReportFull.pdf
39. For details see Amartya Sen, *Development as Freedom*, New York: Knopf Books, 1999.
40. Human Development Centre, *Human Development Report*, New York: Oxford University Press, 1999.
41. Jabeen, n. 5, p. 2
42. H. Zafarullah and A. Haque, 'Public Management in South Asia: Dimensions and Directions of Change', *International Journal of Public Administration,* vol. 21, no. 10, 2003, pp. 1477-8.
43. M. Haque, 'Recent Transition in Governance in South Asia: Contexts, Dimensions, and Implications', *International Journal of Public Administration*, vol. 24, no. 12, 2001, pp. 1405-36.

44. *Ibid.*
45 UNDP, *Human Development Report,* 2001, New York: Oxford University Press, 2001, p. 10.
46. S.P. Osborne and K. McLaughlin, 'From Public Administration to Public Governance: Public Management and Public Services in the Twenty-first Century', in S.P. Osborne and K. McLaughlin (eds.), *Public Management: Critical Perspectives,* vol. 1, London: Routledge, 2002, pp. 1-10; Sarker and Rahman, n. 2, p. 94.
47. UNDP, *Public Sector Management, Governance and Sustainable Development,* New York: Management and Governance Division, UNDP, 1995; Sarker and Rahman, n. 2, p. 96.
48. A. Rahman, S.N. Wadood and M.A. Eusuf, 'Civil Society and Governance', in H.A. Hye (ed.), *Governance: South Asian Perspectives,* Dhaka: University Press Limited, 2000, pp. 421-36; Sarker and Rahman, n. 2, p. 97.
49. D. Kaufmann and A. Kraay, *Issue Paper for Roundtable on Measuring Governance,* World Bank: World Bank Institute and the Development Economics Vice-Presidency, 2007, see Jabeen, n. 5.
50. Kofi Annan, *Partnerships for Global Community: Annual Report of the Organization,* New York: United Nations, 1998.
51. Anwar Shah, 'Tailoring the Fight Against Corruption to Country Circumstances', in Anwar Shah (ed.), *Performance Accountability and Combating Corruption,* Washington, DC: World Bank, 2007, pp. 233-54.

PART 2

GOVERNANCE AND GLOBALIZATION

CHAPTER 2

Macroeconomics of Governance in South Asia

I.P. Khosla

INTRODUCTION

The traditional concept of governance emphasizes rule of law and the satisfactory functioning of political and administrative institutions. Thus, as a fairly typical case, the Development Advisory Committee (DAC) of the Organization for Economic Cooperation and Development defines good governance as 'the rule of law, responsible leadership and effective systems for public management, transparency and accountability'.[1] In a more recent paper, the DAC Network on Governance, which was created in 1995 in response to widespread demand among OECD countries for general principles on the basis of which assistance should be given, linked it also to accountability, and stressed that governments which received OECD funding should help citizens participate in the development process, should preserve fundamental rights and have accountability mechanisms in place so that they answer to the people and their representatives. Some of the literatures on the subject, on the other hand, confuse governance with government. There are a large number of government functions including defence matters, law and order and policing, even economic planning, which are taken as part of governance, though that is not exactly where they belong. There may be some justification for such definitions, though one might be pardoned for believing that this was one way, a rather unsubtle one, of pushing others to conform to OECD's particular brand of values.

ORIGIN AND HISTORY OF THE CONCEPT OF GOVERNANCE

However, overall it does need to be remembered that the concept of governance and its evolution is entirely a product of thinking of the 'West', or the developed world; none of it has originated outside that world, though, of course, this is not to belittle or in any way denigrate the concept. Indeed, in the years since debate on this concept intensified, say roughly after the end of the Cold War, there has been a great deal of contextualization of all the ideas around it and also of the concept itself, responding to the needs of the so-called 'Third World', with South Asia occupying an important place in the debate. Both these points, about its origin and how it was contextualized after 1990, have determined what we talk about today when we mention 'governance' and thus needs to be kept in mind.

If we go back into history, the concept in one sense or another has been in use since roughly the fourteenth century, which is when the term first entered the English language, and from when a host of meanings were attached to it: this included not only the governance of the country but also governance of an estate in private hands, even a household; and it was the act or manner of governing and its offices or power; but also being wise or virtuous in the general behaviour of those who were in authority. In other words, there were two aspects: the exercise of authority; and the need to do this with moral prudence. This was perhaps largely because of the authority of the Church, which did exercise governmental power all over Europe and believed that Christian virtues, based on morality, were important in the exercise of that power, whether it is by the government or by private persons in a more restricted setting. However, after the Peace of Westphalia (1648), as the state system came to dominate the international scene and the influence of the Church faded, it became fully synonymous with government, meaning just rule, the exercise of authority without the need for moral prudence; hence also and by stages it faded out of use and was more or less entirely replaced by 'government'. History moved along; wars came and went; systems of government changed with the changing times, but there was no challenge to the untrammelled authority of the state, so that governance remained synonymous with government, simply, the exercise of authority by the state, often without any pretence at securing moral authority. After the end of the nineteenth century and along with the entry of realism in international relations as the focus of statecraft, the moral connotations of wisdom and virtue which were heretofore attached to the exercise of authority remained lost.

This was true till about 1990, and in the various encyclopaedias and dictionaries published before that there is actually rarely any mention at all of the word, for it was considered throughout as synonymous with government. During the Cold War, and also between 1945-90, the determination of virtue was based on which side a country chose, the West or the Socialists, and it was not important what kind of government the country had, democracy or dictatorship, or whether there was good governance or not, so the word remained synonymous with government. This was, of course, no longer applicable after 1990. In the 1990s the normative aspect of rule over societies and countries came into prominence again after a gap of over three centuries due to the political and economic changes that marked the decade. Only one ideology was left to dominate the international system and its moral stature, which had always been the focus of the Cold War, could now be emphasized and promoted without fear of contradiction or opposition. The end of the Cold War suggested that there was only one truly correct system which needed to be adopted by all nations: a pluralist democracy, which many countries now embraced; the devolution of political power to a spreading number of parties, groups and institutions; and the general abandonment of centrally planned and government-run economic systems in favour of a free market so that the same thing happened to economic opportunity.

An uncontested wave of publicity supporting these aims across the globalized media defined the empirical and normative contours of this route to governance. It became not only virtuous to adopt a pluralist democracy and free market but was also projected as the only way to attain success in socio-economic aims. Governance became once more synonymous with good governance, and there was a package of results which would come as payoff: economic growth and poverty eradication, political stability, improved health and education standards. Among the first to spell out in detail what should be done and how, were the international financial institutions led by the World Bank and the International Monetary Fund, in consultation with donors, economists and non-governmental organizations, who built up a voluminous theoretical literature on the subject, although the ideas have shifted and evolved over the years. In 1993, according to the World Bank, governance comprised three components: the form of the political regime, the process of managing economic and social resources, and the capacity to formulate and implement policies and discharge governmental functions. This suited the international situation of the time; ethical overtones are there, since the end of the Cold War had made the Western institutions rather confident that theirs were the ideals best suited to the human race and there was 'endist' thinking in the air; these overtones are now muted.

Since then the thinking has evolved and more recently prominence has been given to a three-player system of the state, the market and civil society. In this system the role of the state should be pruned for it has often (in the world of developing countries) taken on more than its capability. This mismatch between role and capability can be cured in part by reducing the role of the state and handing over many functions hitherto done by it to the private sector, which needs to be strengthened by the creation of institutional mechanisms, greater public sector procurement, cooperative ventures between the private and the public sector and suitable regulations. Many other functions could be devolved to civil society, including both professional organizations and NGOs, which in turn need to be helped by building social capital, institutional rules and regulations as well as mutual understanding with the government. Given all these precautions, and with time, it could even be envisaged that civil society could take over as the major contributor to the provision of social services like health and education at the national level.

IMPACT OF GLOBALIZATION

In any case, international thinking has been that the capacity of the state needs also to be raised in order to be able to perform the functions of good governance successfully, and this can best be done by greater globalization. The theory is that trade and investment across borders sharpens the competitive edge as well as encourages adherence to international norms, and this adherence is not limited to the economic effects; there is an important spill-over into social value norms including to those of good governance. Thus the partnerships that are built within the nation, between the public and the private sector, between private and private, between civil society networks, all these intra-national partnerships have extra-national effects. Put in a different way, liberalism and democracy at home leads to liberal internationalism.

The effort has been to put the empirical and the normative aspects of governance into a single scientific framework. This would include sets of law like statements about income and poverty, education and health, decentralization and the rights of minorities, apart, of course, from the basic ones about democracy and a free market. These objectives are all linked together, they march forward in synchronous steps; progress in one goes hand in hand with progress in the others. This framework would be above dispute or human intervention, elevated to the status of an objective science, similar to physics or mathematics, more or less determinate, but in any case predictable in its results. The quest for such a framework was carried forward in several stages, only some of which can be cited here, space permitting.

The Asian Development Bank study of 1997 offers a good sampling of the linkage. It cites economic transformation leading to falling death and birth rates, a decline in the average family size, and contends that women's status and opportunities have improved, largely because of rising incomes, demographic change, better education and better household technologies. This, in turn, completing the virtuous circle, helped alleviate poverty by promoting smaller families, leading to greater affluence, with families thereby better able to afford higher standards of nutrition and health care, education and thereby economic growth.

Later studies carried this quest further. A 1999 report on Human Development in South Asia from the MahbubulHaq (he was a pioneer in taking the concept of human development forward) Human Development Centre in Pakistan defined good governance as humane governance, meaning the effective participation of people in state, civil society and private sector activities that are conducive to human development. Explaining this, it then asks states in the region to redirect their priorities towards the basic needs of the poor, stimulate economic growth, revitalize existing state institutions, decentralize power, forge new partnerships between state and civil society and work for government-business cooperation. All these activities have to be sequenced and prioritized for effective implementation.

Another direction was taken by those studies that reduced the problem to charts and indices, to quantitative measures, taking inspiration from the UNDP Human Development Index and going on from there to propose a 'humane governance index', based on a wider range of parameters than that of the UNDP, as also a distance index which is to measure the distance between government bodies and the people, as well as a citizen's survey. The Asian Development Bank has a quality of life measure comprising life expectancy, literacy rates, nutrition, pollution, though it was not possible actually to quantify the last one. So the Bank did not seriously attempt to quantify this, arguing that some aspects of the quality of life are not really susceptible to measurement, being intangible. There are other measures of governance which have been suggested from time to time.

All these ideas were no doubt laudable; every government in our region, as indeed elsewhere in the world, would subscribe to all or most of them. It seems like plain common sense to assert that growth, and an increase in national income, will lead to better education, improved health and greater gender sensitivity, among other factors which go to make for good governance. Furthermore what could be more laudable than to simplify all these things into simpler and more easily measured numbers, which would also go to explain to ordinary citizens how well the whole plan is succeeding, how far good governance has gone? But it is also, and this has, of course, happened, quite as easy to reduce the whole problem to one of getting better looking maps, charts and statistics, to put those forward as the reality and turn away from the fact that, in the field, as the ground surveys consistently show, it is quite clear that education is going nowhere, health among the poorest is deteriorating and gender sensitivity is so low that in some states of India systematic gender weeding before birth has reached epic proportions.

This is not the result of any deliberate effort by governments. Indeed governments in South Asia have really tried to decentralize power, which seems the obvious way to ensure that the needs of the people are reflected in the policies implemented for those needs. Where raising levels of nutrition and of public health are concerned, or ensuring universal primary education and literacy, giving people the right to an adequate livelihood, even the right to work, the Directive Principles enshrined in the Constitution of India, Article 37, are comprehensive. The Constitution of Pakistan has similar provisions, and also unenforceable, like those of India. The Constitution of Sri Lanka has a chapter on Directive Principles of State Policy and Fundamental Duties, which lays down similar targets, and those of Nepal as well as of Bangladesh. Furthermore, there is an effort to ensure that all these are implemented by representatives of the local people at the local level. For this purpose, constitutional provisions as well as legal enactments have been put in place for local bodies, empowered as well as locally elected, so that real progress is made. Unfortunately, no real financial power, no finance really, was given for this purpose, so little was actually achieved (though in theory it was there).

Consequently, the region remained dependent on statistics collected by government agencies to assess how much good governance was around.

NEED FOR A PEOPLE-CENTRIC APPROACH

However, in the South Asian context these top down definitions and collected statistics are too one-sided and generalized; they emphasize the rulers and the government or those that might substitute for them and what is to be done by them; or they are motivated by preconceived ideas generated by the developed countries and their interests.

When field surveys are carried out, however, both the techniques, that of grouping governance aims under a few simple (or even one – such as growth) headings; as well as that of describing it through statistics, do not reflect reality.

As for the first, even a cursory look at the figures show that such grouping does not reflect reality. Poverty, for instance, is not closely linked to health or education. The National Family Health Survey, first carried out in 1992-3, shows that malnutrition has no strong correlation with poverty less than that 0.4 per cent across the region. There are other examples. GNP per capita in the Maldives is the highest in the region, but its human development index, for instance, is lower than that of Sri Lanka, and about the same as that of India. The GNP of Sri Lanka has actually grown much slower than that of its large northern neighbour in the new millennium, but its human development index has improved a great deal faster: in adult literacy, in life expectancy at birth, in maternal mortality, as well as national spending on health, it has consistently out done India. Other examples can be given, but the general truth is that each of these indicators of good governance, health, education, gender sensitivity and so on, have to be looked at separately if we wish to assess it properly.

The second technique, of describing good governance through some simplified statistics, is also of doubtful validity. Such statistics would show the Punjab (India), for example, ahead of Kerala, since growth rates (the usual single figure generally taken to reflect all the reality of welfare in a nutshell) have always been higher, but governance is admittedly much better in the latter: better administered health care facilities, higher literacy and school attendance rates, and certainly a great superiority in gender sensitivity, quite apparent in its sex ratio which, by the 2011 census, was 1084, the highest in the country, compared to 861, among the bottom ten, for the former.

So it is the people's needs in all their aspects that should occupy centre stage in any definition suitable for our region; and since the situations vary from country to country, even within a region such as South Asia, these definitions need to be broadly outlined, and not be too detailed. Generally the rule of law, wide ranging institutional functioning and the tasks of government are extant if not always ideally implemented, but those people's needs, adequate nutrition, provisions for their health and education; and for the rulers and the governing apparatus to be responsive to the people's needs; this is what should be at the centre of any definition.

There are other definitions that underline that it is the needs of the people, starting with the individual and the family, that are to be satisfied for good governance. At the turn of the century, the Centre for Policy Research, New Delhi, undertook a major research project covering governance in each of the South Asian countries and came up with several useful volumes which have now become standard reference books; in a final summing up volume it was said that 'good governance implies that the affairs of state are so managed that the material and social well being of the citizen is effectively looked after within a system of properly organised institutions of governance'.[2] Prime Minister Modi, in a message to the nation on 25 December 2014, also emphasized the idea of citizen first, that good governance means 'bring government closer to the people through technology, as both an empowering tool for citizens and accountability medium for government'.[3]

A reasonable definition of good governance would be 'the responsive provision of human security', on this presumption. There are two elements in this definition: being responsive and providing for human security.

The first element emphasizes the systems through which a nation is ruled or governed and the second, the manner in which these systems are implemented. As we shall see, the second element is the more important one for South Asian countries. Regarding the first element, in general the systems through which a nation is ruled or governed are well known and have been the subject of different definitions of governance, and include properly functioning democratic institutions, regular free and fair elections, an independent judiciary, a responsive parliament, a free press and these go down to the lowest level so as to include empowered and representative local bodies free of political control and which are able to articulate people's needs in a manner free of caste, religions, gender or other prejudices while achieving egalitarian end results. The systems should also include special interest areas, by enabling them to represent their needs in the formulation of policy: Chambers of Commerce; art and cultural societies; academic institutions and think tanks and others which identify and articulate the needs and interests of their members in a similar manner to institutions at a higher level. This is the big picture of how a system can be responsive, and while all these systems do not function ideally in our region, they do function, by and large, and there is a commitment by political leaders to ensure their adequate functioning.

As for the second element, the idea of human security, this includes not only human development in all its parameters with the individual at the starting point, but also peace and the wider idea of security as suggested by General Assembly resolution 66/290 of 10 September 2012, which was a significant milestone for the advancement of human security. In paragraph 3 of that resolution, the Assembly agreed on a common understanding of human security which included the right of people to live in freedom and dignity, free from poverty and despair. All individuals, in particular vulnerable people, are entitled to freedom from fear and freedom from want, with an equal opportunity to enjoy all their rights and fully develop their human potential. In sum it is people-centred, comprehensive, context-specific and prevention-oriented, strengthens the protection and empowerment of all people and all communities; recognizes the inter-linkages between peace, development and human rights, and equally considers civil, political, economic, social and cultural rights; that it does not entail the threat or the use of force or coercive measures; and, importantly, that it does not replace state security and is based on national ownership.

It needs to be noted here that good governance requires a benevolent, humane, social and political system. Its quality needs to be seen directly from how it benefits individuals, those at the lowest rung of the socio-economic ladder in terms of poverty removal, health and nutrition, the opportunities for education and general welfare including employment opportunities, recreation and sports, all measured or estimated in disaggregated form. Just as one cannot understand biology without understanding the gene, nor physics without understanding the atom, so one cannot understand governance without understanding the needs of the individual at the bottom rung of the socio-economic ladder.

Once such a comprehensive definition of governance (emphasizing the second element) is spelled out it is seen that there are many areas in South Asia where remedial action is needed. Some are endemic like high population growth and low savings rates and low growth; social inequalities and prejudices; the misuse of the political system; the lack of properly functioning markets and investment systems. Others like poor health care systems and non-functional schools can be tackled quickly. However, there is one shibboleth about this subject that needs to be laid to rest: that it is the military and political tensions in the region that have been the big obstacle to the achievement of good governance. In fact, India, as an example, spends rather little on defence as a proportion of income, just 2.4 per cent compared to 3.3 per cent for the US, 3.6 per cent for Pakistan. There is very little scope for reduction here.

THE IMPERATIVE NEED FOR RESOURCES

This chapter argues that even if the various above-mentioned obstacles to good governance were to be removed, the biggest one would remain, namely the lack of resources. It is government that has to provide the bulk of the resources needed for good governance; NGOs, civil society, the private sector, can all certainly make useful contributions by way of ideas, manpower, local initiatives and other such efforts, but they can only generate a miniscule fraction of the material resources required; it is government that has to find the bulk. In point of fact governments typically, especially in developing countries, spend some 99 per cent of the total required for the provision of human security to individuals at the very lowest levels of the socio-economic ladder and in South Asian context, governments collect less than half of the resources required for the sum total of the unavoidable tasks they need to perform such as debt repayment, defence, leaving very little over to achieve good governance. Note that even a substantial increase in non-government resources and spending would not make much of a difference here; such a tiny proportion of the total incomes from such resources that is it not useful to rely on them to make up a significant part of the shortfall. In India, the NGOs, Corporate Social Responsibility spending, charities of various kinds, all together account for less than 1 per cent of the total. So it is the government that has to spend almost all the money required and in the region, governments do not have the resources to do so.

Let us look at how much is needed for good governance in terms of percentages of GDP. Most developed countries where good governance can be cited collect some 40 per cent to half of their GDP in terms of revenue to spend on various aspects of government, including good governance. Europeans typically collect these amounts; thus, citing two examples – for Germany it was 45 per cent, for Norway 47 per cent.[4]

Citing the figures given by the World Bank in its 'World Development Indicators' we see that in India the central government collects 17.6 per cent of GDP in total revenue (2013). For the same year, other South Asian economies did even less well: for Bangladesh the figure was 10.5, for Pakistan 14.5.[5]

Second, the resources of governments in South Asia are typically tied down to some unavoidable expenditures like interest payment on debt, defence, civil services and administration as also subsidies. Out of the amount collected, a quarter to one-third goes on payment of interest on debt (in the case of India 4.6 per cent out of the 17.6, or about 26 per cent of the total at the disposal of government), while another sixth of the total or a little less goes on defence; once subsidies and administrative expenses are covered, that leaves little, say around a third or a little more of the total revenue collected, for things like education, health, and the other inputs which are the heart of good governance. In Europe or any developed economy, on the contrary, the exact opposite is true: out of the very large amount collected as government revenue very little is spent on interest payments and defence: for Germany it is about one-twentieth of the total revenue in each case, for Norway the total on both is less than one-twenty-fifth. That leaves a large amount for good governance. Citing an example, India spends 2 to 3 per cent of its GDP on health programmes, while in the case of a developed country like Germany or Norway it is 10 per cent or more. The figures for education are less stark but similar. This is the main problem in achieving whatever targets we set; if there are no resources, the targets can simply not be met.

It is possible to depend on economic growth to raise the figure of total spending on governance-related programmes, but this is necessarily a slow process. There has to be a radical overhaul of the tax structure and regime, if at all the whole process of getting good governance is to be speeded up. So the next point is about the indications whether governments are sincere in wanting a foreseeable future in which these targets are going to be met, which is shown by how egalitarian their policies have been; and how fast have their revenue collection regimes worked to increase the kind of resources that can be used to promote human development and security, as a proportion of GDP and thereby to increase equality. In India certainly they have been the opposite of egalitarian, and a reasonable indication of this is the GINI coefficient which has crept up from 30 to 38 in the past twenty years; inequality has, slowly but surely, increased. Further details can be given about this, based on data given in the India Human Development Survey prepared just before the India Economic Summit, 2016. According to a report by the Johannesburg-based company New World Wealth, India is the second-most unequal country globally (only Russia is more unequal).[6] In India, the richest 1 per cent own 53 per cent of the country's wealth, according to the latest data from Credit Suisse. The richest five per cent own 68.6 per cent, while the top 10 per cent have 76.3 per cent. At the other end of the pyramid, the poorest 50 per cent own only 4.1 per cent of national wealth. What's more, things are getting better for the rich. The Credit Suisse data shows that India's richest 1 per cent owned just 36.8 per cent of the country's wealth in 2000, while the share of the top 10 per cent was 65.9 per cent.[7] Such systems are characterized as 'patrimonial capitalism' due to the steadily increasing importance of inherited wealth, and the return of private capital to dominance especially in the developed but also in the developing world. Inherited wealth, of course, plays its own role in the acceleration of inequality, since more and more people live at the very top of the wealth pyramid without working or increasing growth.

Another sign of egalitarian policies, especially as this is an indicator of the government's intention to spend more on good governance, is that the tax collection regimes should grow faster than the economy as a whole, that the aim should be to reach the figures of 40-50 per cent of the GDP, which are typical of countries where good governance prevails.

In India, to cite a typical case, during 1965-90, GDP increased 2.8 fold or 280 per cent, while revenue collected (as a proportion of that GDP) increased from 10 to 16 per cent, i.e. by 6 per cent; then from 1990-2013 GDP increased 4.8 fold or 480 per cent, while tax collection by only about one per cent to just over 17 per cent of GDP; the government was not only not able to match GDP increases by increases in tax collected; in fact, there was regression, a slowing down of even the pace at which tax collected as a proportion of GDP was rising in the earlier period. A second reflection on egalitarian policies is whether the tax balances are progressive or regressive and in India as in the rest of the region, they are regressive, while no attempt has been made to correct this state of affairs. The best indication of this is the proportion of direct to indirect taxes; the more the indirect taxes the greater the burden of the poor. Direct taxes (progressive) account for some 35 per cent of the total in India, a figure which has remained roughly the same for 50 years; actually it has marginally declined over the last 20 years. No effort has been made to remedy this. The rest is indirect taxes, which are regressive, while for the developed countries in general the ratio is the opposite, 65 per cent direct, 35 per cent indirect. In India there is a total of two million people who pay direct taxes; further the latest figures show that only 20,000 people have incomes of over rupees one crore. Given the kind of luxury spending that we see daily and the kind of advertisements which are popular, this is difficult to believe, easier to believe that it represents under-reporting on a massive scale, with government unwilling or unable to come up with policies to prevent it and to get the taxes that should be due with the kind of incomes that are clearly in the hands of the wealthy.

Then there are the tax breaks provided especially to corporations and rich individuals which enable them to avoid payment of taxes altogether or at least to pay the minimum. The statutory rate of taxation for companies is 33.84 per cent; however, the actual rate collected in 2014-15 was 24.64 per cent. Further it is generally seen that the larger companies paid lower percentages than the smaller ones; those with profits of less than rupees one crore paid an average of 29.37 per cent, while those with profits greater than Rs. 500 crore paid out some 22.88 per cent. In sum, there has been a large amount of revenue foregone because of tax concessions to the richest companies, a total of some 4.5 per cent of GDP had been given in this manner in 2014-15, to give a specific example, but figures are not dissimilar for other years. The proportion of GDP spent on health or education or family welfare schemes is, in each case, less than that.

THE IMPACT OF POLITICO-ECONOMIC CONTROL

We should note that the economic outcomes that these figures represent are not the result of impersonal or objective economic forces over which no one has control; they are the result of decisions taken by conscious agents who are aware of the consequences of their actions, so that politics is ubiquitous in the playing out of these parameters; the way they change is not the result of predetermined or ineluctable processes. We cannot assert that the top one per cent of the most wealthy are able or in fact do manipulate the key economic parameters in such a way as to ensure their income and wealth, compared to the rest of the population, goes on increasing; but it is true that the top centile is a relatively broad elite that plays a central role in shaping the economic, political and symbolic structure of society. In South Asia, the wealthy have over the last three decades since liberalization not only accumulated wealth much faster than the average (as mentioned above) but they have also slowly tightened their grip on the levers of real power; as one example among many, the last (2014) Lok Sabha elections (India) had 48 candidates, including from prominent industrial families, with over Rs. 100 crore worth of assets compared to fourteen the time before, 2009, and surveys have repeatedly shown that wealthy candidates have a much higher chance of being successful.

Here, we can see how aspects of the economy with which we are familiar from reading the daily papers impact the parameters outlined above. Public debt has historically been and is today an instrument that enhances the influence of private wealth; it is most often financed by private savings and this of course takes the total capital stock to higher levels. Further, the return on it has traditionally been higher than the rate of growth, thus acting as a force for divergence. So high levels of public debt, the determination of which is, of course, in the hands of those with influence and financial power, serves the interests of those who lend to the government. The alternative means of financing government expenditure is to increase direct taxation, which will impact, especially in a developing economy where the tax base is low, mainly the wealthy, hence lead to greater egalitarianism, but clearly this is not being done. Indeed, as the above figures show, the very opposite is being done.

Another familiar aspect is the flow of capital, especially from the developed to the developing countries. We have been made aware since the writings of Ivan Ilich and Susan George that this flow impoverished the poor countries, which ended up transferring real resources to the wealthy, which were supposed to be aiding them. Capital mobility from the developed to the developing does not promote convergence between them, since the wealthy end up owning a substantial share of the capital of the latter, leading to a net transfer of income from them to the developed. All major developed countries enjoy a level of national income that is somewhat greater than what they actually produce, the difference being accounted for by the fact that their investments in the developing countries yield net income. Per contra, the balance of payments data compiled by the United Nations, the World Bank and the International Monetary Fund show that the income of, for example, African countries is 5 per cent or, in the case of some countries, even 10 per cent less than their output, meaning that is the amount transferred to the developed. In South Asia, the figure is usually around two to 3 per cent but that is also high, for this kind of movement of capital has increased inequality between the rich and poor countries, in this case between the rich of the developed world and the poor of the developing world. Where there is round-tripping, the rich of a developing country shifting their resources abroad and then investing in their own country to take advantages of the offers made by their government to foreign investors, this also leads to even greater inequality within the country. The record shows that countries that developed fast, financed their own investment in physical capital and, even more so, in human capital, and research shows that this is what holds the key to development.

Here is the clue to the general encouragement of foreign investment by South Asian countries; it goes to create more inequalities rather than be a genuine contributor to development that helps the poor and therefore promotes good governance.

CONCLUSION

There are a number of remedies for what is admittedly the state of poor governance in South Asia, among others the need for political stability, administrative efficiency for timely delivery at the areas of the socio-political spectrum where governance impacts particularly the poor as well as an active civil society which acts as a watch dog while also taking a positive role in activating the receipt of the end products; other groups, business corporation through the corporate social responsibility programmes, lawyers, academics, journalists through objective reporting, all have an important role to play.

However, without the kind of resources that only government can provide, good governance can achieve very few objectives.

In essence this will mean a re-ordering of the priorities governing the politico-economic system which is currently in place in each of the countries of our region. What is being suggested is not a revolution but a great deal of advocacy and even pressure by civil society groups, eminent individuals and the seeking of allies among those with political and/or economic power. For the wealthy will have to yield a great deal more of their income and resources to government in the form of taxes than they have so far. Together with this, of course, is the need for streamlining government procedures and programmes so that the benefits that are supposed to go to the poorest actually do find their way there. A great deal has been done already through local empowerment, raising consciousness among the poorest about what they are entitled to receive. But more is needed.

NOTES

1. Cited in Harry Blair, 'Rural Development and Governance: Can Democracy Rescue a Stalled Enterprise', in Ahmed Shafiqul Huque and Habib Zafarullah, *Handbook of International Development Governance*, New York: Taylor and Francis, 2016, Chapter 45.

2. V.A. Pai Panandikar, 'Democratic Challenges to Governance, in V.A. Pai Panandikar (ed.), *Problems of Governance in South Asia*, New Delhi: Konark Publishers, 2000, p. 27.
3. PM@narendramodi-PMO India@PMOIndia, 25 December 2014.
4. The World Bank, *World Development Indicators, 2014*, Chapter 4, Economy Table 4.12, 'Central Government Finances', gives the percentages in terms of GDP that are collected by various countries as revenue.
5. *Ibid.*
6. Nisha Agrawal, CEO, Oxfam India, on 4 October 2016, writing on 'Inequality in India: What's the Real Story?'. See https://www.weforum.org/agenda/2016/10/inequality-in-india-oxfam-explainer/
7. Press Trust of India, London, 24/11/2016, citing *Global Wealth Report, 2016*, compiled by the Credit Suisse Research Institute, Credit Suisse, Zurich, Switzerland. The share of the richest one per cent in 2016 was 58.4 per cent, showing the way the gap between rich and poor is increasing very rapidly.

CHAPTER 3

Governance in Contemporary South Asia

Regional and Global Dimensions

Prithvi Ram Mudiam

INTRODUCTION

The concept of governance has been generally associated with the rise of the modern nation state and its subsequent universalization in the international system over the last four centuries. Historically, while the idea of governance benefited from the direction and supervision of a centralized and cohesive modern state, it was also tied down by its angularities and limitations. However, the collapse of the USSR and the subsequent end of the Cold War, which accelerated the processes of globalization, particularly in the economic sphere, has eroded the authority and role of the state in the contemporary world. This, in turn, has resulted in the emergence of non-state and non-territorial forces like market, civil society and multilateralism creating a new context for revisiting and redefining the idea of governance. This is particularly relevant and important for South Asia as a region, given its history of colonial rule and social and linguistic diversity.

The idea of governance has been traditionally co-terminus with institutions, processes and practices at the national level, particularly with the emergence of the modern Westphalian state in the middle of the seventeenth century in Western Europe with territoriality and sovereignty as its defining features. This process of centralization of state authority was the outcome of social cohesion based on common religion, language, ruler and definite territory and fierce economic and military competition among states of Western Europe which, in turn, transformed them into powerful and aggressive states.

The Westphalian state of Western Europe spread its political footprint to almost all corners of the globe through imperialism and colonialism, resulting in the rise of 'colonial state' in Africa and Asia with all its weaknesses and vulnerabilities. The most consequential feature of colonial state was territorial demarcation and 'such an exclusive emphasis upon geographical boundaries was bound to contain an element of artificiality'. Since 'the lines of demarcation were, as often as not, drawn right across pre-existing ethnic and cultural groupings' the colonies so created 'had to rely almost exclusively upon the legitimacy of territory, and invest their boundaries with an almost sacred character. . . .'[1] This is particularly true of South Asia which is one of the most naturally delineated regions in the world but divided arbitrarily by the British colonial rulers with all the attendant complications.

Further, colonial rule resulted in

> the creation of colonial administrative units by the imperial powers in near-total disregard for the populations' precolonial affinities and loyalties. Political boundaries drawn for purposes of administrative convenience or as a result of territorial trade-offs among imperial powers arbitrarily cut across ethnic, tribal, religious, and linguistic ties; dismembered established political units; and linked more than one precolonial political entity in uneasy administrative unions.[2]

Consequently, fixation with territorial boundaries and the fact that these boundaries cut through natural geographical features, religious, ethnic and linguistic groups created a deep sense of vulnerability and insecurity among post-colonial states in the Third World and made any cross-border cooperation in their eyes potentially destabilizing and detrimental to their efforts towards national consolidation and state-building. The political, economic and security implications of bifurcation of pre-Independent India's two largest and most populous provinces, namely Punjab and Bengal, to create a separate state for Indian Muslims, for India-Pakistan relations hardly needs any elaboration.

After decolonization, the Third World states as a collective, which constituted the largest group of states in the international system, started putting a premium on their sovereignty and territoriality as the only way to safeguard their autonomy vis-à-vis the more established, powerful and meddlesome Western states. They were in no mood to dilute their hard won sovereignty by accepting the ideological lead of some other country in favour of communism or capitalism or allow the violation of their territory by offering military bases to an external power as a subordinate partner. As a corollary, these countries also decided to largely protect their national economies from the world economy by following insular economic policies and by focusing on the domestic market and minimizing their interactions with the world economy dominated by the West. This has further hardened and deepened the state system across the globe.

The Cold War tensions and rivalries after the end of the Second World War, though they did lead to the creation of some transnational organizations in the military sphere like the North Atlantic Treaty Organization (NATO) and the Warsaw Pact in the military sphere and the European Economic Community (EEC) and the Comintern in the economic sphere in Europe, they largely reinforced the state system in many ways.

In other words, till 1991, international relations, whether in politics, economics or security, remained largely state-centric. This, in turn, has made interactions, initiatives and cooperation across state-boundaries rather difficult, sporadic and often superficial, particularly in the Third World. However, the collapse of the USSR and the end of the Cold War and the momentum they imparted to the processes of globalization, particularly in the economic sphere, completely transformed this global picture. This, consequently, has had four significant and far-reaching consequences for the world order. They are as follows:

First, the ideological divide between capitalism and socialism simply dissolved. In the neo-liberal upsurge that followed, the capitalist market-oriented economic model became almost universal. At the national level, the strategy of integrating the national economy with the world economy and export-led growth has more or less become the norm. Consequently, the role of the state in the running of the economy has become substantially downgraded.

Second, the threat of war, particularly the threat of nuclear war, has significantly reduced. Moreover, the rise of non-conventional threats like terrorism and environmental degradation questioned state's monopoly over security issues and its competence and commitment in dealing with them.

Third, the democratic wave that swept the post-Cold War world saw the emergence of democratic regimes across Eastern Europe, Asia, Africa and South America which were hitherto largely governed by right-wing, left-wing or military dictatorships. The upsurge in democratic spirit and popular institutions created the political environment conducive for an active citizenship and civil society initiatives within and across national boundaries.

Fourth, given the increasing globalization of national economies and the rise of non-conventional threats, most of which have been transnational in nature, there has been a general shift of emphasis in international diplomacy from bilateralism to multilateralism. That is because even 'By the middle of the twentieth century, the international arena had become too big and too complex for traditional bilateral diplomacy, unleashing the unprecedented drive of the past fifty years to build international and regional organizations … and gradually shifting the emphasis in diplomatic method from traditional bilateralism to multilateralism.'[3] The onset of globalization gave a further fillip to this process.

In other words, globalization has unleashed global, transnational and sub-national forces which are above, beyond and below the nation states necessitating the emergence of supranational, transnational and sub-national institutions and mechanisms to deal with them. The state, therefore, is no longer the sole actor or arbiter in international relations. It has been forced to cede space to non-state and non-territorial forces like market and civil society and focus more on multilateralism rather than bilateralism as its preferred mode of diplomacy.

Moreover, even if institutionalization has not been able to keep pace with politico-economic changes at global and regional levels, what is increasingly being witnessed at these levels is 'governance without government'. As Anthony Giddens succinctly puts it, "Government" hence becomes less identified with the government – national government – and more wide-ranging. "Governance" becomes a more relevant concept to refer to some forms of administrative or regulatory capacities. Agencies which either are not part of any government-non-governmental organizations – or are transnational in character contribute to governance.'[4] In other words, 'Globalizing processes have transferred powers away from nations and into depoliticized global space'.[5] And this complex and fascinating process is largely taking place through the agencies of market, civil society and multilateralism. States have been trying to adapt themselves to this new reality in world politics partly as a result of realizing their own limitations in coping with a globalizing world and partly in expectation of some benefits for themselves in economic and security terms.

Changes at the Global Level

At the global level, there is a broad ideological homogeneity because of the acceptance of the neo-liberal ideology by most states. As a result, there is similarity in the economic ideas and strategies of states across the board. Common membership of multilateral organizations like the World Trade Organization makes the states adhere to the same economic rules and regulations. The multinational corporations are the most important agents of economic globalization and the terms for attracting them are similar to all states. Consequently, the best practices can also be borrowed from anywhere in the world.

The two important international consequences of these developments at the global level have been a general shift of emphasis from geopolitics to geo-economics and the rise of 'new regionalism' in the 1990s.

GEO-ECONOMICS

It is quite clear that there has been a global shift of emphasis from geopolitics to geo-economics after the end of the Cold War. The two concepts, of course, cannot be and need not be seen as separate and independent categories. They are, in fact, two sides of the same coin. However, the issue here is one of emphasis. In the post-Cold War milieu, there is a general de-emphasis and decline in the use of military force. As a consequence, geography is being increasingly perceived as a basis for economic gain and commercial advantage rather than military gain or strategic advantage.

As Edward N. Luttwak observes, 'methods of commerce are displacing military methods'. According to him, capital is replacing firepower, market penetration is seen as more important than bases and garrisons and civilian innovation is preferred over military technical advancement.[6] This is so because while war is a zero-sum game, commercial relations are not.[7] In other words, economic ties tend to create a win-win situation for all participant states. It is argued that in the contemporary world of accelerating economic globalization and interdependence, it is possible and profitable to build geo-economic bridges across countries, regions and continents and geo-economic blocs are increasingly perceived as building blocks of the future world order.

Now let us turn our attention to the second consequence of changes at the global level namely the emergence of 'new regionalism'.

NEW REGIONALISM

The changes at global level have given a new salience and thrust to regionalization in the post-Cold War world and it has been christened 'new regionalism'. According to Norman D. Palmer,

> the new regionalism was a more truly worldwide phenomenon. It had more linkages with both nationalism and transnationalism, and it developed in more of the world's regions than any previously organized forms of cooperation. Moreover, this new regionalism was more outward than inward-turning and its external links seemed to strengthen it, rather than undermine its regional effectiveness.[8]

The processes of globalization, particularly in the economic realm, which picked up momentum in the post-Cold War context, imparted a new momentum and urgency to economic regionalism.

> As countries have turned toward global markets, a paradoxical consequence has been the development of pressures toward increased regional integration. Increased global competition has led multinational firms to develop regional strategies to compete globally. To be internationally competitive, firms must have access to key inputs at the lowest prices. This leads to sourc-

ing from nearby trading partners whose comparative advantage lies in such inputs. Similarly, firms seek to enjoy scale economies by selling to large regional trading partners.[9]

The 'new regionalism' that emerged in the post-Cold War world in the early 1990s has been very different from the 'old regionalism' of the 1950s and the 1960s. While the old regionalism was restricted to Western Europe and Southeast Asia, the new regionalism almost encompassed the whole world. The former followed the strategy of import substitution and withdrawal from the world economy, export-oriented growth and integrating with the world economy characterized the latter. Old regionalism followed planned and political allocation of resources whereas new regionalism involved market allocation of resources. Old regionalism dealt with just border barriers, new regionalism aimed at deeper integration. Further, old regionalism was largely confined to industrial products, new regionalism encompassed all goods and services as well as investments. Most importantly, old regionalism was initiated by governments but new regionalism has been driven by private firms.[10]

It is against this background of increasing geo-economic linkages across the globe and the rise of new regionalism driven by market forces, which has more or less become a universal phenomenon in the post-Cold War world, that we need to address the issue of governance in South Asia and the possibility and potential of market, civil society and multilateralism in contributing to it.

Changes at the Regional Level: South Asia Role of Market

The advantages of operation of market in South Asia as a region are innumerable. Markets will treat South Asia as a natural geographic unit which will ensure the optimum utilization of water resources and facilitate geo-economic linkages across the region and beyond. Economic activities are a non-zero-sum game and will benefit all participants. Evolution of regionalism in South Asia is necessary to deal successfully and effectively with similar trends elsewhere. Economic Confidence Building Measures are easier to implement and quick to yield results. Markets enable economies of scale, permit structural integration and common regional currency, facilitate commercial exchanges and save foreign exchange.

Markets can be successful even in the absence of adequate institutionalization and even if there is no general improvement in governance. This is because markets can operate in a piece-meal fashion in the form of Special Economic Zones (SEZ) and generate spill-over effects which could help the overall economy over a period of time. SEZ refers to 'designated areas in countries with special economic regulations that differ from other areas in the same country'. SEZs are zones intended to facilitate rapid economic growth by leveraging tax incentives to attract foreign investment and technological advancement. Many mainstream economists believe that China's SEZs helped liberalize the once traditional Chinese state and it was able to use the SEZs as a way to slowly implement national reform that would have been otherwise impossible.[11]

Thus, markets can overcome the limitations of the Westphalian state and circumvent its rigidities in terms of sovereignty and territoriality to its economic advantage without endangering the state itself. Internationally, this can lead to a more liberal and economy-oriented foreign policy facilitating more dense and durable commercial transactions across state boundaries, both regionally and globally.

Most importantly, the unchaining of market forces in South Asia can create economic constituencies in the states of the region which could act as catalysts for further regional economic cooperation and integration. According to one analyst,

> Recent programmes of liberalization and economic reform in India and Pakistan have led to the emergence of a growing class of young professionals, private entrepreneurs, business consultants and technical experts in both countries. The burgeoning class of energetic and forward-looking business professionals in India and Pakistan needs to be recruited into the confidence-building process. The enormous potential of this constituency for influencing public opinion and political leaders, as well as for mobilizing business resources, still remains to be tapped.[12]

Civil Society

The democratic wave that swept across the world in the post-Cold War world did not leave South Asia untouched. For the first time in its post-colonial history, South Asia can boast of democratic governments in all the states in the region. While democracy is not yet deep-rooted and irreversible in the region, the direction of change towards popular rule and institutions is unmistakable.

In broader terms, democratic governments are representative of the people and are more likely to be sensitive and responsive to their aspirations. Hence they are likely to get their priorities right. Elected governments also tend to follow foreign policies which are relatively more restrained and responsible because they are accountable to the people. Most importantly, democratic institutions tend to foster civil society organizations which can develop into a regional supranational force facilitating people-to-people contacts and eventually forging a sense of regional identity. It is, therefore, fair to say that

> A flourishing civil society typically depends on the security and predictability provided by an effective democratic state that is controlled by a government that ensures the rule of law and policies that respond to the needs of the population. . . . Thus, civil society and democratic states are highly complementary and even interdependent. Furthermore, civil society groups can help to monitor and constrain the arbitrary exercise of state power and increasingly, the behaviour of private businesses and even multinational corporations. Therefore, civil society enables different groupings in society to debate differences; to reach compromise; to form priorities and to develop consensus on a higher common purpose.[13]

The existence and operation of civil society in South Asia is of particular political and economic significance for issues of governance.

Since civil society is transnational in nature, it does not threaten the existing political boundaries in the region. This is of importance for the states in South Asia in order to protect their national identity and cohesiveness. As civil society represents soft power, the enormous asymmetry in power capabilities of states in South Asia becomes less of an issue for regional governance.

Contemporary civil society can also play a role in the economic development and security of states in South Asia. In economic terms, the role that the Indian diaspora, located particularly in North America, West Asia and Southeast Asia, has been playing in India's economic development since Indian economy was liberalized in the early 1990s has been significant. It is interesting to note that institutionalization regarding the economic utilization of Indian diaspora for achieving India's developmental goals in the form of establishing Ministry of Overseas Indians and Pravasi Bharatiya Diwas followed the realization by the Indian government of the crucial importance of the remittances to Indian economy by the Indian diaspora rather than being their cause.

In security terms, in recent times, the people of Indian origin in the United States lobbied successfully against the sale of American F16 fighters to Pakistan.[14]

There can hardly be any doubt that market, civil society and multilateralism are no substitutes for states and in fact they depend on states for their own existence and effective functioning. Nevertheless, they can help to get over and circumvent the weaknesses and limitations of a state-centric approach particularly in South Asia without undermining the state system for the larger good of the region.

States in South Asia are likely to support these forces because for most of them economy has been their top priority given that the largest number of poor people in the world live in this region. The broadening and deepening of the idea of security and the contemporary focus on 'human' rather than 'state' security have made these states alert to non-conventional security threats. They naturally perceive market and civil society as more appropriate diplomatic tools in the changed post-Cold War milieu. These states have also learned through experience that multilateralism is more effective than bilateralism in dealing with most issues in the contemporary world, particularly the ones related to the economy.

It is in this context that India's major regional economic initiative in the 1990s known as the 'Gujral doctrine' needs to be appreciated. I.K. Gujral, the then Foreign Minister of India, introduced an important element, namely, 'non-reciprocity' into India's dealings with the South Asian region in 1997. The objective of the exercise was to improve the political climate in South Asia and move the region towards greater economic cooperation. The principle of non-reciprocity meant that with neighbours like Sri Lanka, Bangladesh, Bhutan, Maldives and Nepal, India 'does not ask for reciprocity but gives all that it can in good faith and trust'. The reasoning behind this was that given the asymmetry that existed between India and most of its neighbours, India ought to make concessions wherever it could. As Gujral himself explained, 'India is the biggest country in the region. Demanding reciprocity with countries like Bhutan or Maldives is an unfortunate way of looking at things.' The move also reflected India's desire to de-emphasize the power asymmetry that existed among states in the region by imparting a more positive context and content to its ties with its smaller neighbours.[15]

CONCLUSION

Generally speaking, at international level, institution-building has always been problematic because of the implications carried by concepts like sovereignty and territoriality. At the regional level in South Asia, institution-building has been even more difficult because of the asymmetry in the power capabilities between India and other states in South Asia, the deep and perennial nature of India-Pakistan bilateral disputes and India's testy and frictional relations with other smaller states of the region.

One way of dealing with these complex set of problems is to envisage South Asian Association for Regional Cooperation (SAARC) without Pakistan. Alternatively, the mode of decision-making in SAARC can be changed to the principle of majority rather than one of unanimity with dissenting states free to opt out of a particular course of action. Greater focus on and impetus to Bangladesh, India, Myanmar, Sri Lanka Technical and Economic Cooperation can largely take Pakistan factor out of India's regional aspirations and initiatives and add substance to India's Act-East policy. Free Trade Agreements (FTA) between individual countries is another option that needs to be pursued more vigorously.

Be that as it may, similar ideology, i.e. neo-liberalism and greater economic cooperation and interdependence at national, regional and global levels provide a broad and effective framework for market, civil society and multilateralism to operate and contribute to good governance at all the three levels. Therefore, good governance need not and cannot be confined to national boundaries nor can the states be seen as the sole providers of good governance anymore.

In other words, governance has grown beyond national boundaries and states have been compelled to work towards creating regional and global mechanisms favourable for the achievement of their national goals on the one hand, and reform the national order to suit the requirements of the regional and global orders, on the other.

Therefore, focusing on governance at the national level is no longer feasible or adequate for the states of South Asia to achieve their national goals. It is imperative that they extend their attention and energies to governance at regional and global levels as well even in the absence of adequate institutionalization. In trying to do so, it is necessary for them to explore the potentialities and possibilities of non-state and non-territorial forces like market, civil society and multilateralism for improving governance at global and regional levels which, in turn, would help them improve governance at national level as well. This is a critical and inescapable requirement for states in South Asia to achieve their crucial goals of national economic development and national security in the post-Cold War strategic and economic milieu.

NOTES

1. Anthony D. Smith, *State and Nation in the Third World: The Western State and African Nationalism*, Brighton, Sussex: Wheatsheaf Books, 1983, p. 27.
2. Mohammed Ayoob, *The Third World Security Predicament: State Making, Regional Conflict, and the International System*, Boulder, Colorado: Lynne Rienner Publishers, 1995, p. 34.
3. James P. Muldoon, Jr., 'Introduction', in James P. Muldoon Jr., JoAnn Fagot Aviel, Richard Reitano and Earl (Tim) Sullivan (eds), *Multilateral Diplomacy*, Cambridge, MA: Westview Press, 2005, p. 5.
4. Anthony Giddens, *The Third Way: The Renewal of Social Democracy*, Cambridge: Polity Press, 1998, p. 33.
5. *Ibid.*, p. 141.
6. Edward N. Luttwak, 'From Geopolitics to Geo-Economics: Logic of Conflict, Grammar of Commerce', *The National Interest*, vol. 20, 1990, p. 17.
7. *Ibid.*, p. 23.

8. Norman D. Palmer, *The New Regionalism in Asia and the Pacific*, Lexington, Mass: Lexington Books, 1991, p. 2.
9. Robert Z. Lawrence, 'Regionalism, Multilateralism, and Deeper Integration: Changing Paradigms for Developing Countries', in C. Roe Goddard, Patrick Cronin and Kishore C. Dash (eds), *International Political Economy: State-Market Relations in a Changing Global Order*, New Delhi: Viva Books, 2005, p. 396.
10. *Ibid.*, p. 398.
11. See http://www.investtopedia.com/terms/s/sez.asp.
12. Poonam Barua, 'Economic CBMs between India and Pakistan', in Michael Krepon and Amit Sevak (eds), *A Crisis Prevention, Confidence Building, and Reconciliation in South Asia*, London: Macmillan, 1995, p. 155.
13. Catherine Barnes, 'Weaving the Web: Civil-Society Roles in Working with Conflict and Building Peace', in Paul van Tongeren, Malin Brenk, Marte Hellema and Juliette Verhoeven (eds.), *People Building Peace II: Successful Stories of Civil Society*, New Delhi: Viva Books, 2007, pp. 7-9.
14. See epaper.brecorder.com/m/2016/11/16/20-page/613777-news.html.
15. Prithvi Ram Mudiam, 'The Democratic Developmental State: The Indian Experience', in Daniel A. Omoweh (ed.), *The Feasibility of the Democratic Developmental State in the South*, Dakar: Council for the Development of Social Science Research in Africa (CODESRIA), 2012, pp. 98-9.

CHAPTER 4

Role of Good Governance on Growth of Per Capita Income in South Asia

A Debate on Means and Ends

Ramesh Chandra Das

INTRODUCTION

Governance has twin roles in economic systems. The first is the positive role where it guides administrators in an organized manner to shift the administrative practices from the bureaucratic state to third party government. Governance is redefined as a combination of lateral and inter-institutional relations in administration in a phase where the economies are going to minimize the territorial differences in view to prosper more in a competitive world.[1] Governance is self-organizing inter-organizational networks where different economic agents of different institutions are interdependent, one's decision is contingent upon the others and the question of economic sovereignty vanishes.[2] The second is the normative role where it is assumed that good governance can be a precondition to economic growth and development. This particular concept of good governance has been propounded by the World Bank in 1992 under the backdrop of its failure to revive the African economies despite plenty of foreign assistance. According to the World Bank, economic development in Africa cannot be sustained because of deficiency in good governance in this area.

There have always been debates between two groups of policy makers all over the world on the issue of whether good governance is the means or ends in determining the growth and development of countries. One group dominated by the Western thinkers and associates of World Bank opines that good governance is a necessary precondition to growth and development of countries, particularly from the Asian and African continents. On the basis of this plea, the developed countries led by US have started investing, rather intervening into the internal managements of the African countries to ensure good governance and hence the growth of incomes of these countries. Another group, led by the countries from the developing countries, has opined that good governance should not be the means of growth and development; rather it should be the end of development. In other words, they meant that growth and development will push up the levels of governance in developing countries. Although the concept of governance is a normative term and the growth of income is a positive term, it is very difficult to link of the positive factors with the normative factors. Hence, the linkage between governance and growth is like an impracticable attempt. To make the normative factors of governance into quantitative nature, the World Bank has put hard effort to survey across the countries through a number of agencies worldwide and imposed values upon different governance indicators.

The World Bank concept of good governance has three broad categories.[3] Category 1 captures the process by which a country's governments are selected, monitored and replaced by the power of citizens. It has two sub-categories: (1) Voice and Accountability (VA) that tries to capture the perceptions of the extent to which a country's citizens are able to participate in selecting their governments as well as freedom of expression, freedom of association and a free media. (2) Political Stability and Absence of Violence (PSAV) that tries to capture the perceptions of the likelihood that the ruling government will be destabilized or overthrown by violent means including politically motivated violence and terrorism. Category 2 captures the ability of the government to formulate and implement effective policies that covers two more sub-categories – (3) Government Effectiveness (GE) that reflects the perceptions of the quality of public services, the quality of the civil services in implementing policies with the degree of independence from political pressures and the credibility and commitment of the government towards such policies. (4) Regulatory Quality (RQ) that reflects the perceptions of the ability of the government to formulate policies and regulations that permit and promote private sector and implement sound development. Category 3 captures the respect of citizens and the state for the institutions that govern economic and social interactions among them that has two sub-categories – (5) Rule of Law (RL) that reflects perceptions of the extent to which economic and social agents have confidence in and abide by the rules of the society, and in particular the quality of contract enforcement, property rights, the police, and the courts, as well as the likelihood of crime and violence and (6) Control of Corruption (CC) that reflects the perceptions of the extent to which public power is exercised for private gains (that is the rent seeking activities) including small and large volumes of corruption as well as gripping of the state by the few elites for private interests. These six broad categories of good governance are quantitatively measured by the tool of unobserved components that are scaled from -2.5 (worst governance) to +2.5 (superior governance) which are distributed around a mean zero. The zero value of the indicators can be treated as the world average value of the governance indicators. One report claims that the countries can derive a very large dividend in their development fronts if they possess good governance.[4] The report points out the estimate that a country that improves its governance from a relatively low level to an average level could almost triple the income per capita in the long run and similarly reduce infant mortality and illiteracy.

The present chapter aims to examine the role of good governance on growth of per capita income in South Asia under the debate on whether good governance is the means or end in determining growth of the countries. If any indicator of governance influences the growth rate of any economy, then we say that governance is a means to growth and if the reverse happens then we can say it is an end.

The chapter has been organized in the following sections: survey of the existing literatures on the related topic, data and methodology, graphical and empirical results and followed by concluding observations and policy prescriptions.

SURVEY OF RELATED LITERATURE

Before examining the link between growth and governance in South Asian countries, we shall try to highlight the relation between growth and governance of the world economies that is accessible from the existing literature. One such study is of Hussain[5] which tried to indicate that not only is the incidence of absolute poverty higher than in any other region of the world but the number of people deprived of basic services such as safe drinking water, health and sanitation is even greater than those in poverty. At the same time, the analysis proposes that the nature of governance currently being practised in South Asia precludes certain resource allocation and economic policy initiatives. Another study by Kaufmann et al.[6] showed the interrelationship between growth and governance in terms of rule of law indicator for 175 countries. The study observed that governance and per capita incomes of the countries are positively and strongly correlated. Also they found a positive causal link from governance to growth of per capita incomes but find a negative causal link from growth of per capita income to governance. A critical study by Chang[7] claims on the basis of historical evidence that the newly-industrialized countries have experienced higher growth rates despite bad quality of governance and also that improvements in growth of per capita incomes lead to improvements in governance. Criticizing Kauffman's findings of a positive correlation between growth and governance, a study by Pritchett[8] argues that the estimates of such a positive relation are biased in the sense that they fit well for the developed countries where the bilateral causalities could also happen. Another criticism is that the positive correlation works for the developed countries that operate under already established good governance systems.[9] On the other hand, Dixit[10] showed that the growth governance relation for the developing country is kink shaped in the sense that at low levels of governance the country can have positive and rising growth rates but after a certain level of growth was attained then governance had to be improved to manage the rising growth profile. After the kink point, the positive relation between the two could appear. The important lesson from the fast growing countries like China and India that even with poor degrees of governance these two countries have maintained a sizeable growth rates in their territories.[11] The reason for such high growth rates is that China and India were able to leverage policy reforms into sustained fast growth because of their large markets and abundance of low cost labour. Khan studied the existence of association between growth and governance in China, India and Bangladesh. According to the study, China, having a below average level of governance indicators during the last two decades performed very well in the growth front. Only government's effectiveness has improved that may not cause growth rate to rise to such a level. At the same time, India with more or less parity in governance indicators with China maintained a rising trend of growth rates. The same, although the growth rate is low but rising, observations were made for Bangladesh as well. In the recent past, Das[12] tested whether good governance is a necessary prerequisite for growth and development of 44 countries in the world. The chapter observed that inverse signs of causations worked for the developing countries and direct or positive signs of causations happened in case of most of the developed countries.

DATA AND METHODOLOGY

The empirical findings have been derived by using the World Bank data on worldwide governance indicators and the growth rates of per capita incomes of the eight South Asian countries for the period 1996-2015. Since the data on per capita growth rates as well as aggregate income of Afghanistan is not available from the same source, we have analysed for the said country for the period 2002-15.

Primarily we have donegraphical and basic statistical analyses like correlation, ranking of the countries and then carried out appropriate econometric analyses like the stationarity test in line with Augmented Dickey-Fuller technique.

Primarily we have used the graphical presentation of the data on growth and governance indicators and basic statistical analyses like correlation, ranking of the countries to view the overall scenario of the growth and governances of all the countries. We have classified the countries by means of growth and governance. Since the data set is of 20 years length, they may suffer from non-stationary or unit root problem and as we know the regression analysis upon the non-stationary variables always give spurious results.[13] Hence, primarily we have tested for stationarity of the given growth and governance indictors' series by means of Augmented Dickey-Fuller[14] test. The equation for the same is as follows:

$$\Delta y_t = \alpha + \beta y_{t-1} + \sum_{j=1}^{p} \gamma j \Delta y_{t-j} + u_t \ldots\ldots\ldots\ldots(1)$$

After that we ran the Granger[15] causality test for the countries using EVIEWS for all six indicators of governance separately for a lag up to 3. Suppose *X* be the growth variable for the set of countries *j* = 1, 2, …., 8 for the time period lag *t-j*, *j* = 1, 2, …., 20 (1996 to 2015) and *Y* be the governance indicator, then Granger causality tests are done by estimating the following two regression equations:

$$y_t = \sum_{j=1}^{n} \alpha_{1j}.y_{t-j} + \sum_{j=1}^{n} \beta_{1j}.x_{t-j} + u_{1t} \ldots\ldots\ldots\ldots(2)$$

$$x_t = \sum_{j=1}^{n} \alpha_{2j}.y_{t-j} + \sum_{j=1}^{n} \beta_{2j}.x_{t-j} + u_{2t} \ldots\ldots\ldots\ldots(3)$$

The decision rules are given in the following six criteria:

(i) If $\beta_{1j} = 0$, for all *j*, *x* may be said not to *Granger cause y*. (ii) If $\alpha_{2j} = 0$ for all *j* and $\eta_{xy} = 0$, *y* may be said not to *Granger cause x*. (iii) If (i) holds but (ii) does not, *Granger causality* may be said to be *unidirectional from x to y*. (iv). Conversely, if (i) does not hold but (ii) does, *Granger causality* may be said to be *unidirectional from y to x*. (v) If both (i) and (ii) do not hold *Granger causality* between *x* and *y* may be said to be *bi-directional or it is termed as feedback causality*. (vi) If both (i) and (ii) hold, *Granger causality* between *x* and *y* may be said to be absent, or there is no causality.

EMPIRICAL RESULTS AND DISCUSSION

Before giving details of the empirical results and discussion we would like to see the trends of all the six governance indicators and growth of per capita incomes of all the countries of the South Asia. Figures 4.1 to 4.7 present the time series data on the said variables.

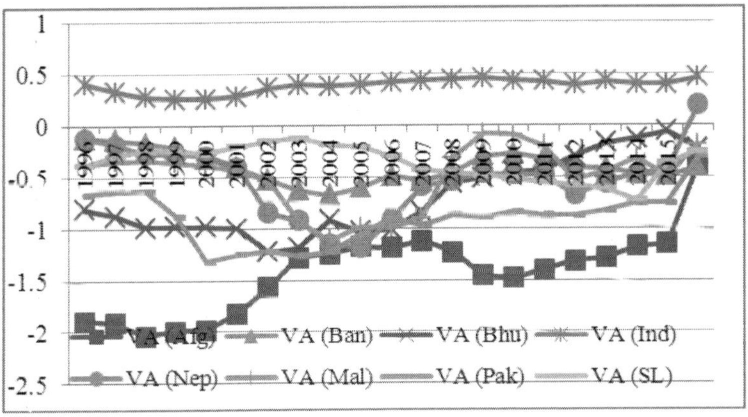

Source: The World Bank, https://data.worldbank.org/indicator/NY.GDP.MKTP.KD.ZG and https://data.worldbank.org/data-catalog/worldwide-governance-indicators

FIGURE 4.1. VOICE AND ACCOUNTABILITY ACROSS THE COUNTRIES FOR 1996-2015

We observe from Figure 4.1 that India leads the group in voice and accountability and Afghanistan is at the bottom position, although the country is improving significantly over time after the end of the Taliban regime with cooperation of countries like the US and India in its restructuring activities. Most of the countries started improving after 2006.

In respect to political stability indicator (Figure 4.2) we observe that Bhutan and Maldives dominate the region but the latter has been slipping from its intial leadership position. Afghanistan and Pakistan are at the bottom level.

Government's effectiveness (Figure 4.3) in clearing projects is still good comparatively in Bhutan, Maldives and India but the latter maintains a stable position whereas Afghanistan is still lagging.

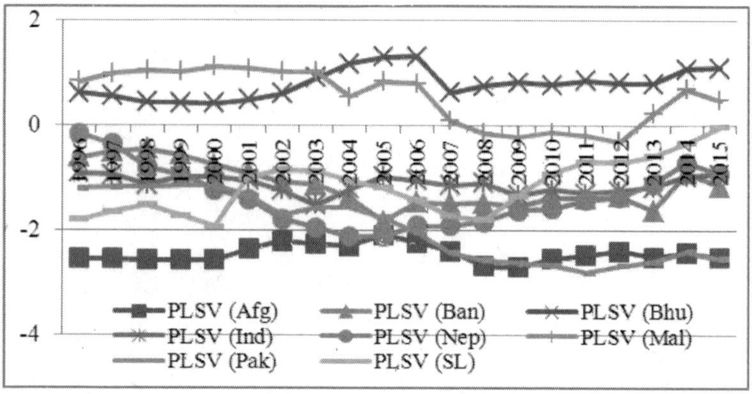

Source: The World Bank, https://data.worldbank.org/indicator/NY.GDP.MKTP.KD.ZG and https://data.worldbank.org/data-catalog/worldwide-governance-indicators

FIGURE 4.2. POLITICAL STABILITY AND ABSENCE OF VIOLENCE ACROSS THE COUNTRIES FOR 1996-2015

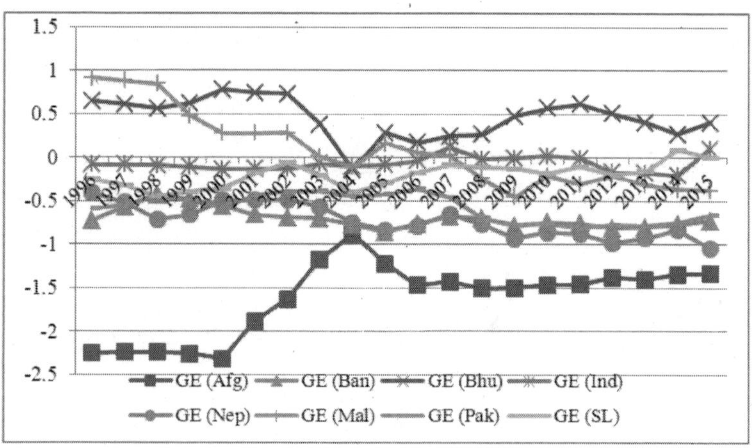

Source: The World Bank, https://data.worldbank.org/indicator/NY.GDP.MKTP.KD.ZG and https://data.worldbank.org/data-catalog/worldwide-governance-indicators

FIGURE 4.3. GOVERNMENTS EFFECTIVENESS ACROSS THE COUNTRIES FOR 1996-2015

There are steep degradations in the regulatory quality in Maldives, Sri Lanka, Bhutan, Nepal and Pakistan. Afghanistan is growing at a higher rate starting as lowest in the region. India still maintains a stable level of regulatory quality over the years (Figure 4.4).

There is a clear distinction of Bhutan, Maldives, India and Sri Lanka from Nepal, Bangladesh, Pakistan and Afghanistan in the sense that the first four maintained positive values in rule of law for their countries in most of the years and the second group has negative values for all the years (Figure 4.5).

When we talk about good governance by means of control of corruption, Bhutan surpasses all the countries in the region with an increasing trend of the estimated values of the governance factor. All the countries except Bhutan and Afghanistan maintained declining trends in the control of corruption, meaning the countries are getting more and more corrupt over time (Figure 4.6).

Now let us come to the final part of the indicators, which is the per capita growth rates of incomes of all the countries in the region. All the countries maintained around 5 to 6 per cent of growth rate

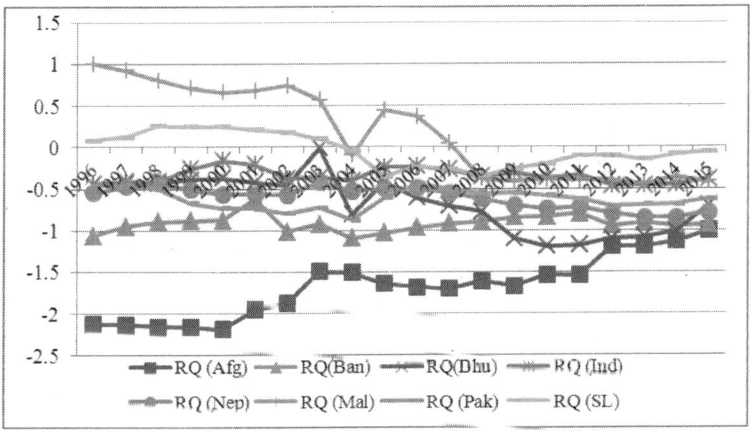

Source: The World Bank, https://data.worldbank.org/indicator/NY.GDP.MKTP.KD.ZG and https://data.worldbank.org/data-catalog/worldwide-governance-indicators

FIGURE 4.4. REGULATORY QUALITY ACROSS THE COUNTRIES FOR 1996-2015

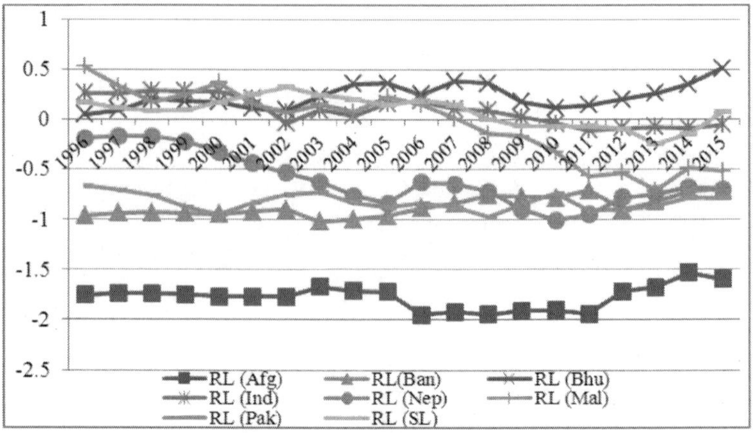

Source: The World Bank, https://data.worldbank.org/indicator/NY.GDP.MKTP.KD.ZG and https://data.worldbank.org/data-catalog/worldwide-governance-indicators

FIGURE 4.5. RULE OF LAW ACROSS THE COUNTRIES FOR 1996-2015

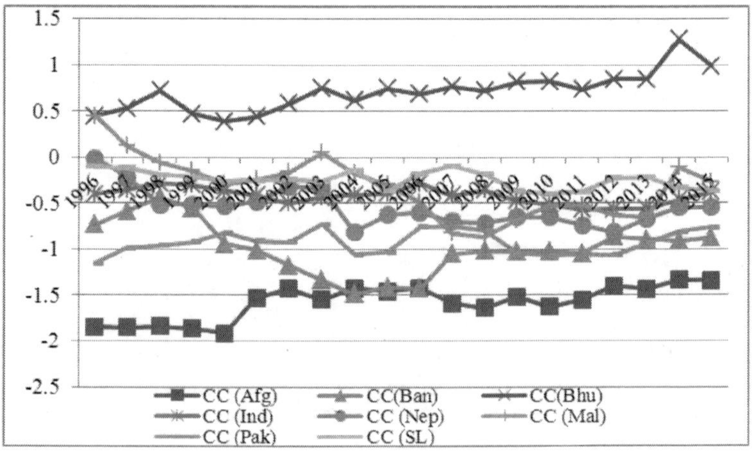

Source: The World Bank, https://data.worldbank.org/indicator/NY.GDP.MKTP.KD.ZG and https://data.worldbank.org/data-catalog/worldwide-governance-indicators

FIGURE 4.6. CONTROL OF CORRUPTION ACROSS THE COUNTRIES FOR 1996-2015

on an average across the years. No country is found to be the absolutely leader or follower in this respect (Figure 4.7).

Tables 4.1A and 4.1B present the changes of values of all governance indicators and per capita GDP growth rates of the countries for the period 1996-2015. Most of the countries in all the indicators have performed poorly over time. We point out them briefly.

- VA increased for Afghanistan, Bhutan and Sri Lanka and decreased for the remaining
- PSAV increased for Afghanistan, Bhutan and Sri Lanka and decreased for the remaining
- GE increased for Afghanistan, Bangladesh, India and Sri Lanka and decreased for the remaining
- RL increased for Afghanistan, Bangladesh and Bhutan and decreased for the remaining
- RQ increased for Afghanistan, Bangladesh and India and decreased for the remaining

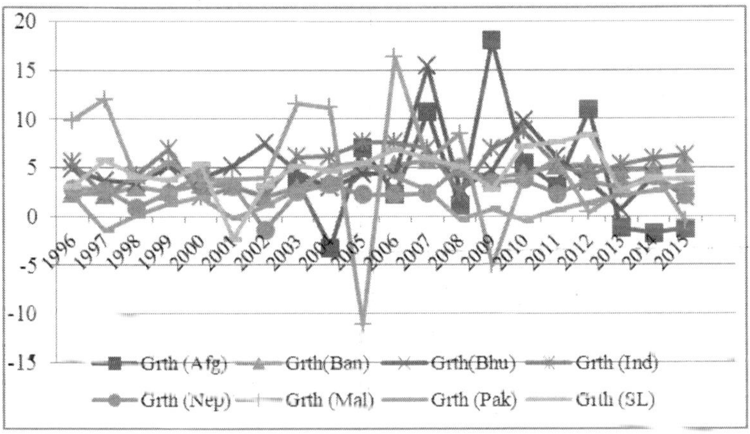

Source: The World Bank, https://data.worldbank.org/indicator/NY.GDP.MKTP.KD.ZG and https://data.worldbank.org/data-catalog/worldwide-governance-indicators

FIGURE 4.7. GROWTH RATES OF PER CAPITA INCOMES ACROSS THE COUNTRIES FOR 1996-2015

TABLE 4.1A: CHANGES IN GOVERNANCE INDICATORS FROM 1996 TO 2015 ACROSS COUNTRIES

Country	*VA*	*VA*	*Change*	*Sign*	*PSAV*	*PSAV*	*Change*	*Sign*	*GE*	*GE*	*Change*	*Sign*
	1996	*2015*			*1996*	*2015*			*1996*	*2015*		
Afg	-1.89	-1.15	0.7444	+	-2.54	-2.502	0.0372	+	-2.25	-1.336	0.9187	+
Ban	-0.12	-0.49	-0.37	-	-0.612	-1.155	-0.543	-	-0.72	-0.728	0.0012	+
Bhu	-0.81	-0.06	0.7491	+	0.6136	1.099	0.4854	+	0.64	0.406	-0.24	-
Ind	0.40	0.39	-0.014	-	-0.911	-0.921	-0.01	-	-0.08	0.101	0.1823	+
Nep	-0.12	-0.43	-0.308	-	-0.152	-0.925	-0.774	-	-0.40	-1.043	-0.635	-
Mal	-0.37	-0.5	-0.118	-	0.8356	0.478	-0.357	-	0.91	-0.382	-1.292	-
Pak	-0.66	-0.76	-0.088	-	-1.203	-2.544	-1.341	-	-0.58	-0.661	-0.074	-
SL	-0.38	-0.37	0.0143	+	-1.801	-0.03	1.7709	+	-0.25	0.009	0.2639	+

Source: The World Bank, https://data.worldbank.org/indicator/NY.GDP.MKTP.KD.ZG and https://data.worldbank.org/data-catalog/worldwide-governance-indicators

TABLE 4.1B: CHANGES IN GOVERNANCE INDICATORS FROM 1996 TO 2015 ACROSS COUNTRIES

Country	*RL*	*RL*	*Change*	*Sign*	*RQ*	*RQ*	*Change*	*Sign*	*CC*	*CC*	*Change*	*Sign*	*Grth*	*Grth*	*Change*	*Sign*
	1996	*2015*			*1996*	*2015*			*1996*	*2015*			*1996*	*2015*		
Afg	-1.76	-1.6	0.163	+	-2.13	-1.01	1.117	+	-1.85	-1.34	0.506	+	19.12	-1.3	-20.38	-
Ban	-0.36	-0.7	0.261	+	-1.06	-0.93	0.132	+	-0.73	-0.88	-0.142	-	2.311	5.28	2.971	+
Bhu	0.05	0.51	0.460	+	-0.44	-0.71	-0.264	-	0.44	0.984	0.540	+	4.84	1.95	-2.903	-
Ind	0.26	-0.1	-0.316	-	-0.44	-0.39	0.049	+	-0.4	-0.38	0.022	+	5.52	6.28	0.750	+
Nep	-0.19	-0.7	-0.512	-	-0.55	-0.79	-0.239	-	-0.01	-0.55	-0.534	-	2.86	2.13	-0.734	-
Mal	0.53	-0.5	-1.046	-	1.002	-0.42	-1.426	-	0.44	-0.27	-0.715	-	9.86	-0.5	-10.37	-
Pak	-0.67	-0.3	-0.123	-	-0.45	-0.62	-0.17	-	-1.15	-0.76	0.391	+	2.26	3.37	1.107	+
SL	0.17	0.07	-0.104	-	0.08	-0.05	-0.132	-	-0.1	-0.37	-0.269	-	3.02	3.81	0.786	+

Source: The World Bank, https://data.worldbank.org/indicator/NY.GDP.MKTP.KD.ZG and https://data.worldbank.org/data-catalog/worldwide-governance-indicators

- CC increased for Afghanistan, Bhutan, India and Pakistan and decreased for the remaining
- Growth rates increased for Bangladesh, India, Pakistan and Sri Lanka and decreased for the remaining

We have also presented the rankings of the countries in different indicators in 2015 vis-à-vis 1996. We observe from Figure 4.8 that Afghanistan remains in the last rank, i.e. 8th in the group in all indicators across two time points while Bhutan leads the list in most of the cases.

To have a brief view on the degrees of associations between growth of per capita GDP and each of the governance indicators across the countries, we have calculated the product moment correlation coefficients out of the values of the two-year points –1996 and 2015 – and rank correlation coefficients of each of the indicators across these two time points. The results are given in Table 4.2.

The extracts from the table are as follows:

- In majority of the indicators, there is insignificant degree of association between any governance indicators and growth rate of the countries.

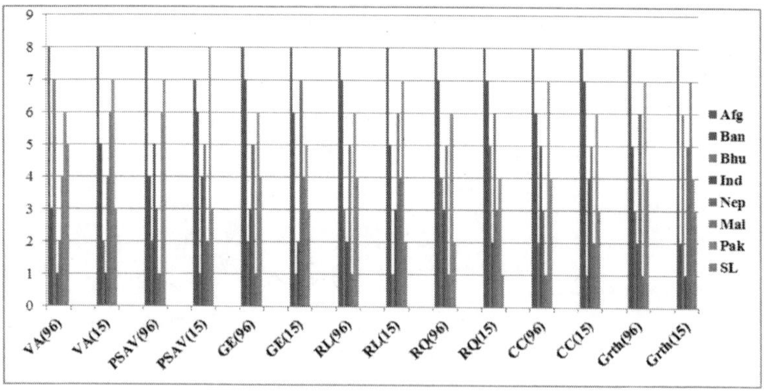

Source: The World Bank, https://data.worldbank.org/indicator/NY.GDP.MKTP.KD.ZG and https://data.worldbank.org/data-catalog/worldwide-governance-indicators

FIGURE 4.8. RANKINGS OF GOVERNANCE INDICATORS AND GROWTH RATES ACROSS THE COUNTRIES FOR 1996 VIS-À-VIS 2015

TABLE 4.2: CORRELATION COEFFICIENTS (MOMENT AND RANK) BETWEEN DIFFERENT GOVERNANCE INDICATORS AND GROWTH ACROSS THE COUNTRIES

Country	*VA*	*PSAV*	*GE*	*RL*	*RQ*	*CC*	*Grth*
Afg	**-0.57952**	0.243522	**-0.51638**	-0.13751	**-0.57226**	-0.00743	1.00
Ban	**-0.41**	**-0.72271**	**-0.5647**	**0.605402**	0.067259	**-0.3142571**	1.00
Bhu	-0.23163	-0.22444	0.075184	-0.10579	-0.05076	-0.0531	1.00
Ind	**0.460007**	-0.13106	**0.399117**	-0.20522	0.041093	-0.05001	1.00
Nep	0.189292	0.049369	-0.21707	-0.22866	-0.3163307	-0.3281928	1.00
Mal	-0.19669	0.221595	0.282546	0.280282	**0.269616**	**0.267272**	1.00
Pak	-0.30783	0.004639	**0.3384093**	-0.09906	-0.24382	0.154992	1.00
SL	-0.25787	-0.05057	-0.04238	-0.22711	**-0.3946655**	-0.05168	1.00
Rank Correlation	**0.91**	**0.93**	**0.96**	**0.95**	**0.97**	**0.98**	**0.86**

Note: Bold figures and small bold figures respectively represent significant results at 5 and 10 per cent levels. Rank correlation has been calculated for 2015 with respect to 1996.

Source: The World Bank, https://data.worldbank.org/indicator/NY.GDP.MKTP.KD.ZG and https://data.worldbank.org/data-catalog/worldwide-governance-indicators

- There are negative and significant moment correlations observed for Afghanistan (in VA, GE and RQ), Bangladesh (in VA, PSAV, GE and CC), Nepal (in RQ and CC) and Sri Lanka (in RQ).
- Positive correlations are observed for Bangladesh (in RL only), India (in VA and GE) and Pakistan (in GE only).
- The rank correlation results show very high and significant outcomes across all the governance as well as growth indicators, meaning the position of the countries mostly remain same in 1996 (2003 for Afghanistan) and 2015.

Presence of correlation among the variables does not necessarily mean the existence of causations. Hence, we need to analyse whether there are significant causations from governance to growth (i.e. good governance as means), from growth to governance (i.e. good governance as ends) and both way causations (i.e. good governance as both means and ends). To test for causality in a statistical way, we have used the Granger (1969)[16] method which is to make estimations of two regression equations (2 & 3) as mentioned in the methodology section. Before going into that we need to test whether the series of all the seven indicators (six for governance and one for GDP growth rate) are stationary. We have tested the coefficient by means of eq. (1) in the methodology section in line with ADF test technique. The results of stationarity or unit roots tests are given in Table 4.3.

We observe from Table 4.3 that almost all the indicators are non-stationary (or suffer from unit root problems) at their level values but are stationary (or free from unit root problems) at first or second differences of the series. Since estimation of an equation with at least two variables under the non-stationary natures produces spurious results in the sense of very low value of R^2 or a very low value of Durbin-Watson statistics, meaning the presence of autocorrelation among the error terms, we ran the pair-wise Granger causality test for both the variables in first difference or second difference at a time. The results are given in Tables 4.4A, 4.4B and 4.5.

The key results on directions of causality are given below:

- Governance is a cause of growth in Afghanistan and India for VA, Bangladesh for PSAV, GE, RQ and CC and for Sri Lanka in

TABLE 4.3. UNIT ROOT TEST RESULTS OF GOVERNANCE INDICATORS FOR 1996-2015

	At Levels							At First Differences						
Country	*VA*	*PSAV*	*GE*	*RL*	*RQ*	*CC*	*Grth*	*VA*	*PSAV*	*GE*	*RL*	*RQ*	*CC*	*Grth*
Afg	NS	NS	NS	NS	NS	NS	S	S*	S**	S (2nd diff)	S (2nd diff)	S (2nd diff)	S	S
Ban	NS	NS	NS	NS	NS	NS	NS	S (2nd diff)	S (2nd diff)	S	S*	S*	S**	S*
Bhu	NS	NS	NS	NS	NS	NS	S*	S*	S**	S**	S*	S*	S*	S
Ind	NS	S*	NS	NS	NS	NS	S*	S*	S	S (2nd diff)	S*	S**	S (2nd diff)	S
Nep	NS	NS	NS	NS	NS	S*	S*	S (2nd diff)	S (2nd diff)	S	S*	S*	S	S
Mal	NS	NS	NS	NS	NS	NS	S	S**	S*	S*	S*	S	S**	S
Pak	NS	NS	NS	S	NS	S*	NS	S**	S*	S*	S	S**	S	S (2nd diff)
SL	NS	NS	NS	NS	NS	S*	NS	S (2nd diff)	S*	S	S*	S	S	S

Note: * for 5 per cent and ** for 10 per cent levels of significance, the remaining at 1 per cent for the stationary cases only

Source: The World Bank. https://data.worldbank.org/indicator/NY.GDP.MKTP.KD.ZG and https://data.worldbank.org/data-catalog/worldwide-governance-indicators

TABLE 4.4A: GRANGER CAUSALITY TEST RESULTS FOR AFGHANISTAN, BANGLADESH, BHUTAN AND INDIA

Country	*Hypothesis*	*F*	*P*	*Remarks*
Afghanistan	**VA does not cause Grth**	11.82	0.006	**Yes**
	Grth does not cause VA	0.89	0.36	No
	PSAV does not cause Grth	0.089	0.77	No
	Grth does not cause PSAV	0.000	0.98	No
	GE does not cause Grth*	8.58	0.01	**Yes**
	Grth does not cause GE*	3.53	0.09	Yes
	RL does not cause Grth*	0.05	0.82	No
	Grth does not cause RL*	0.88	0.37	No
	RQ does not cause Grth*	6.77	0.02	**Yes**
	Grth does not cause RQ*	5.86	0.03	**Yes**
	CC does not cause Grth	0.54	0.47	No
	Grth does not cause CC	1.72	0.21	No
Bangladesh	VA does not cause Grth*	1.19	0.29	No
	Grth does not cause VA*	2.53	0.13	No
	PSAV does not cause Grth*	4.96	0.04	**Yes**
	Grth does not cause PSAV*	0.000	0.99	No
	GE does not cause Grth	3.26	0.09	**Yes**
	Grth does not cause GE	1.26	0.27	No
	RL does not cause Grth	0.13	0.72	No
	Grth does not cause RL	7.39	0.01	**Yes**
	RQ does not cause Grth	5.32	0.03	Yes
	Grth does not cause RQ	0.01	0.89	No
	CC does not cause Grth	4.84	0.04	**Yes**
	Grth does not cause CC	2.05	0.17	No
Bhutan	VA does not cause Grth	0.43	0.51	No
	Grth does not cause VA	3.24	0.09	**Yes**
	PSAV does not cause Grth	1.82	0.19	No
	Grth does not cause PSAV	0.04	0.83	No
	GE does not cause Grth	0.37	0.55	No
	Grth does not cause GE	0.05	0.81	No
	RL does not cause Grth	0.01	0.90	No
	Grth does not cause RL	0.02	0.89	No
	RQ does not cause Grth	0.03	0.87	No
	Grth does not cause RQ	0.02	0.88	No
	CC does not cause Grth	0.00	0.94	No
	Grth does not cause CC	1.61	0.22	No

India	**VA does not cause Grth**	3.03	0.09	**Yes**
	Grth does not cause VA	0.03	0.86	No
	PSAV does not cause Grth	3.41	0.08	**Yes**
	Grth does not cause PSAV	3.07	0.09	**Yes**
	GE does not cause Grth*	0.06	0.79	No
	Grth does not cause GE*	0.84	0.37	No
	RL does not cause Grth	2.00	0.17	No
	Grth does not cause RL	0.05	0.82	No
	RQ does not cause Grth	1.14	0.30	→
	Grth does not cause RQ	0.31	0.58	No
	CC does not cause Grth	0.01	0.9	No
	Grth does not cause CC	0.00	0.95	No

Notes: All the results are at first differences except the * marks representing it at for second differences. The number of lags in each country is 1.

Source: Computed by the author and the World Bank, https://data.worldbank.org/indicator/NY.GDP.MKTP.KD.ZG and https://data.worldbank.org/data-catalog/worldwide-governance-indicators

TABLE 4.4B: GRANGER CAUSALITY TEST RESULTS FOR NEPAL, MALDIVES, PAKISTAN AND SRI LANKA

Country	*Hypothesis*	*F*	*P*	*Remarks*
Nepal	VA does not cause Grth*	0.03	0.86	No
	Grth does not cause VA*	0.09	0.75	No
	PSAV does not cause Grth*	0.41	0.53	No
	Grth does not cause PSAV*	1.8	0.20	No
	GE does not cause Grth	2.13	0.16	No
	Grth does not cause GE	0.60	0.45	No
	RL does not cause Grth	2.13	0.16	No
	Grth does not cause RL	0.60	0.45	No
	RQ does not cause Grth	0.94	0.34	No
	Grth does not cause RQ	3.37	0.08	**Yes**
	CC does not cause Grth	1.43	0.25	No
	Grth does not cause CC	0.04	0.84	No
Maldives	VA does not cause Grth	0.45	0.51	No
	Grth does not cause VA	0.00	0.93	No
	PSAV does not cause Grth	4.27	0.05	**Yes**
	Grth does not cause PSAV	2.07	0.17	No
	GE does not cause Grth	4.02	0.06	**Yes**
	Grth does not cause GE	0.15	0.70	No

	RL does not cause Grth	3.12	0.09	**Yes**
	Grth does not cause RL	0.11	0.74	No
	RQ does not cause Grth	8.13	0.01	**Yes**
	Grth does not cause RQ	0.25	0.61	No
	CC does not cause Grth	3.73	0.07	**Yes**
	Grth does not cause CC	0.92	0.35	No
Pakistan	**VA does not cause Grth***	3.22	0.09	**Yes**
	Grth does not cause VA*	4.78	0.04	**Yes**
	PSAV does not cause Grth*	0.01	0.89	No
	Grth does not cause PSAV*	2.87	0.11	No
	GE does not cause Grth*	1.14	0.30	No
	Grth does not cause GE*	0.00	0.98	No
	RL does not cause Grth*	0.06	0.80	No
	Grth does not cause RL*	0.36	0.55	No
	RQ does not cause Grth*	6.99	0.01	**Yes**
	Grth does not cause RQ*	5.00	0.04	**Yes**
	CC does not cause Grth*	0.20	0.65	No
	Grth does not cause CC*	1.97	0.18	No
Sri Lanka	VA does not cause Grth*	0.44	0.51	No
	Grth does not cause VA*	4.76	0.04	**Yes**
	PSAV does not cause Grth	1.92	0.18	No
	Grth does not cause PSAV	0.16	0.68	No
	GE does not cause Grth	1.40	0.25	No
	Grth does not cause GE	0.39	0.53	No
	RL does not cause Grth	0.19	0.66	No
	Grth does not cause RL	6.11	0.02	**Yes**
	RQ does not cause Grth	3.19	0.09	**Yes**
	Grth does not cause RQ	0.09	0.76	No
	CC does not cause Grth	1.65	0.21	No
	Grth does not cause CC	0.59	0.45	No

Notes: All the results are at first differences except the * marks representing it at second differences. The numbers of lags in each country are 1.

Source: Computed by the author and the World Bank, https://data.worldbank.org/indicator/NY.GDP.MKTP.KD.ZG and https://data.worldbank.org/data-catalog/worldwide-governance-indicators

TABLE 4.5. KEY RESULTS ON MEANS AND ENDS

Indicators	*Means*	*Ends*	*Means and Ends*
VA	Afghanistan, India	Bhutan, Sri Lanka	Pakistan
PSAV	Bangladesh		India
GE	Bangladesh		Afghanistan
RL		Sri Lanka	Bangladesh
RQ	Bangladesh, Sri Lanka	Nepal	Afghanistan, Pakistan
CC	Bangladesh		

Source: Computed by the author.

RQ, i.e. total of five indicators have roles on growth. That means governance is a means.

- Bangladesh is a country where four governance indicators work for growth.
- Growth is the cause of good governance in Bhutan, Sri Lanka and Nepal. Growth influences three indicators, viz., VA, RL and RQ. That means governance is ends.
- Bilateral causality works for Afghanistan, Bangladesh, India and Pakistan. That means governance is both means and ends.
- For Afghanistan and Pakistan, the 'means and ends roles' work for two indicators; GE and RQ for the former and VA and RQ for the latter.
- In overall assessment, governance indicators have worked as means in seventeen cases and as end in eight cases.

CONCLUSION

This chapter aimed to examine the role of good governance on growth of per capita income in South Asia – whether good governance was the means or end in determining growth of the countries. Applying the Granger Causality Test on World Bank data on six governance indicators and growth of per capita income of eight South Asian countries for the period 1996-2015, the study has observed mixed results in the sense that most of the governance indicators except VA for Bangladesh and Maldives are causing their growth of Income to change. Political stability and absence of violence has a bilateral causality with growth of income in India only and RQ has the same role in Afghanistan and Pakistan economies. Government's effectiveness has both means and ends roles to growth for Afghanistan only. Control of corruption has been the driving force of growth in Bangladesh and Maldives. In case of Sri Lanka, growth has influenced its VA and RL to change. In overall assessment, governance indicators have worked as means in 17 cases and as ends in 8 cases. Hence, it is prescribed further improvements in the quality of governance in the region to exploit inclusive growth and development of the associated countries.

NOTES

1. H.G. Frederickson and K.B. Smith, *The Public Administration Theory Primer*, Boulder, Colorado: West View Press, 2003.
2. R.A.W. Rhodes, *Understanding Governance, Policy Networks, Governance Reflexivity and Accountability*, Buckingham: Open University Press, 1997.
3. D. Kauffman, A. Krray and M. Mastruzzi, 'The Worldwide Governance Indicators: Methodological and Analytical Issues', *World Bank Policy Research Working Paper*, Washington D.C.: World Bank, 2010.
4. D. Kauffman, 'Back to Basics: 10 Myths about Governance and Corruption', *Finance and Development*, vol. 42, no. 3, 2005.
5. A. Hussain, 'Poverty, Growth and Governance in South Asia', in V.A. Panandiker (ed.), *Problems of Governance in South Asia,* New Delhi: Konark Publishers, 2000.
6. Y.J. Kaufman, T. Didier and B. Olivier, 'A Satellite View of Aerosols in the Climate System', *Nature*, vol. 419, no. 6903, 2002, pp. 215-23.
7. H.J. Chang, *Kicking Away the Ladder-Development Strategy in Historical Perspective*, London: Anthem Press, 10 June 2002.
8. Lant Pritchett, 'It Pays to be Ignorant: A Simple Political Economy Model of Rigorous Program Evaluation', mimeo, Kennedy School of Government, April 2002.
9. M.H. Khan, 'Governance and Development', in N. Islam and M. Asaduzzaman (eds.), *Ship Adrift: Governance and Development in Bangladesh*, Dhaka: Bangladesh Institute of Development Studies, 2008.
10. A.K. Dixit, *Lawlessness and Economics : Alternative Modes of Governance*, Princeton: Princeton University Press, 2004.

11. P. Keefer, *Governance and Economic Growth in China and India*, World Bank Working Paper, January 2007.
12. R.C. Das, *Is Governance a Precondition to Growth? : A Study of Selected Countries in the Globalized World,* Conference Proceedings, Madrid, Spain: GOGEP Complutense, 2013.
13. G.S. Maddala & K. Lahiri, *Introduction to Econometrics*, New Delhi: Wiley India, 2012.
14. D.A. Dickey and W.A. Fuller, 'Distribution of the Estimators for Autoregressive Time Series with a Unit Root', *Journal of the American Statistical Association*, vol. 74, no. 366, 1979, pp. 427-31.
15. C.W.J. Granger, 'Investigating Causal Relations by Econometric Models and Cross Spectral Methods', *Econometrica*, vol. 37, July 1969, pp. 424-38.
16. *Ibid.*

CHAPTER 5

Changing Global Power Constellation

China's Rise and Its Implications for South Asia

M.J. Vinod

INTRODUCTION

The world has moved from bipolarity to unipolarity to multipolarty. These changes have posed challenges to the international governance system and impacted on global governance. The rise of India and China has been a topic of intense discussion, debate and strategic review. India and China as two non-Western countries are home to one-third of the world's population. Their rise poses challenging questions/issues which impacts on development policy, global governance and the strategic climate.

The purpose and goals of global governance is to evolve new mechanisms of international cooperation that makes it possible to deal with the global challenges and trans-boundary developments and realities. The new forms of governance pose new challenges and threats to the international community. Many of these challenges need to be dealt with beyond the nation state system. The future world order could be influenced by the reality of a turbulent multilateralism. China's rise in particular poses a challenge to the development projects of the West. China as a non-liberal, non-democratic state functioning on the basis of a market economy poses major challenges to the Western notions of 'legitimacy' of global governance. Along with this the expanding military capabilities of the PLA are a major factor for the changing military balance in the Asia-Pacific region. Chinese leaders have described the initial decades of the twenty-first century as a '20 year period of opportunity'.[1] China would like to build a force structure commensurate with its status.

Against this backdrop, one should not be surprised that China's interest in South Asia has increased considerably. In this context one needs to look at the following dimensions: (1) The reasons for China's ventures into South Asia; (2) How this impacts on China's mode of governance? and (3) How India is affected by these developments?

China's growing presence in South Asia is part-and-parcel of its global economic and strategic reach. China's entry into the region has major geopolitical implications. The fact is China's power and influence impacts on the regional politics of South Asia. The security/insecurity in the region largely depends on the choices that China makes. China's growing power has created unease among many Asian countries including India.

THE INDIA FACTOR

The geopolitical rise of India is a factor in the region cannot be ignored. India also has been maneuvering its interests by encompassing the diplomatic, economic, cultural and diplomatic dimensions. The Indo-Pacific region has been central to achieving its foreign policy goals.

The maritime silk route (MSR) which commences in Fujian and winds up in Venice is a clear indication of China's attempt to redefine the world order and its role in it. India is conscious of the regional maritime dimensions and impact of the MSR for it. It tends to perceive the MSR as a strategic move to dominate the maritime domain through economic, cultural and naval influence in the Indian Ocean region. The issue is the extent to which the MSR could radically alter the strategic balance in the Indian Ocean and the Bay of Bengal, though China argues that its interests in the Indian Ocean region are purely economic.

However, China too is developing an expeditionary naval capability and it is likely that the Indo-Pacific maritime environment will be the test of the potential for co-existence or clash between players in this strategic triangle.[2] As of now China does not possess the capability to sustain the expeditionary blue water naval presence of the United States. In the long run, a peaceful and stable South Asia is possible only if India and China are able to manage their difference and work in relative tandem. In spite of common principles of peaceful co-existence, India and China have an array of national and regional concerns. Both India and China want influence. A struggle will inevitably ensue if India chooses to contest/balance China's growing influence. India has to face the reality of a complex geopolitical map that is constantly shifting. While China has moved ahead, India aspires to achieve its destiny in the Indo-Pacific region.

ONE BELT ONE ROAD

The 'One Belt One Road' initiative proposed by China are plans for the Silk Road Economic Belt on the land and the twenty-first century MSR on the sea. This is an infrastructure investment that will take decades to build involving 65 countries and 4.4 billion people or 63 per cent of the world's population.[3] The reach and expanse of MSR has been expanding, which could see Chinese influence spread from Bali to the Baltic. The MSR which will begin near Guangdong on the South China Sea, will move through the Malacca Strait and Indian Ocean, make its way around the Cape of Good Hope, onto the Red Sea and the Mediterranean, and wind up in the historic city of Venice. The route represents the dominant link between southern China and the Mediterranean with a network of Southeast Asian and South Asian ports in between. President Xi's concept works on dual tracks both land and sea. China has in recent times clearly stepped up its maritime diplomacy in the Indian Ocean littoral.

Technically, MSR is an ambitious oceanic trade route linking China and Europe via Southeast Asia, India and Africa. Analysts argue that the New MSR (see Map 5.1) and the Silk Road Economic Belt, along with the new Suez Canal, will be three mainstays to world trade and the global economy.[4] It will also traverse through the disputed parts of the South China Sea. The project envisages a network of linked ports, infrastructure projects and special economic zones. The proposal has attracted enormous interest among policy makers and scholars. Though the Silk Road symbolizes China's connectivity

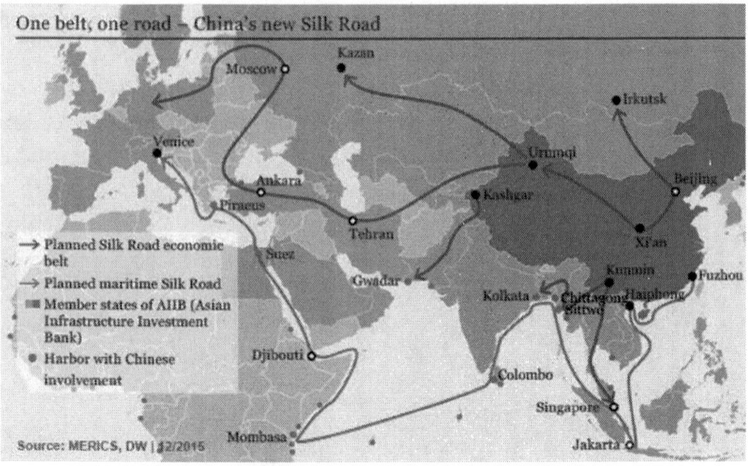

Source: https://www.google.co.in/search?hl=en&tbm=isch&source=hp&biw=1366&bih=662&ei=GkgQWob9HIn9vgSNm5rABg&q=obor+map&oq=OBOR+&gs_l=img.1.1.35i39k1j0l9.8108.9

MAP 5.1: ONE BELT, ONE ROAD – CHINA'S NEW SILK ROAD

with the whole world, yet it has raised geopolitical anxieties in many countries. Though most of the ports are technically civilian ports, New Delhi is anxious that they may portend a permanent Chinese presence in the Indian Ocean.

The dilemma before India is whether it should chart out its own course or become part of what is essentially a China-dominated Asian economic system, whether one calls it the Pacific Age or a New Silk Route or a pan-Eurasian system. India, while displaying some reservations concerning 'One Belt, One Road', agrees with the premise of linking up its strategy of economic development with the projects, which means China's advantages and India's development demands will be closely integrated. At the same time, it promises to facilitate the construction of the BCIM Economic Corridor.[5] Some argue that the Asian order has already been established by China, and hence India has few options. China's location and economy is perceived as the hub which connects to the rest of Asia.

The reasons for China's compulsions to emerge as a maritime power in the region are many. Chinese strategists, including

President Xi, have highlighted the role of China's international trade, its merchant fleet, and its naval task forces – especially China's first aircraft carrier, Liaoning, deployed in 2012. China's economy relies on a steady flow of seaborne cargo: oil and natural gas, soyabeans and grains, and raw materials from the Middle East, South America, and Africa. The Chinese merchant fleet is essential for these imports and for exporting Chinese goods to foreign markets; the vulnerability of such transport links, the 'Malacca Dilemma,' is a fundamental consideration driving China's quest for true maritime power and for the naval strength that it requires.[6] Hence, from President Xi's perspective, China's maritime core national interests can be best secured through exercising maritime power to defend its national interests and state sovereignty.

THE CHINA-PAKISTAN AXIS

The evolving ties between China and Pakistan spans over 60 years and encompasses the political, economic, military dimensions and dynamics. China is Pakistan's largest arms supplier. China has helped Pakistan take forward its nuclear and missile programmes, forcing India to focus on the Pakistan threat. China has built the nuclear power plant in Chasma in the Minawali district of Punjab province for example. The Karokaram Highway that links both the countries is strategically significant. China continues to shore up Islamabad's economic and strategic position in the region. This perhaps explains why China is reluctant to put pressure on Pakistan to crack down on terrorists who contribute to instability in the region, including the former.

THE CHINA-PAKISTAN ECONOMIC CORRIDOR

Beijing contends that it has only two altruistic objectives in promoting MSR, viz., to ensure the security of the sea lanes ofcommunication and to ensure economic dividends. Beijing consistently argues that MSR has no strategic or military dimension, and that it is purely commercial and developmental, and hence it can be a game changer. Economic success has been central to Beijing's emergence as a regional and global power.

The China-Pakistan Economic corridor (CPEC) connects Gwadar to China's north western city of Kashgar in the Xinjiang region (see Map 5.2). Gwadar, the crown jewel of CPEC, is at the foot of the Arabian Sea; the mouth of the Persian Gulf; and only 200 miles from the Strait of Hormuz. For China, Gwadar is a geopolitical asset. China's energy supply chain could avoid the thousands of miles of sea lanes that are dominated by the US navy. It could also strengthen Pakistan's economy – with new infrastructure projects and jobs.

The Gwadar Port provides China the following advantages:

(a) To monitor the sea-lanes of the Persian Gulf
(b) Observe Indian and US naval activities
(c) Guarantee its 'blue-water navy' in the Indian Ocean region, maintenance and supply and
(d) Gwadar as a 'supply location for the PLA Navy is key to China's foreign policy goals.

One wonders whether we are seeing the Chinese version of the Monroe Doctrine. The issue is whether China's emergence as a mari-

Source: https://www.google.co.in/search?hl=en&biw=1366&bih=662&tbm=isch&sa=1&ei=P0gQWq6uH8vSvwS_lb3IAw&q=cpec+road+map&oq=CPEC&gs_l=psy-ab.1.5.0i67k1j0j0i67k1j0

MAP 5.2: CHINA-PAKISTAN ECONOMIC CORRIDOR

time power will be commensurate with its geostrategic vision. It includes construction of roads, laying railway lines and pipelines to carry oil and gas. Once complete it will cut short the trade route for oil imports by 9,656 km. At present almost 80 per cent of China's oil requirement is shipped via the Malacca Strait to Shanghai – a distance of almost 16,000 km. It is also expected to open a brand new strategic gateway for China to tap into African, West Asian, South Asian and Eurasian trade. It helps China to access fuels and minerals from these regions. China's installed capacity in steel, cement, bulk chemicals and heavy machinery can also be fully utilized. Needless to say, OBOR creates new export markets.

The CPEC is the flagship programme of OBOR linking Eurasia in the form of connectivity and cooperation. CPEC consists of the corridor as well as the projects. The former estimated at 11 billion dollars and the latter 34 billion dollars. It involves the surface route through the Karakoram Highway and the link to the Arabian Sea through the coastal town of Gwadar. Various other projects of the CPEC include among others the upgradation of the Karakoram Highway and the motorway project between Lahore and Karachi. Many critics in Pakistan have termed the CPEC as the China-Punjab Economic Corridor, raising larger issues pertaining to the projects being undertaken in Punjab, Sindh, Baluchistan, Khyber Pakhtunkhwa and POK. Let us not forget that since Baluchistan is one of the least populated provinces in Pakistan blessed with immense natural resources, it tends to attract a large number of people from other parts of Pakistan. If one were to take the population of Gwadar, for example, its population is currently 0.1 per cent and among them 20 per cent are non-locals. The non-locals are mostly from Kech district who have moved in search of jobs. The expansion of economic activities in the southern part of Baluchistan especially Gwadar, Turbat and Khuzar is likely to increase such a trend. Baluchistan must get its share of the economic corridor.

CPEC has not just regional but also global trade implications. It will physically connect China to the markets in Asia, Europe and beyond. Whether Pakistan will be able to bear the debt burden accruing from the CPEC only time will tell. However, most Pakistanis tend to believe that the partnership with China is crucial for the future.

The CPEC also helps China to maintain its growth momentum. Given the Malacca dilemma, the corridors that are being developed carry great strategic value for Beijing. OBOR also enables China to position itself in the Indian Ocean and Arabian Sea.

CHINA-AFGHANISTAN RELATIONS

Historically, China has stayed out of Afghanistan's 'great game' politics. When former President Karzai was in power, he tried to persuade China to use its influence with Pakistan to restrain the Talibans, but to no avail. President Ghani made his first official visit abroad to China. The conflict in Afghanistan has also radicalized China's Uighur community which comprises at least 43 per cent of the population of Xinjiang province. The use of Uighurs in the Islamic jihad movement in Afghanistan has been a matter of low-lying tension between China and Pakistan as China believes that Pakistan is not doing enough to control them. China also fears that many Uighurs have left Xinjiang and joined ISIS in Iraq and Syria.

China has multiple interests in Afghanistan: which can be listed as follows:

(a) Exploiting its untapped natural resources, including iron and copper
(b) A commitment to $330 million in aid
(c) Building a closer economic relationship
(d) China has agreed to build a railway line between Kabul and Xinjiang and
(e) Afghanistan could become a larger transportation hub for OBOR, as well as 'market for its goods'.

China hopes that stability in Afghanistan would enable it to build roads, railways and other infrastructure projects as part of OBOR. As indicated above, Beijing is already a major investor in Afghanistan, especially the development of the Aynak copper mines. Other investments are in Afghanistan's rich mineral and oil sectors. There are major physical barriers between China and Afghanistan. At present much of the bilateral trade passes through third countries like Iran and Pakistan. The rugged terrain in Wakhan, Badakhshan, the part of Afghanistan bordering China is a major hurdle for trade. Some Afghan scholars argue that if building the Karakoram highway in Pakistan is possible why not the Wakhan corridor in Afghanistan. This would help boost trade enormously between the two countries which has crossed the $1billion mark since 2014.[7]

China needs to do a lot more to get its ally Pakistan to crack down on such militant groups that Islamabad cultivates to promote its regional interests. The need for a China-Pakistan-Afghanistan trilateral has gained in momentum. Afghanistan Finance Minister Eklil Ahmad Hakimi highlighted the importance of the Belt Road Initiative (BRI) for his country when he said, 'China's One Belt One Road (OBOR) project could provide hope and opportunities for war-torn Afghanistan'. But to make this a reality, Afghanistan's inclusion in CPEC is perhaps necessary which could also benefit Pakistan.[8] Pakistan can also gain easier access to Central Asia through Afghanistan. Since October 2016, Kabul has expressed a strong desire to join the CPEC. China would also like to see a low key Indian role in Afghanistan which suits its close ally Pakistan.

CONCLUSION

China is engaging with the South Asian countries bilaterally that tends to exclude India. Beijing is today Sri Lanka's largest donor and has made a $1 billion investment to develop the southern port of Hambantota. China has also constructed a refinery in Colombo, an international airport and an international trading hub. A container terminal is also coming up in Colombo. Despite India's displeasure, a nuclear-powered submarine had docked in Colombo port. Beijing is not only a source of military hardware for Bangladesh, but is also Dacca's largest trading partner. Beijing's efforts in modernizing the Chittagong port needs to be emphasized.

Balancing Chinese power across the Indian Ocean would necessitate close ties with the littoral states and powers like Japan and the US. Both US and China are interested in shifting power alignments in South Asia for economic and political reasons. The China factor has to be complementary to India's neighbourhood policy. China's strategic partnership is a way to offset US and Indian influence in the region. At the same time bolstering Pakistan is a way for China to counter India's growing influence. The rise of China's influence in South Asia need not have to be a story of India's weakness but can remain a story of China's strength.

China's rise has clearly impacted on the balance-of-power in the Asia-Pacific region. Beijing's unitary strategies like in the South China Sea are also fraught with concerns. Much as India seems to have a sense of its pre-eminent position in the Indian Ocean, so too does China within the South China Sea. It has to deal with unresolved border disputes with Japan and India. Japan, for example, sees a direct link between the Chinese strategies in the South China Sea and the East China Sea.

As far as MSR is concerned, at this point of time, it tends to be more of a strategic concern than an economic opportunity for India. China's maritime power is central to its foreign policy outlook and its grand strategy. This cannot be possible from Xi's perspective without balancing the land and sea. China offers both challenges and opportunities to the international community. Countries like India will have to both engage and compete with China. The challenge is to strike a pragmatic balance. China is central to Asian and global geopolitics. Gone are the days when China would prefer to have a subdued profile. India cannot and need not stop the neighbouring states from cooperating with China on infrastructure development. Though India has its own reservations and concerns which it is entitled to, yet some thought need to be given to see how India could perhaps participate and shape its agenda. Rather than trying to keep China out of the Indian Ocean region, India needs to think of ways and means of reconnecting with the countries in the Indian Ocean region. Let us not forget the stakes are too high in the great game being played in the Indian Ocean region. Recently the Chinese have launched their second aircraft carrier after the Liaoning which was brought from Ukraine. China has its own version and perception of regional security backed up by a new geo-strategic plan for the future. OBOR is clearly an initiative in this direction.

India remains wary of Beijing's overtures to its neighbours, and also Beijing's conscious efforts to widen and strengthen its military presence in the Indian Ocean. South Asia provides China economic opportunities and strategic benefits. China is clearly trying to increase its military foothold in South Asia. China's expanding foothold in the region also puts added pressure on India and also counters India's eastward expansion. While China has ties with many countries in the Asia-Pacific region, its ties with India and the US are bound to impact on regional stability.

NOTES

1. Annual Report to the Congress, *Military Power of the People's Republic of China 2007*, Washington D.C.: Department of Defense, Office of the Secretary of Defense, 2008, p. 7.
2. Robert Gates, Speech to the United States Military Academy West Point, New York, 25 February 2011, archive.defence.gov/speeches/speech.aspx?SpeechID=1539
3. Ruby Tsao, 'Maritime Silk road One Belt Route', *Chinese American Forum*, July-September 2015, vol. 31, no. 1, 2015, p. 12.
4. Mohamed Noman Galal, 'Visions of the Maritime Silk Route', *Beijing Review*, 5 February 2015, see http://www.bjreview.com
5. Lin Minwang, *China's New Diplomatic Blueprint for South Asia*, vol. 63, no. 11, November 2014, p. 45.
6. Ian Storey, 'China's Malacca Dilemma', Jamestown Foundation, *China Brief*, vol. 6, no. 8, 12 April 2006, see www.jamestown.org/.
7. Ahmed Bilal Khakil, 'The Blueprint for China-Afghanistan-Pakistan Cooperation', 29 June 2017, see http://thediplomat.com/2017/06/the-blueprint-for-china-afghanistan-pakistan-cooperation/
8. Anurag Ram Chandran, 'Why Afghanistan should join CPEC', 5 May 2017, see http://thediplomat.com/2017/05/why-afghanistan-should-join-cpec/

PART 3

GOVERNANCE, POLITICS AND VIOLENCE IN SOUTH ASIA

CHAPTER 6

Governance and Conflict in South Asia

P. Sahadevan

INTRODUCTION

Conflict is an abnormal phenomenon that typifies 'breakdown of normal politics' in society.[1] In contrast, peace symbolizes normalcy, order and stability. Whereas conflict stems from a single or multitude of grievances leading to ruptured relations between the state and communities, peace is achieved through a difficult process of changing their perceptions, attitudes, interests and goals. Generally, there is a tendency to view social conflict as an extraneous event, caused principally by competing interests and aspirations of actors, occurring within a polity and society. This chapter argues that conflict essentially originates from bad governance policies and lopsided functioning of state institutions, resulting in their inability to manage and resolve the competing demands and interests of groups. Hence, conflict is as much a problem of governance as a challenge to governance. Peace is contingent upon privileging good governance as an inviolable state policy. Given the intricate link between governance, conflict and peace, the state and its elites should primarily bear the responsibility for outbreak of conflict and, at the same time, are entitled to take maximum credit for building peace and stability.

This chapter focuses on some of the major internal conflicts in South Asia to underscore their primary causal links to (bad) governance and show how far the governance agenda of states have incorporated the task of preventing and managing conflicts and building peace. In the process, the nature of governance and the shared experience of people in the region are revealed. This exercise is conducted by advancing a set of conceptual arguments on the role of governance in conflict and peace.

CONFLICT AS GOVERNANCE PROBLEM

In the contemporary period, governance is a buzzword used by the global community, informed citizens, credible national leaders and active civil society. Yet, there is little agreement on what constitutes governance and what its elements are. It is conceived both in minimalist and maximalist terms, and used in a specific context to promote a set of goals. Initially, in the 1980s, some international financial and development institutions such as the World Bank, International Monetary Fund (IMF) and United Nations Development Programme (UNDP) took the lead in defining the concept from the standpoint of their organizational mandate. Considering governance as a process, their definitions commonly emphasized some key elements such as authority, power, control and management. In their perspective, governance is an exercise of power and authority to manage a country's public affairs and control society. It denotes capacity of government to frame policies and implement them while discharging its functions to satisfy the needs of citizens. Further, it entails effective management of a country's social and economic resources for progress and development, and tasks to achieve its core national objectives.[2] In summary, governance is a 'process through which power is exercised to manage the collective affairs of a country, achieve the core national objectives and uphold certain principles, norms and values'.[3] This definition and the elements therein make governance a technocratic affair, entailing a process based on the principles of control and compliance, with the purpose of achieving development, order and stability. In this framework and conception, interests and goals of citizens are hardly factored, thereby creating an impression that governance inevitably results in peace and conflict is banished in society. That conflict is an integral part of life and governance holds the key in preventing and managing it was not recognized earlier.

This lacuna is addressed by the concept of good governance under which the agenda is expanded. Also, the prefix 'good' to governance indicates that governance by itself may not necessarily be good, and good governance carries a set of additional tasks for the authorities aimed at producing a variety of 'good things' to benefit the governed – people. Good governance, thus, incorporates a democratic governance system drawing on most, if not all, of the following principles: democracy, representative institutions, rule of law, transparency, accountability, inclusivity, equity, participation, pluralism, human rights, efficiency, competence, responsiveness, effective public management, etc.[4] Good governance, therefore, refers to representative institutions and democratic processes that are transparent, inclusive, efficient, competent, responsive, effective and accountable; promote rule of law, inclusivity, equity, pluralism and participation; and uphold the principles of just social and political order and coexistence among the citizens. These principles, so comprehensive, constituting good governance make it appear an absolute phenomenon or goal. Yet, in reality, it is difficult to envisage that all good governing systems would be able to incorporate or adopt all these principles. Therefore, there is no such thing called 'absolutely' good governance.

The point pertinent to our analysis is that good governance tends to create a conflict-free society by removing disaffection among citizens and preventing fissures between communities. It does not allow grievances to accumulate and be institutionalized; if at all a section of the population genuinely feels aggrieved or nurtures grievances, the existing political structures provide suitable avenues and means to redress them on a timely basis. Reversely, in the absence of the core good governance principles such as pluralism, inclusivity, equity, participation and development particularly in culturally plural or divided societies, identity groups tend to perceive discrimination or develop a sense of deprivation if the states build majoritarian tendencies into their structures and pursue ethnic partisan policies. This creates propitious conditions for conflict as aggrieved identity groups become inclined to mobilize their members for collective action demanding 'inclusion' and 'equality'. In such a situation, adoption of other good governance principles such as democracy, representation, transparency, competence, efficiency, accountability and effective public management may not help prevent a conflict situation. The argument is that conflict becomes inevitable if good governing systems are 'good to some' and 'not to all' citizens and, having adopted partially some of the core principles, if they cause a deep sense of alienation and deprivation among a section of population.

This suggests that as an interest-driven event, conflict is fundamentally a governance problem produced by a long period of malgovernance. A widely accepted definition describes conflict as a 'situation' in which two or more entities or parties perceive that they possess 'mutually incompatible goals'.[5] Goals are the much-desired outcomes or end-state, which hold a huge intrinsic value for parties. They are framed in objective conditions created by the functioning of governing systems, which generate potential causes of conflict. Generally, the causes are linked to institutionalization of *inequality* as a state policy, pursued more openly than discreetly in many cases, to disadvantage one group and privilege another. This is majorly manifested in three Ds – deprivation, discrimination and denial (of basic needs). Deprivation is defined as a situation when an identity group perceives a major discrepancy between its expectations and what it is actually capable of attaining.[6] This is an undesirable outcome of the state policy of neglect or indifference to a targeted group's interests aimed at depleting its strength and capabilities. According to Ted Gurr, 'discontent arising from the perception of relative deprivation is the basic, instigating condition for participants in collective violence'.[7]

Similarly, discrimination is an issue that directly involves the state and a group of its citizens. Here again, the state plays a key role in making unequal citizenry, who can be classified in political terms as privileged and deprived. While multi-national states invariably accept inclusive citizenship as a core policy choice, majoritarian states tend to develop their own nationalist agenda based on the principles of exclusion of ethnic minorities from power structures and inclusion of majority community as the sole or principal stakeholder. When the state at large determines the policy and systems of governance in a parochial and ethnic partisan manner, there is little or no chance for the targeted group to escape from the regime of discrimination. Often, discrimination entails restriction on the cultural and linguistic rights of ethnic minorities, denial of political autonomy and unequal distribution of economic resources and benefits to them.

One of the principal tasks of governance is to satisfy the basic human needs (BHN) of people. BHNs, as postulated by various authors, are a long list of the most desired goals in life. They include power, resources, identity, respect, autonomy, self-esteem, dignity, welfare, freedom, etc.[8] All of these are important for everyone, but some are more important than others. Thus, BHNs could be ranked, in terms of importance, as crucial, essential, marginal and peripheral, in accordance with the desire, preference and requirement of people. Generally, there are three major noticeable trends in how governing systems work: they either fulfil or partially satisfy or deny BHNs. Denial of BHNs is the most potent cause for conflict which, if not prevented or managed, tends to seriously challenge or threaten the state. This is because people cannot make compromise on their BHNs; rather, they show strong determination to achieve some or all of them to ensure their survival as equal citizens.

The arguments made in this section are, thus, summarized: cumulatively, 3Ds create a structure of inequality as a source of conflict. They are located in governing systems, state policies, competitive politics, and lack of credible political institutions as forums for reconciling differences, moderating interest-laden positions and prevention and management of conflict. Second, 3Ds form negative indices of bad or mal-governance that produces a conflict situation where political entrepreneurs take up the cause by organizing the concerned demand-bearing group against the state.

GOOD GOVERNANCE AS CONFLICT MANAGEMENT

The next relevant conceptual concern is to explore how good governance works as an effective conflict management strategy. 'Governing is conflict management' which in essence characterizes the 'nature of governance', says Zartman.[9] Good governance has a dual function of preventing as well as managing conflict. The assumption is that progressive principles of governance generally work good to prevent conflict, yet it is not always certain. As 'society plays its role in the conduct of normal politics', it is possible that conflict of interests develops among groups which put their demands on government. In such a situation good governance entails 'continual effort to handle the ordinary conflicts' by taking measures required to meet their demands and counter-demands. It is government's job to manage these conflicts effectively. Otherwise, as Zartman rightly cautions, they possibly 'threaten to escalate, leading to a variety of debilitating outcomes: blockage of the governing process, a widening split between state and society, outbreaks of violence, and collapse of the state'.[10] Not surprisingly, hence, conflicts are prevalent even in societies where good governance is established.

As the tasks of good governance expand to include conflict management along with conflict prevention, governing systems need to be strengthened by certain additional attributes – norms, principles and practices. In the context of conflict management, we argue that good governance is not good *enough* governance unless it is made quite liberal democratic in functional terms. Here, the emphasis is not just on adherence to the liberal principles listed earlier, but also their strict implementation as part of the process of good governance. This underlines the need for a normative framework and structural mechanisms. At the normative level, political system should promote an unwritten 'social contract' among all sections of society to reject inequality, and also a similar kind of 'political contract' between the competing political elites to end it forthwith. They should further commit themselves to de-politicize the issue by de-linking it from electoral politics and support to the politics of consensus as the basic values of democracy. While opposition parties are needed to function as responsible actors in conflict management, it is important that the regime pursues popular and not populist policies, and the ruling elites should be benign, strong, sensitive and creative in responding to conflict. In this context, Zartman offers an insightful explanation. According to him,

> Effective governance depends on the establishment of a national consensus on norms, the reinforcement of those norms and values as a legitimizing regime, and the establishment of new institutions and principles as a replacement regime if the former values and institutions prove inadequate. The first element in a national consensus on values is the development of

national traditions growing out of critical junctures in individual countries.'[11]

The second element in Zartman's schema pertains to a 'central normative code about the way conflicts should be managed'. In his view, in a conflict situation, the state should adopt coherent political strategies rather than 'simple repression', 'a legitimizing institutional structure', and 'resources for allocation'. These attributes contribute to a successful management of conflicts.[12]

At the structural level, good governance fosters a range of institutional mechanisms for problem-solving and building peace in divided societies. For instance, parliament provides a mediating forum where negotiations over competing group interests and demands are held. The judiciary functions in an independent way as the custodian of rights and adjudicates the critical questions over constitutionality. Other institutions that provide peace, order, security and resource allocation are built on the principles of representation, transparency and accountability. And, the state accepts civil society's constructive role in conflict management.

It is thus clear that good governance as a conflict management strategy encompasses a wide variety of norms, principles and functional attributes. Together they add some liberal democratic features to good governance to make it virtually liberal democratic governance (LDG). Critiques may see LDG as an unattainable framework or approach as the task of arranging or rearranging society and polity to meet the requirements of conflict management is practically difficult. While appreciating such concerns, at the conceptual level, we make an argument that LDG is a relevantly useful approach even though it may not be easy to frame and adopt in every society. It is also underscored that if LDG as a conflict management tool contributes to peace, the latter as the most desired outcome in turn strengthens LDG.

SOUTH ASIA: A REGION OF CONFLICT

The conceptual arguments in previous sections provide a useful guide to evaluate the state of governance in South Asia and assess how far it has been able to prevent and manage conflicts. It is puzzling why has the region experienced a plethora of internal conflicts? And, what does their protraction signify? In undertaking this exercise, we shall focus on five countries – India, Pakistan, Bangladesh, Sri Lanka and Nepal – where the systems of governance are varied in significant ways. However, the task, here, is not to present a detailed empirical account of each conflict but to identify the characteristics of governance and trends in conflict management.

It must be noted that the countries under discussion are different in terms of political history and the nature of governance. India and Sri Lanka have long been established democracies with certain structural and functional deficiencies that make them weak. Having maintained an impressive record of holding regular elections and transferring power smoothly from one party (loser) to another (winner), both countries are known as electoral democracies. In contrast, Pakistan and Bangladesh began their political journey as democracies but slipped into military dictatorship before transiting again to democracy in the recent period. Whereas democracy is yet to be fully stabilized in Pakistan, it has not become strong and entrenched in Bangladesh. Nepal's experience is altogether different from all the other countries. Originally a monarchy that entrenched itself for many decades, the landlocked country had experimented limited democracy (under party and party-less Panchayat system) for forty years until the parliamentary system was established in 1990.[13] Nevertheless, all four countries share a common social structure characterized by deep cultural plurality and complex multi-ethnicity.

In the absence of a strong democracy and institutionalization in many of the states in South Asia, governance has faced huge challenges. It is largely interpreted in a typical technocratic manner as a process of exercising state power and authority over, and to control, the society. If the states in structural terms are weak,[14] ideologically they find themselves in contrast. Secularism is the fundamental ideological base of the Indian state, which has factored certain progressive principles and norms in policymaking to protect the interests of deprived social groups and linguistic and religious minorities. At least under the Constitution, no one particular identity group is privileged to solely own or control the state; rather the stakeholders are a large number of communities inherently and deeply divided along the lines of multiple but cross-cutting identities based on caste, class, religion, language and region. In contrast the states in Pakistan, Sri Lanka and Bangladesh present a different picture. Theocracy is the foundational principle of both the Pakistani and Bangladeshi states where Islam forms the bedrock of both Constitutions. Yet, religion is not a unifying force in Pakistan since ethnicity has assumed a preponderant position in defining the people's relationship with the state. This has led to the Pakistani state's emergence as a Punjabi-dominated majoritarian entity that has chosen to pursue policies of exclusion of other ethnic groups, such as Baluchis, Sindhis, Pakthuns, etc., from its power structure. In Bangladesh, the Islamic state is an exclusivist institution that believes in and promotes the supremacy of the Bengali Muslims as against the Hindu Bengalis and the Buddhist Chakmas. Although Sri Lanka has not declared itself a theocratic state, its Constitution gives the foremost place for Buddhism to make it a *de facto* state religion. Other religions – Hinduism, Islam and Christianity – are virtually accorded a secondary status. The state's strong association with Buddhism and Sinhalese language has fostered its parochial nature of being a Sinhalese-Buddhist majoritarian entity that has undermined the legitimate aspirations of the ethnic minorities. The Nepali experience denotes a unique case of a longstanding Hindu state transforming itself into a secular entity in recent times. Yet, in practice, it has not completely dispensed with its majoritarian character. Rather, it has added regional and caste dimensions to its majoritarian identity. In simple terms, the Nepali state largely identifies with, and is dominated by, the Nepali-speaking high caste groups settled in the hill region.

The sectarian or ethnic nature of states in South Asia has affected the structure and process of governance in the region. There is severe institutional deformity in most of the South Asian states; the exception is India where, however, violations and tardy implementation of policies have undermined governance and weakened its structure. In this context the main arguments based on a general survey are the following: First, though the societies are recognized as plural, pluralism is not the guiding principle of state policy in most of the countries. Second, democracy in all states has enforced the electoral representative character of institutions, but in most cases participation in decision-making is skewed along ethnic lines. This has given rise to an acute sense of powerlessness among a section of population in each state. Third, the rule of law is enshrined in all constitutions, but in practice the ruling elites have no qualms about undermining it when their regime interests are challenged. Transparency is an issue in many societies as the regimes are keen to maintain secrecy in the name of national security and interest. Accountability is hard to establish on matters like, for instance, human rights abuses if they directly involve the state and its core institutions like the military. Above all, it is widely believed that governance has not seriously addressed the issues of inequity and exclusivity, thereby entrenching 3Ds in societies across the region. As discussed below, these issues have formed the principal causes of many of the internal conflicts in South Asia.

There have been about 20 internal conflicts in South Asia; India accounts for half of them in the post-Independence period.[15] In almost all cases, relative deprivation has been a principal causation factor. Members of various identity groups have invariably developed high expectations and uncompromising goals regarding power, autonomy, position, social and economic progress, peace and security. They have considered all of these as their legitimate aspirations, and sought to achieve them by all means. But in reality, what they have achieved are far below their expectations, thereby revealing their inherent weakness or incapacity as compared to other group members who have been more successful in realizing their goals. The basic grievances of the Sri Lankan Tamils, Pakistan's ethnic minorities (Baluchis, Pakhtuns, Sindhis and Mohajirs), the Janajatis and Madheshis of Nepal, the tribal groups in Bangladesh's Chittagong Hill Tracts (CHT), and various ethnic communities in India's northeast, particularly in Assam, Nagaland, Mizoram and Manipur, have originated from their deep sense of 'powerlessness' created either by ethnic hegemony of the majority communities or centralization of powers by the states. In this context, the states are seen to be playing a partisan role or indifferent to the minority grievances either under compulsions of narrow nationalism or pressure from their respective majority communities, such as the Punjabis of Pakistan, the Sinhalese of Sri Lanka, the high-caste Hindu Nepalese of central hill region, and the Bengali Muslims of Bangladesh. In all these cases, since deprivation has a long history, it is deeply entrenched in societies, making the states' half-hearted measures to change the condition of life of the deprived communities ineffective. It must be noted that the issue of deprivation goes beyond political power in many cases to include a fair or equitable share of development benefits. A glaring case in hand is the acute problem in India's tribal societies where underdevelopment is perpetuated by resource crunch accompanied by exploitative 'corporate and political greed' and 'indifference' of the Indian state.[16] Governance, in this case, has done little to remove the fundamental sources of deprivation among the tribal communities.

Discrimination has accentuated relative deprivation in societies where ethnic policies of most of the states are guided by majoritarian nationalism. There are strong built-in structures of discrimination that the states have maintained in the face of resistance from ethnic rebels demanding their total reform. Typically, the main areas where the states have openly applied their discriminatory policies include language, education and employment. Thus, in the 1950s, the Sri Lankan and Pakistani states adopted a policy of homogenization by declaring Sinhalese and Urdu as their only national and official languages respectively. What followed were policies to deny equal educational and employment opportunities for the Sri Lankan Tamils, and the East Bengalis and other ethnic minorities in Pakistan. Resource allocation has also been an instrument of discrimination whereby the states have wilfully neglected development concerns in regions concentrated by the minorities. Development has, thus, not been inclusive and participatory in both countries. Similarly, in the CHT, the Bangladeshi government's lopsided development programmes have benefitted more the Bengalis than the tribal groups whose access to economic and employment opportunities is limited. In Nepal, communities in the Terai region have perceived political discrimination at the hands of the Kathmandu-based ruling elites who under the new Constitution have sought to marginalize them by adopting a geographical approach to delineate the federal units. While the citizenship provisions have sought to create an unequal citizenry by mainly disadvantaging women in the Terai region, the communities concentrated there have feared that the new electoral system would tend to make their representation in the national parliament disproportionate to their population.[17] Thus, even when there is a process of designing governing systems under a new Constitution, the Nepali ruling elites have failed to prevent conflict. By embedding the sources of conflict in the new constitutional framework, they have failed to seize the opportunity to establish good governance.

Further, the process of governance has not satisfied BHNs of the minorities in many South Asian states. While some of them suffer from fear of assimilation, losing ethnic identity and marginalization, others have developed a sense of insecurity in the face of entrenched majoritarianism.[18] They have sought the states to protect their material interests, fulfil their emotional needs and ensure freedom from fear. Human rights and peace with justice and dignity are other critical needs that not all the states have fulfilled, so much so that violence has become endemic and institutionalized in many cases. The record of reconciliation involving the violence-affected communities and the states is poor. Given all these, the goals of ethnic groups have ranged from autonomy to secession, depending upon the nature and magnitude of their problems and the extent of support they have mobilized against the state. Importantly, while many conflicts have remained low-intensity civil strife, some of them have attained a civil war dimension, causing killing of civilians and destruction of their habitat. In conflict situation death and destruction are the main negative indicators, and by far the worst outcomes, of bad governance. Clearly, South Asia scores high on conflict-related violence and low on peace, which indicates that the institutions of governance have not firmly dealt with the issues of deep-rooted disaffection in societies. It also shows that though all the South Asian states are now electoral democracies, they lack a strong liberal base for good governance. Many of them are weak or fragile and their institutional capacity is very limited. The larger political agenda has given priority to state-building over forging or strengthening cross-national unity through a political contract between different stakeholders and the states in the region.

A curious question is why India has, with a better record of governance in South Asia, experienced several internal conflicts. The answer primarily lies in the complex nature of society and strategies of nation-building. Being a secular state, it has been successful to a larger extent in protecting the cultural rights of minorities and thereby fulfilling their identity needs. But the state has not adequately assured them of power and satisfied their basic development needs. Despite being a quasi-federal entity, the state has shown centralization tendencies by making the provinces dependent on the centre. The successful process of integration of territories of the post-colonial state is not accompanied by the integration of its citizens particularly from the borderlands. They still question the manner in which their territories have been incorporated into the Indian state. Further, ethnic and communal relations are so complex that it has become a difficult task for the state to create and maintain peace within and between groups, which have developed competing interests over cross-cutting social, economic and political goals and shown their determination to achieve them. Mechanisms and strategies to address the manifold problems are quite inadequate and ineffective. In the process, the state's capacity for resolving conflicts has come to be questioned even while its coercive capability has increased over the years.

TRENDS IN CONFLICT MANAGEMENT

Generally, the governments in South Asia do not consider governance as a process or strategy of preventing conflict. Hence, prevention is not incorporated into their policy framework and goals of governance. There is also a lack of political will on the part of the ruling elites to adopt suitable measures to prevent conflict. Rather, mostly their tendency is to ignore disaffection in society until violence breaks out and then deal with it mainly as a law and order problem. As violence intensifies, they respond with the aim of managing the conflict. Again, resolving it does not occupy their core political agenda. Some of the major trends in conflict management are as follows:

PRIMACY OF COERCION

In a conflict management process, coercion does not serve as a credible strategy. Yet, it could at best be accepted as an undesired means to create propitious conditions – termed as 'ripe moments' – for political negotiations when the original goal of adversaries for a zero-sum victory (win-lose) becomes unattainable.[19] Coercion, therefore, should be seen as an instrument to soften one party's demands or make another to give up its tough goals and uncompromising position on negotiated peace. In South Asia, however, this strategy is given utmost importance over political engagement for peace. It means that the fundamental aim of parties has been to use coercion to end conflict militarily or pressurise each other to make negotiated peace. It is a strategy preferred by all states and non-state actors alike until a military victory is secured or its limitations are exposed.

The Indian state has never been averse to use of coercion against political dissidents and insurgents. Since the late 1940s, it has used military and paramilitary forces for operations against insurgents in the north-east, Punjab, Kashmir and tribal areas to counter challenges to its sovereignty. While the purpose in most cases is to force the insurgents to come to a negotiating table and accept a solution within the framework of the Indian Constitution, successive governments in Delhi have also sought to defeat them militarily when they have refused to accept India's sovereignty or peace offered under an accord. Except in the case of Maoists who have rejected the state's demand for abjuring violence, use of coercion has had a strategic aim of converting militants into peaceniks. Similarly, successive governments in Sri Lanka sought to rely on war as an instrument to defeat the Liberation Tigers of Tamil Eelam (LTTE). When their military strategy did not yield a victory, the state leaders altered their goal in favour of negotiated peace but returned to the original goal when the militant group took an intransigent position on peace and eventually was decimated in May 2009. Nepal shares this regional trend, where coercion against the Maoists was intended as much to defeat them as forcing them to accept a peace deal. However, state coercion against the agitating Janajatis and Madheshis is not only aimed at countering their violence but also subduing them to accept the contested constitution. Similarly, the Chakmas had experienced the same at the hands of the Bangladeshi state for over two decades until they negotiated a peace agreement in December 1997. In case of Pakistan, use of coercion is intended not just to weaken the insurgents but also to destroy them at the end.[20]

Coercion and counter-coercion by both the state and non-state forces have produced militarism as a powerful ideology and strategy in pursuit of their competing interests. Thus, there are two types of militarism in South Asia: while state militarism is seen as a legitimate phenomenon, militarism by ethnic or sectarian groups is condemned to be an illegitimate countervailing force. Both have jointly made a debilitating impact on societies and challenged or undermined governance. Militarism as a consequence of conflict has emerged as a new cause of bad governance in South Asia, which has in turn added a complex dimension to the same conflict and, thus, made peacemaking a daunting task.

NEGOTIATED PEACE

Good governance provides a huge space for political dialogue and negotiations over contentious issues. Institutions are expected to lend support to this process. However, political engagement between contending parties without reaching an understanding or agreement on the accepted principles of conflict management is not a sufficient indicator of good governance. Further, peace created this way should not only hold but also satisfy all the key stakeholders. For peace to be popular, it should be of high quality based on the principles of justice and fairness. Not all governments tend to deliver just peace even if they have readily engaged some or all disaffected leaders in political negotiations.

Most of the governments in South Asia have engaged moderate and militant leaders in negotiations at different stages of conflict. While some of them have shown enough commitment to find a political settlement, others have sought to use negotiations as a tactical opportunity to strengthen their position. Of all, India has maintained a better record of conflict management as successive governments have chosen to hold talks with the rebels and political dissidents, leading to signing of peace accords in many cases (in Assam, Nagaland, Mizoram, Punjab, etc.). However, not all accords have achieved their stated objectives: While the conflicts in Assam and Nagaland continue without a definite end, peace has returned to Mizoram even though a section of the Mizo society seems to be unhappy with the 1986 peace accord. The same can be said about the CHT where negative peace is established under the 1997 accord, but the Chakmas remain dissatisfied and alienated. The Sri Lankan government's intermittent peace talks with the Tamil militants since the mid-1980s failed to yield peace, but its brutal military strategies resulted in defeat of the LTTE and eventual end of the civil war in 2009. At one level, Nepal marks a case of successful conflict management as the 2006 peace accord has ended the Maoist insurgency forthwith. At another, the government is reluctant to redress the grievances of the agitating Janajatis and Madheshis in the Terai region. Finally, Pakistan remains a case in itself, where successive governments have shown least interest in a negotiated settlement of internal conflicts.

LIMITED STRUCTURAL CHANGES

If conflict is an integral part of society, governance holds importance for managing it. Governance is not just about controlling or managing society in normal times; it also involves reordering it in a way to overcome an adverse condition. Particularly, in conflict situations, governance entails a process of creating new institutions or restructuring the existing ones in response to demands of people who have questioned and challenged the structures of governance and state policies. This exercise is carried out through negotiated peace deals, which provide the basic framework and principles of institutional restructuring and innovation. In most cases in South Asia, unfortunately peace accords largely hold a symbolic value. They do not trigger off any significant systemic changes; not does it lead to reforming the state. Resistance to state reform has been strong in the region where those who control or wield power of state seek to maintain its institutional *status quo*. Experiences in Sri Lanka, Bangladesh, Pakistan, and even in India substantiate this argument. A notable exception is Nepal where the 2006 comprehensive peace accord to end the Maoist insurgency has brought about the state's total restructuring under a new secular and federal constitution.

LACK OF BIPARTISANISM

Managing conflict is a collective task of all stakeholders in a democratic polity; it underlines the need for a bipartisan approach under which both the ruling elites and opposition leaders come together to partner a peace process. Thus, conflict gets a national dimension and peace becomes a national goal. This approach enables both the government and opposition leaders to share credit for their success in conflict management; however, often the former alone faces criticism for their failure to end violence and establish peace. On this, South Asia presents a disappointing trend. Conflict and peace are politicized as the parties in power and opposition use them for advancing their electoral interests. Since these issues are part of competitive electoral politics, most of the South Asian polities are unable to develop a bipartisan approach. In Sri Lanka, for instance, two mainstream Sinhalese parties – United National Party and Sri Lanka Freedom Party – have always stood against each other's policy on peace and conflict. Similarly, in Bangladesh, the CHT peace accord has fuelled the political rivalry between the Awami League and the Bangladesh Nationalist Party. Nepal has a similar trend where political consensus among different parties is hard to arrive at on a solution to the problems of various communities. India is an exception, where internal conflicts are hardly used for electoral purpose. Being a diverse polity where issues are plenty, conflicts hold a limited political value and appeal at the national level, even if they are relevant to regional politics to some extent. Further, India has developed a political culture of getting the mainstream parties to agree on an approach to peace or a united response to the issues of national security and integration.

CONCLUSION

Conflict poses serious challenges to governance even as failure of governance tends to create propitious conditions for conflict. This link is clearly seen in South Asia where conflicts are endemic and concerns over violence are strong. Governing systems in the region are grappling with the adverse effects of violent conflicts without, however, accommodating the forces of change and reforms. The reform resistance by the state has led the dissidents and rebels to redouble their challenges even while the state has, in response, shown greater determination to defeat them. Such exchanges of violence and counter-violence with impunity have further weakened governance. Thus, failure of governance is redoubled in South Asia.

This chapter underscores the need not only to remove governance deficits but also to leverage LDG to build positive peace by pursuing progressive policies and creating or strengthening institutions. As conflict is an interest-driven activity, its resolution is contingent upon addressing the root causes. Ideally a framework of solution needs to be built in governance policies and structures to make peace-building an integral part of the same systemic processes. In South Asia, there are intra-regional variations in quality of governance, but an overall assessment is that it ranks poor in LDG as an approach to building peace.

NOTES

1. William I. Zartman, 'Dynamics and Constraints in Negotiations in Internal Conflicts', in W.I. Zartman (ed.), *Elusive Peace: Negotiating an End to Civil Wars,* Washington, DC: Brookings Institutions, 1995, p. 5.
2. See the review of definitions in Rachel M. Gisselquist, 'Good Governance as a Concept, and Why this Matters for Development Policy', *UNU-WIDER Working Paper No. 2012/30,* Helsinki, 2012, pp. 1-5.
3. *Ibid.*, p. 4.
4. These principles are culled from the definitions offered by the United Nations, the UNDP and the World Bank, which are analysed in Gisselquist, n. 2, pp. 5-27. Also see, Thandike Mkandawire, 'Good Governance: The Itinerary of an Idea', *Development in Practice,* vol. 17, nos. 4-5, August 2007, pp. 679-81; 'Governance Challenges', http://www.governancereport. org.en/home/governance-challenges/
5. Christopher R. Mitchell, *The Structure of International Conflict,* London: Palgrave Macmillan, 1981, p. 17.
6. Ted Robert Gurr, *Why Men Rebel,* 40th anniversary edition, Boulder, US: Paradigm Publishers, 2011, p. 24.
7. Ibid, p. 13.
8. Johan Galtung, 'International Development in Human Perspective',

in John Burton (eds), *Conflict: Human Needs Theory*, London: The Macmillan Press Ltd., 1990, pp. 301-35.

9. William Zartman, Governance as Conflict Management in West Africa', in I.W. Zartman (ed.), *Governance as Conflict Management: Politics and Violence in West Africa*, Washington, DC: Brookings Institution Press, 1997, p. 9.
10. *Ibid.*, p. 1.
11. *Ibid.*, p. 2.
12. *Ibid.*, p. 3.
13. For comprehensive analysis of experience in democratization, see Maya Chadda, *Building Democracy in South Asia: India, Nepal and Pakistan*, New Delhi: Vistaar Publications, 2000.
14. See T.V. Paul (ed.), *South Asia's Weak States: Understanding the Regional Insecurity Predicament*, New Delhi: Oxford University Press, 2010.
15. See P. Sahadevan, 'Ethnic Conflict and Militarism in South Asia', *International Studies*, vol. 39, no. 2, 2002, pp. 103-38.
16. See Nandini Sundar, *The Burning Forest: India's War in Bastar*, New Delhi: Juggernaut, 2016.
17. See Julia Strasheim, 'The Politics of Institutional Reform and Post-Conflict Violence in Nepal', *GIGA Working Papers No.296*, February 2017.
18. See Sahadevan, n. 15, pp. 105-12.
19. The concept of ripeness is explained in William I. Zartman, *Ripe for Resolution: Conflict and Intervention in Africa*, 2nd edn., New York: Oxford University Press, 1989.
20. Role of coercion in conflict management in select South Asian countries is analysed in P. Sahadevan, 'Managing Internal Conflicts in India, Nepal, Sri Lanka and Myanmar: Strategies and Outcomes', in V.R. Raghavan (ed.), *Policy Choices in Internal Conflicts: Governing Systems and Outcomes*, New Delhi: Vij Books, 2013, pp. 77-189.

CHAPTER 7

Uneasy Partnership

Political Parties and Governance in South Asia

N. Manoharan

INTRODUCTION

If democracy is understood, in the famous words of Abraham Lincoln, as 'government of the people, by the people, and for the people', the importance of political parties in a democratic system is inevitable. Schattschneider, in this regard, rightly observes, 'Modern democracy is unthinkable save in terms of parties'.[1] In other words, while there are parties without democracy, there can be no democracy without political parties. The imperativeness of parties is because of their multitudinal role in a democratic system, especially in the parliamentary form. Political parties broadly perform seven categories of functions:

1. As intermediaries, 'linking the institutions of government to economic, ethnic, cultural, religious and other societal groups'.[2] This is otherwise known as 'political socialization'.
2. As activists, by placing the local concerns of citizens and other inhabitants of the country in a national context and also in influencing public policy. They aggregate interests and communicate them to the political and government institutions for further actions.
3. As compromisers, by organizing differences on issues and creating grounds for conciliation.
4. As feeders, by training and nominating political leaders, who will take part in the governance process. In the words of Antony

Downs, 'A political party is a team of men seeking to control the governing apparatus by gaining office in a duly constituted election'.[3]

5. As educators, by creating a better understanding of the issues and possible solutions to the common man through debates, potentially leading to new insights or workable solutions.
6. They act as the opposition thereby presenting themselves as the alternative to voters to choose, as against the existing government. This also acts as a pressure for the incumbent government to better address the people's interests.
7. They also help in the legislative process by rallying support for or against a particular legislation.

In short, political parties can be understood as 'permanent associations of citizens that are based on free membership and a programme, and which are anxious to occupy through the path of elections, the politically decisive positions of the country with their team of leaders, in order to materialize suggestions for resolving outstanding problems.'[4]

However, political parties, especially in the developing countries, do not always perform the above functions comprehensively and effectively. They, of course, face different set of problems unlike their counterparts in the developed world. As a scholar observes, in the Indian context,

> If the society is as diversified and skewed as in India, the political entrepreneurs would have an uphill task of negotiating with the complex array of constituents whose aspirations/constituents may not be harmoniously aligned and thus a set of interplay of pulling and pushing forces will keep the free market of democracy volatile as regulated by the Constitution of governance as adopted by the society.[5]

Yet, there is no excuse for them not to do what they are supposed to do in the interest of democratic polity.

Since the political parties fail to respond to citizens' concerns, they are widely distrusted by the public, thus disrupting the entire democratic process. The political parties may see themselves as 'a group of people united for the good of their country' and are seen as such by their followers.[6] Yet, in practice, they are perceived by the common man as a group of people united for the good solely of themselves. Lincoln's observation is twisted like: 'off the people, buy the people and far away from the people'. Parties in South Asia are no exception.

However, despite the perceptions and shortcomings, as Alexis de Tocqueville observed, 'Parties are a necessary evil in free governments'.[7] It is in this analytical framework the relevance and interaction of political parties in governance in South Asia is looked into. The chapter intends to find answers to the following questions: What is the nature of political parties of South Asia? How important are they in taking the governance process forward? Despite dwindling reputation, what factors make them to sustain in the political system? How far has the ideological orientation of political parties of the region impacted the governance? Have the assertiveness of civil society increased the accountability of political parties in the region? How far internal democracy of parties has reflected on the larger governance process?

NATURE OF POLITICAL PARTIES IN SOUTH ASIA

According to the *Human Development in South Asia* report,

> South Asia presents a fascinating combination of many contradictions. It has governments that are high on governing and low on serving. It has parliaments that are elected by the poor but aid the rich; and society that asserts the rights of some but perpetuates exclusion for others. Despite a marked improvement in the lives of a few, there are many in South Asia who had been forgotten by formal institutions of governance. These are the poor, the downtrodden and the most vulnerable of the society, suffering from acute deprivation on account of their income, caste, creed, gender or religion. Their fortunes have not moved with those of the privileged few and this in itself is a deprivation of a depressing nature.[8]

Yet, South Asia has the distinction of being the largest democratic region in the world. Surprisingly, despite low human development index, the region could maintain democracy for long falsifying the common notion that democracies could sustain only in developed industrialized countries. The countries of South Asia are young in the Westphalian sense of modern states; most of them emerged out of colonial rule or shadow of colonialism in the late 1940s. Political parties in some of the countries like India have emerged as anti-colonial national movements, but later turned political parties. Parties in countries like Afghanistan, Bangladesh, Bhutan, Maldives and Nepal had origins in the democratization of the respective polities.Interestingly, in the present context, almost all countries in the region are under democratic regimes.

Given the plural nature of the society, the countries in the region is characterized by the presence of multiple political parties. Unlike their European counterparts, parties in South Asia operate in different socio-economic and political contexts. The nature of party system in the region clearly reflected differences in the system of governments, state structures, socio-cultural milieu, economic conditions and historical moorings.[9]

The parties of the region have different shades of ideological orientation: Left, Centrist and Rightist. Caste is another identity factor predominantly seen especially in the case of Indian political parties. However, in the recent decades, religious ideology is gaining ascendency among political parties in the region either that be Hindutva in the case of India, Islamic radicalism in the case of Pakistan and Bangladesh or Buddhism in the case of Sri Lanka.[10] At the same time, these religious-oriented parties did not remain unchallenged either by opposing ideological parties or the so-called 'secular' parties. Notably, vote bank is the main consideration behind ideological narratives or counter-narratives of these parties.

Parties of South Asia are by and large leader-centric, giving rise to the phenomenon of 'dynastic politics'. Dynastic politics is common in almost all countries of the region. Notable family names in politics include Nehru-Gandhi family in India; Bhuttos in Pakistan; Koiralas in Nepal; Bandaranaikes in Sri Lanka; and Zia and Sheikh in Bangladesh. People in the region tend to trust noted personalities and their heirs rather than new entrants.[11] It is this tendency that has brought women political leaders to the fore, despite the region known for patriarchal domination in every field, especially when it comes to power politics. Interestingly, South Asia is second only to Scandinavia in having had more number of women head of the state or governments, though women presence in the political parties is proportionately low.[12]

The dynastic politics has impacted on intra-party democracy. Elections to the party leadership are usually a formality: a single candidate is elected unopposed. And the party leadership, in turn, selects other leaders of the party. Key positions are filled usually with the kin. Given the position of the party leadership in awarding seats to contest for national and provincial legislatures and later government formation, party leaders are powerful and are not shown any dissent. Those who fail to confirm to the party position have no choice but to leave the party.[13]

The political parties of South Asia are broadly classified as national parties, regional parties and ethnic parties. Their support base depended on under which category they fell. Proportional Representation (PR) electoral system led to the increase in the number of parties contesting for power. At the same time, it does not fully confirm to Duverger's law. Despite, First Past the Post System (FPTP) system, multiple parties continue to exist in South Asian countries.[14] Similarly, two dominant parties (UNP and SLFP) formed governments in Sri Lanka despite the proportional representation system.

Some groups, who were involved in militancy in the past, have turned to political parties. Maoists in Nepal, Tamil groups in Sri Lanka, few Communist groups in India and Sri Lanka fall in this category. In some cases like Bangladesh and Pakistan, military dictators found political parties to legitimize their rule. Bangladesh Nationalist Party by Gen. Zia ur Rehman, Jatiya Party by Gen. Ershad and All Pakistan Muslim League by Gen. Pervez Musharraf are few notable examples.

Funding is important for running political parties and to contest elections. The political parties of the region raise funds from varied source. But, all sources of income are not transparent. Though rules and regulations are being strengthened to regulate funding the political parties, they have been not so effective. State funding of the parties has been under debate, but not been implemented in any of the countries of the region.[15] These trends are reflected in the character of the political parties of the region.

POLITICAL PARTIES AND THE GOVERNANCE PROCESS IN SOUTH ASIA

Simply speaking, governance is 'the process of decision-making and the process by which decisions are implemented'.[16] In other words, governance involves 'identification of both the rulers and the ruled, as well as the various processes by which they are selected, defined, and linked together and with the society generally'.[17] It is the extent to which a state delivers to its citizens the desired benefits of government at acceptable costs.[18] According to the United Nations Development Programme (UNDP), the essential characteristics of governance are: participation; rule of law; transparency; responsiveness; consensus orientation; equity; effectiveness and efficiency; accountability; and strategic vision.[19]

Government is the predominant actor in a country's governance. In a democratic set-up, political parties form governments and hence they play an important role in the governance process. The UN Democratic Governance Group's *Handbook of Working with Political Parties* set forth the rationale, saying that 'political parties are an essential part of the apparatus of governance'.[20] The observation is based on the contributions of political parties in aggregating interests, mobilizing the electorate, shaping public policies, holding politicians accountable, and fostering future leaders.[21] Political parties themselves as group of people united for the good of their country. They are perceived by the followers not just as political organizations, but also as social and moral agents of change. In the South Asian context, this is more than true. Moreso, the high level of participation in party-related activities could be because of clientelism as people see parties as access points for state benefits.[22]

World Bank's 'Worldwide Governance Indicators' has clearly established the linkage between the quality of party system and governance in over 200 countries surveyed.[23] It is found that countries with political parties have better governance than countries without parties, and those with competitive and stable party systems have better governance than those with less competitive and less stable systems.[24] However, the central question is: How far the quality of the political parties affects the quality of governance?

Some scholars opine that 'South Asia is united by a common thread of misgovernance'.[25] The 'essence of governance lies in delivering to the citizens the rights, privileges, and provisions enshrined in the constitution of each of these countries with respect to political, economic and social life'.[26] Achieving these goals, however, is not without challenges. Fifteen major problems are identified: population growth, poverty and deprivation, slow economic development, high illiteracy, high infant mortality, poor health care and sanitation, inadequacy of democratic processes, poor quality of institutions of governance, failure of political parties, politicization of armed forces, rise in ethnic conflict, rise in violence, growth of urbanization, degradation of the environment and corruption in public life.[27] Though failure of political parties is identified as one of the problems, it is the principal issue due to the centrality of parties in democratic regimes in the region. At the same time, it is important to identify certain challenges faced by the political parties of South Asia in general in the process of governance.

First, popular expectations and consequent demand for good governance has increased in the region. This is due, to an extent, to the rise of middle class, who are educated with significant socio-political awareness. Called as 'Square People', the new middle class emerged as a 'third party', who took to streets and squares to make the ruling regimes know of the failings in the governance process.[28] The polit-ical parties could not afford to ignore such articulations. The civil society organizations have also played a significant role in this regard by creating consciousness on the people's right to good governance. At times, opposition parties join civil society organizations in criticizing the governments on the governance and provide alternatives.

Second, there is a marked shift in the process of public governance in the region. Market-oriented policies like privatization, deregulation, downsizing and liberalization have started replacing state-centric policies. Sri Lanka was the first country to open its market followed by other countries. State got 'reinvented'; three major trends emerged in the governance process:

1. Involvement of more private sector as against the public sector;
2. Transformation of public sector management; and
3. Participation of civil society groups in the process of governance.[29]

As the role of the state diminished in the governance process, political parties found it hard to sustain the motivation of its cadres; lessor state institutions means limited 'goodies' available for distribution among the party loyalists. With the emergence of vibrant civil society groups having the benefit of liberalized international funding, the political parties of the region are no longer the sole agents of interest articulation. But, the civil society in South Asia is fragile in nature as compared to other regions.[30] The governments also try to constrain them in the name of security and sovereignty.

Third, there is a dwindling role of national parties and the rise of regional parties, especially in federal systems like India and Pakistan.[31] There has been differing electoral behaviour in national and provincial elections. Provincial elections attracted more electoral turnout compared to the national/federal elections. This clearly reflects the local governance concerns of the people rather than the larger issues of the state. The political parties are, therefore, forced to tune themselves to the new trend. This tilt away from the centre towards the periphery is, however, a cause for concern for the nation-building process of the countries of the region.[32]

Fourth, unlike in the past, formation of governments through coalitions has become normal in various countries of the region. However, this trend has posed two problems to the governance process: (1) political instability due to inability of a single party to gain majority on its own or unease coalitions falling apart before completing the terms of governments; and (2) compromises on the quality of governance in the name of 'coalition dharma'.[33]

Fifth, impact of dynastic politics on the quality of governance cannot be ignored. South Asia is known for dynastic politics, which has witnessed a new dynamics in the recent past. Traditional political families are no more the sole proprietors of political power; new families have entered politics at various levels: national, provincial and base. Some call them as 'Democratic Dynasties'.[34] Some of the new entrants are Rajapakses in Sri Lanka, Yadavs in Bihar and Uttar

Pradesh, Abdullahs of Jammu & Kashmir, the Scindias of Madhya Pradesh, and the Thackerays of Maharashtra. As a result, patron-clientelism has flourished leading to rent-seeking, nepotism, cronyism, arbitrariness, and secrecy.[35]

With these challenges faced by the parties of the region, the essential characteristics of governance, viz., participation, rule of law, transparency, responsiveness, consensus orientation, equity, effectiveness and efficiency, accountability, and strategic vision come under immense stress. Due to dynastic politics and paternalistic character of the parties, participation, transparency, consensus and accountability are in question. Due to vote bank politics, the rule of law, equity and accountability are undermined. Political parties strive to gain and sustain power. Else, they risk desertions at both cadre and leadership levels. The strategic vision on governance is oriented towards achieving immediate goals of the parties rather long-term objectives of the country.

CONCLUSION

South Asia is home to not only 'one of the oldest civilizations of the world but having large population, growing poverty, weak governance structures and feeble democratic institutions, increasing militarization and sectarianism'.[36] The role of political parties is essential for functioning of representative democracy. They perform five major functions: (1) the integration and mobilization of citizens; (2) the articulation and aggregation of interests; (3) the formulation of public policy; (4) the recruitment of political leaders; and (5) the organization of parliament and government. During election campaigns, political parties promise good governance through manifestos However, how far these promises are carried out is a critical question. Though the level of trust on democracy as a system of government is high in the region, trust on political parties is dismally low

Governance, as a result, has suffered. However, there is a hope in some countries of the region where governance is getting better. To attain a common minimum agenda for governance in South Asia, focus is required on eight areas: recognizing the sovereignty of the citizens, controlling population growth, economic growth with equity, restructuring institutions of governance (executive, legislative and judicial), redefining the role of the state, social development, emphasizing common culture and South Asian regional co-operation.[37] Of these, institutions of governance are important. Reforms in the political system have to start with reforms in the party politics in the region. Reforms in political parties have to be made so that the key objectives of elimination of clientelism, transparent party funding, zero criminal record, minimum literacy, fixed tenure for party leadership, gender parity in party positions and intra-party democracy are achieved.

On the positive side, the number of educated persons entering politics has increased due to two reasons: overall increase in the literacy level and politics seen as a career option and to bring in reforms. This is a positive development. But the party system, which has dominantly *status quoist* tendency, tries to push the emerging reformist elements out or to transform them to suit their interests. Hence, reforms in how political parties have to be formed and functioned must be regulated to bring in a positive change in the governance process. Else, political parties and governance will continue to remain as uneasy partners severely impacting on the quality of life of the people of South Asia.

NOTES

1. E.E. Schattschneider, *Party Government in the United States*, New York: Rinehart, 1942, p. 1.
2. The National Democratic Institute, 'Political Parties', see https://www.ndi.org/political-parties.
3. Anthony Downs, *An Economic Theory of Democracy*, New York: Harper & Brothers, 1957, p. 25.
4. Wilhelm Hofmeister and Karsten Grabow, *Political Parties: Functions and Organization in Democratic Societies*, Singapore: Konrad Adenauer Stiftung, 2011, p. 12.
5. M.M.K. Sardana, 'Addressing Naxalism and Left Wing Extremism through Good Governance, Development, Security Action, and Readiness to Talk', see http://isidev.nic.in/pdf/DN1309.pdf.
6. Subrata K. Mitra and Mike Enskat, 'Introduction', in Subrata K. Mitra,

Mike Enskat and Clemens Spieb (eds.), *Political Parties in South Asia*, Westport: Prager Publishers, 2004, p. 2.

7. Alexis de Tocqueville, *Democracy in America*, New York: Doubleday, 1969, p. 174.
8. The Mahbub ul Haq Human Development Centre, *Human Development in South Asia: The Crisis of Governance*, Karachi: Oxford University Press, 1999, p. 112.
9. International Institute for Democracy and Electoral Assistance, *Political Parties in South Asia: The Challenge of Change*, Stockholm: International IDEA, 2007, pp. 19-20.
10. Riaz Hassan, 'Religious Fundamentalism in South Asia: Some Preliminary Considerations', *ISAS Working Paper*, no. 238, September 2016, p. 10.
11. Inge Amundsen, 'Dynasty or Democracy? Party Politics in Bangladesh', *CMI Brief*, vol. 12, no. 6, November 2013, pp. 1-2.
12. For detailed exposition on the aspect of women in South Asian politics, see Amrita Basu, 'Women, Political Parties and Social Movements in South Asia', *Occasional Paper 5*, Geneva: United Nations Research Institute for Social Development, July 2005.
13. Angad Singh, 'Dynasty and Democracy in South Asia', *The Gate*, February 2015, see http://uchicagogate.com/2015/12/02/dynasty-and-democracy-in-south-asia/.
14. Duverger's law suggests a nexus between a party system and an electoral system. It asserts that an election system based on the plurality principle leads to a two-party system, while proportional representation discourages the emergence of a two-party system. It also holds that the plurality system marginalizes small parties. Although there can be several counter-examples to Duverger's law, the Indian example stands out as the most significant one.
15. International Institute for Democracy and Electoral Assistance, *Funding of Political Parties and Election Campaigns: A Handbook on Political Finance*, Stockholm: International IDEA, 2014.
16. UNESCAP, 'What is Good Governance'?, see http://www.unescap.org/sites/default/files/good-governance.pdf
17. The World Bank, 'What is Governance?', see http://web.worldbank.org/WBSITE/EXTERNAL/COUNTRIES/MENAEXT/EXTMNAREGTOPGOVERNANCE/0, contentMDK:20513159~pagePK:34004173~piPK:34003707~theSitePK:497024,00.html.
18. Kenneth Janda, 'Do Party Systems Matter?: Governance through

Modern Political Parties,' *Harvard International Review*, vol. 34, no. 4, Spring 2013, pp. 58-62.
19. United Nations Development Programme (UNDP), *Governance for Sustainable Human Development: A UNDP Policy Document*, New York: UNDP, 1997.
20. UNDP, *Handbook of Working with Political Parties*, New York: UNDP, 2006, p. 9.
21. Ibid.
22. See n. 9, p. 30.
23. The Worldwide Governance Indicators (WGI) project reports aggregate and individual governance indicators for over 200 countries and territories over the period 1996-2015, for six dimensions of governance: Voice and Accountability, Political Stability and Absence of Violence, Government Effectiveness, Regulatory Quality, Rule of Law and Control of Corruption. For details see http://info.worldbank.org/governance/wgi/#home.
24. Janda, n.18, pp. 59-60. Also see, Kenneth Janda and Jin-Young Kwak, *Party Systems and Country Governance*, New York: Routledge, 2016.
25. Sobhan Rehman, 'Governance and Development in South Asia', in V.A. Pai Panandiker (ed.), *Problems of Governance in South Asia*, New Delhi: Konark Publishers, 2000.
26. V.A. Pai Panandiker, *Problems of Governance in South Asia*, New Delhi: Centre for Policy Research, 2000.
27. Ibid.
28. Mahbub ul Haq Human Development Centre, *Human Development in South Asia 2015: The Economy and the People*, Lahore: Mahbub ul Haq Human Development Centre, 2015, p. 15.
29. Shamsul Haque, 'Reinventing Governance for Performance in South Asia: Impacts on Citizenship Rights', *International Journal of Public Administration*, vol. 26, nos. 8-9, 2003, pp. 941-64.
30. Michael Aagaard Seeberg, 'Democracy against the Odds? : The Impact of a Vibrant Civil Society and Institutionalized Political Parties', paper prepared for the Annual meeting of the Danish Political Science Association, 27-8 October 2016, see http://dpsa.dk/papers/Democracy%20against%20the%20Odds%20Civil%20Society%20and%20Party%20Institutionalization%20v.3%2019%2010%2016.pdf.
31. James Chiriyankandath, 'Parties and Political Change in South Asia', *Journal of Commonwealth & Comparative Politics*, vol. 52, no. 1, 2014, pp. 1-6.

32. Elisabeth Leake, 'At the Nation State's Edge: Centre-Periphery Relations in post-1947 South Asia', *The Historical Journal*, vol. 59, no. 2, pp. 509-39.
33. Irfan Nooruddin, *Coalition Politics and Economic Development: Credibility and the Strength of Weak Governments*, New York: Cambridge University Press, 2011.
34. For incisive analyses of dynastic politics in the Indian context, see Kanchan Chandra (ed.), *Democratic Dynasties: State, Party and Family in Contemporary Indian Politics*, New Delhi: Cambridge University Press, 2016.
35. G. Wood, 'Prisoners and Escapees: Improving the Institutional Responsibility Square in Bangladesh', *Public Administration and Development*, vol. 20, no. 3, August 2000, p. 222.
36. Sajjad Hassan, 'Minority Rights in South Asia: Rough Road to Citizenship,' in South Asia Collective (ed.), *South Asia State of Minorities Report 2016: Mapping the Terrain*, New Delhi: Books for Change, 2016, pp. 1-2.
37. Panandiker, n. 26.

CHAPTER 8

Securitization of Nation-building

Scope and Limits of State Coercion against Insurgent Violence

Uttara Sahasrabuddhe and Gayatri Lele

INTRODUCTION

New nation states began to emerge across Asia and Africa, as the colonial powers began to withdraw from their possessions after the end of the Second World War. The retreating colonial powers delineated the territorial boundaries of these new states. Thus, the British left the Indian subcontinent after a partition of the British Indian territory and withdrew later from their Southeast Asian possessions after creating the Federation of Malaysia combining Malay Peninsula, north Borneo and Singapore. Similarly, Dutch colonies in Southeast Asia comprising Java, Sumatra, Bali, South Borneo, Sulawesi, West Papua and hundreds of other islands, became independent forming the largest archipelagic modern state of Indonesia. In most cases, boundaries of the new states did not coincide with either the ethnic divisions within them or with the boundaries of the historical, pre-colonial states. The ethnic, religious and linguistic diversities within these states meant that these were not cohesive societies.

In Europe, nationalism as a unifying force emerged to integrate societies on the basis of language/ethnicity, leading subsequently to the demarcation of state boundaries. In contrast, Asian nationalisms have evolved with reference to, and within the boundaries of, states created by the colonial powers. Thus, the new states faced a massive challenge of nation-building, that is, the challenge of creating material and ideational structures of a modern nation state.

In most of these states, the diverse ethnic identities questioned the mainstream national discourse. Many of these identities also evolved into counter-nationalisms and separatist insurgencies, making the challenge of nation-building even more formidable. As the focus of nation-building was the territory of the state, territorial integrity became the fundamental requirement for the success of nation-building. Post-Independence narratives of national identities evolved around territorial states. Thus, securing territorial integrity became an essential part of post-Independence governance processes of these states. Preventing fragmentation of territory became the objective of nation-building processes, leading to the 'securitization' of nation-building. Consequently, use of the coercive power of the state was preferred over other means of nation-building, such as dialogue, democratic political process and institution-building.

One such case of securitization of nation-building in the context of India is the issue of Naga separatism. Naga identity has emerged as a competing narrative to the dominant narrative of Indian national identity; and Naga separatism has posed an existentialist challenge to the Indian state. The response of the Indian state has been 'securitization' of governance of the threat to security; and the use of coercive power of the state to maintain territorial integrity. This chapter analyses the scope and limits of coercion in the context of Naga separatism.

UNDERSTANDING 'SECURITIZATION'

Security can be defined as 'freedom from threat', both objectively and subjectively. The two ideas contributed by the Copenhagen School, namely sectoral analysis of security and the concept of securitization are widely used to show how in a society either the political elite or their audiences construct security.[1] Barry Buzan identifies five categories or 'sectors' of security, namely military security, environmental security, economic security, societal security and political security. For each sector of security, there are certain 'securitizing actors' and certain 'referent objects'. Securitizing actors are those who declare something as existentially threatened. Referent objects are those that are existentially threatened and have a legitimate claim to survival.

An issue can be plotted on a spectrum ranging from non-politicized, to politicized to securitized. A non-politicized issue does not appear in public debates. A politicized issue can be resolved through standard political process. A securitized issue requires emergency action beyond the standard political process. A certain issue can be securitized through a 'speech act', that is, when the securitizing actors publicly articulate it as an existential threat.[2] Within this framework, Naga separatism and insurgency fall in the first sector of security, i.e. traditional military security. The securitizing actor in this case is the Government of India. The Government of India articulated the threat from Naga separatism to the existence of the state of India and its territorial integrity by emphasizing the need for an emergency response beyond normal political process, i.e. the need for deploying military vested with extraordinary powers through an act of the parliament.

However, the discourse on securitization as developed by Ole Waever deviates somewhat from the sectoral analysis of Buzan. Waever argues in favour of a more traditional concept of security. He is opposed to any move from a strict focus on security of the state toward a broader focus on security of the people. The securitization discourse argues against the inclusion of issues like environment, welfare, immigration or refugees in the agenda of security. Waever claims that at the heart of the concept of security 'we still find something to do with defence and the state. As a result, addressing an issue in security terms evokes an image of threat-defence, allocating the state an important role in addressing it. This is not always an improvement.'[3] Thus, speaking of environmental problems in terms of environmental 'security' would mean allowing the state extraordinary power to meet the problem; which according to Waever, is not always good. According to him, security problems 'are developments that threaten the sovereignty or independence of a state in a particularly rapid or dramatic fashion and deprive it of the capacity to manage by itself. This, in turn, undercuts the political order. Such a threat must, therefore, be met with the mobilization of the maximum effort.'[4] Thus, anything that does not primarily threaten the political order or survival of the state is not regarded by Waever as a security problem. Waever further says, operationally securitization means, '*In naming a certain development a security problem, the "state"can claim a special right*, one that will, in the final instance, always be defined by the state and its elites.'[5] Thus, a security problem is what the political elite calls it to be so. Waever claims that securitization is a 'speech act'. By declaring something to be a security issue, the state – or in operational terms, its political elite – moves a certain issue into an area where it claims the special right to use whatever means to block it. In other words, a speech act of the political elite of declaring an issue as security issue results in securitization of that issue.

The concept of securitization has also met with varied criticism. For example, Matt McDonald argues that securitization defined as a speech act neglects the historical and social contexts in which designations of security and threat become possible, and the question of how particular voices within political communities are empowered or marginalized in *speaking* security.[6] He claims that 'the failure to elaborate on the context of the speech act, in particular the role of audiences, ultimately leaves such questions outside the framework itself'.[7]

We seek to argue that the conceptual framework of securitization helps understand the scope and limits of the coercive measures of the Indian state, i.e. the Armed Forces Special Powers Act (AFSPA), vis-à-vis Naga separatism.

BEGINNING OF NAGA SEPARATISM AND ITS SECURITIZATION

North-east India is not a homogeneous construct. Every state in this region has its own unique history and culture that is strikingly distinct from the mainstream Indian cultural components. Problems faced by every north-eastern state have multiple facets and dimensions. Hence, convincing the population of this region to recognize themselves as a part of the Indian state has been a strenuous national programme.

Since ages, the Nagas in various states of India's north-eastern region have carried a unique identity. The study of Naga identity has remained difficult due to inadequate literature and poor records. Further, the origin of the word 'Naga' is also controversial. Nagas are considered as sub-tribe of the Kiratas, who are mentioned in the Vedas and epics like *Mahabharata*. It is said that Arjuna, the great warrior of Mahabharata, had fallen in love with the Naga princess Ulupi and had lived in Nagalok for a short span of his life. Even in the battle of Kurukshetra, Nagas are believed to have played an important role similar that of other Indian tribes. According to some accounts, the word 'Naga' literally means 'naked people' of the hills. Each Naga tribe bears a unique name and culture as well as distinct history and characteristics. Eventually, the 'Nagas' became a political identity during the British era. The British had intervened in the governance of Naga-dominated regions and also made some military expeditions to the areas inhabited by the Nagas. In the later stage, they followed a policy of non-intervention in internal matters of the Nagas. The British were responsible for regulating administration of Naga Hills district on which they had complete control till the end of the nineteenth century. The Battle of Kohima in the Second World War was a turning point for the Nagas, in which they not only resisted the Japanese troops from entering India but also showed their allegiance with British.

Nagas thought of themselves as a separate nation and never wished to become a part of the independent Indian state. They always perceived themselves to be different from mainstream India. They resented the imposition of foreign laws and customs upon themselves. This fact is well depicted from a report submitted by the Nagas to the Simon Commission. An excerpt from it states:

> Our Country is poor and it does not pay for its Administration. Therefore if it is continued to be placed under the reformed Scheme, we are afraid that new heavy taxes will have to be imposed and in the long run we shall have no share in the land of our Birth and life will not be worth living then. Though our land at present is within the British Territory, government have always recognized our Private Rights in it, but if we are forced to enter the Council, the majority of those members is sure to belong to other districts. We also much fear the introduction of Foreign Laws and customs to suppress our own customary laws which we now enjoy. For the above reasons, we pray that the British government will continue to safeguard our rights against all encroachments from other people who are advanced than us by withdrawing our country from the Reformed Scheme and placing it directly under its own protection.[8]

The Memorandum clearly stated that no foreign rule can govern and represent them; and it also urged the British government to safeguard the rights of the Nagas against the encroachment from others who are way too advanced than them.[9]

An important development in the period leading to the independence of India is the formation of the Naga National Council (NNC). This organization was established by a famous Naga leader Angami Zapu Phizo. The NNC declared Nagaland as an independent sovereign state in 1947. It also conducted a plebiscite in the year 1951 on the issue of granting Nagaland a status of an independent nation state and claimed to be have secured the support of 99 per cent of Nagas for this proposition. Due to all these events, the Indian state increased its counter insurgency activities and gave more powers in the hands of paramilitary forces like that of Assam Rifles. The said intention was securing the region from the threat of rising violence and bringing back normalcy in Naga areas. As a result, the Assam Disturbed Areas Act was imposed in Naga-inhabited areas in 1955, which in the year 1958, became the Armed Forces Special Powers Act.[10]

Holding plebiscite in Naga areas and formation of the Federal Government of Nagaland (FGN), by the NNC in 1956 caused existentialist threat to the Indian state. This action threatened the territorial integrity of the Indian state and could lead to its disintegration. AFSPA can be regarded the 'speech act' of the ruling elite in Delhi, that securitized Naga separatism. Currently, the AFSPA is in operation in various states of north-east India and also in the state of Jammu & Kashmir. Failure of the states' police and paramilitary forces to curb the violent activities undertaken by insurgent groups has created led the Government of India to use the armed forces for the purpose. To handle such situations, special powers have been given to the armed forces. This act gives warrant to the Commissioned Officers in army deployed in areas declared as 'disturbed' under this act, to use force against the people suspected to be acting in contravention of any law and order. Such officers are empowered to destroy any arms dump or fortified position or shelter, arrest any suspicious person, and can also enter and search any suspicious property without a warrant.[11]

There can be no doubt that imposition of AFSPA in the then Assam state in 1950s, and ever since, has prevented physical disintegration of the Indian state. In that sense, AFSPA is a successful Act and its imposition can be justified within the discourse of securitization.

INSURGENCY, PARALLEL GOVERNMENT AND AFSPA

While the NNC was trying to pursue the goal of a separate Naga nation, the peace process had already taken off with the Hydari Agreement signed in the year 1947.[12] Both these processes were going on simultaneously and were having conflicting objectives. Sakhrie, a Naga leader who shaped the Hydari Agreement, was assassinated in 1955 which was suspected to be undertaken by one of Phizo's loyalists. On its part, the Government of India continued efforts to further integrate the Nagas with the Indian Union. A decade after the Independence of India, the Naga Hills District was separated from Assam in 1957 and it became a part of the Union Territory named as Naga Hills Tuensang Area. In 1963, this Union Territory was transformed into the state of Nagaland, which became the sixteenth state of the Union of India. Phizo escaped to London via the then East Pakistan, but the NNC continued its separatist insurgency and the FGN continued to operate in the Naga areas. However, a delegation of the NNC signed an accord – known as the Shillong Peace Accord – with the government of India in November 1975. This led to a split within the NNC leadership.

A group of disenchanted individuals separated from NNC to form the National Socialist Council of Nagaland (NSCN) to pursue the goal of independent Nagaland. Later on, this group too was divided into NSCN(IM) and NSCN(K). The former group led by Issak and Muiva is based in Naga Hills in India, while the latter, led by Khaplang, operates from it base across the border in Myanmar. NSCN(IM) and NNC-FGN have created their own areas of influence as well as their separate governance mechanisms which co-exist with the institutions of the state and the union governments.

The NSCN(IM) has successfully managed to set up its own parallel governmental bodies and taxation policies within the Naga-inhabited region. There are four ministries of NSCN(IM) – Defence, Home,

Finance and Foreign Affairs. The Home Ministry is considered to be important and has influence over nearly eleven Naga administrative regions.[13] The Home Minister is called as *Kilo Kilonser*, to which the officers in these eleven regions submit reports. These institutions work parallel to the institution of village panchayats created by the Indian Government under the Constitution of India. The village panchayats in Nagaland play a significant role in all these eleven Naga-dominated regions. The state of Nagaland has been exempted from the 73rd Amendment of the Constitution due to the existence of traditional local self-government through the village panchayats and Village Development Boards. Hence, these regions do not follow the regulations under the Panchayati Raj system. The village councils are established under the Nagaland Village and Area Councils Act, 1978, who look after almost all the important facets of governance such as law and order, courts, civil matters like marriage and divorce, disputes between villages, drinking water, roads and footpaths, land encroachment issues, etc.[14] In almost all the Naga villages, the GPRN has made the system of *Sakhan* mandatory. Under this, the villagers are expected to carry the belongings of all the revolutionary groups that arrive in the village. Even girls as young as twelve or thirteen years are expected to carry their baskets from one village to another. The GPRN has also developed a 'rotating system' under which almost each of the household has to provide a shelter to the members of rebel groups by turn and carry their belongings to the next destination. It is observed that the revolutionary groups are polite and extremely careful while dealing with the villagers.[15]

The AFSPA was expected to resolve the problem and curb the violent activities undertaken by insurgents. But as the entire governance went under military surveillance, the aggression and activities of FGN and other underground groups further increased in number and volume. They not only drafted their separate constitution but also established their own supreme court. The demand for Nagalim (the integration of all Naga inhabited areas in Nagaland, Assam, Arunachal Pradesh and Manipur) is still prevalent. Interestingly, it is often endorsed also by the Legislative Assembly of the state of Nagaland. Thus, while AFSPA did prevent disintegration of the Indian state, it has not been able to prevent insurgency and periodic violence. It has also not been able to prevent the violence between different insurgent Naga groups. Many people argue that armed forces are still needed to pacify the factions within the Naga community, as well as to save the Naga population from the atrocities committed by the insurgent rebel groups. AFSPA has also proved ineffective in curbing the influence of the parallel governing institutions of the rebel groups. This clearly shows the limit of AFSPA and that of state coercion against insurgent violence.

IDENTITY AND AFSPA

In the current scenario, NSCN(IM) is an organization which is mostly involved in achieving ceasefire agreements and peace accords with the Indian state. On the other hand, NNC and FGN have constantly opposed this position. They claim that they are the only nationally mandated bodies who are committed to support Naga sovereignty and independence. They refuse to call the Nagas 'secessionists', as according to them, Nagas were always an independent nation and are fighting for it. For them, Indo-Naga conflict has remained unresolved due to the continued occupation of their land by aggressors.[16] In their recent statement, they have criticized the Indian government for wrongfully occupying Naga regions through AFSPA and brutal atrocities it has committed to the Naga people. They have further stated that the issue of Nagaland is not a 'political problem', the real problem is unprovoked military aggression by India.[17] They often condemn the NSCN(IM) and proclaim that it does not represent the real will of the Naga people. These two groups accuse that the NSCN(IM) has never sought prior approval of the Naga people for making agreements with the Indian government. Indeed, they warned that 'No agreement between the GOI and the NSCN(IM) should infringe the rights and the interest of the Naga people'.[18]All these groups celebrate Naga Independence Day on 14 August every year and vow to preserve and protect the rights of the Nagas in their own land. This is an indication of perhaps the biggest limitation of state coercion in general and AFSPA in particular.

AFSPA helped in protecting territorial integrity of the Indian state. However, it could not help in enhancing the integrity of the

Indian nation. It has not, and perhaps will not, be able to convince the Nagas that they are not a separate nation, but are a part of the Indian nation. While proving to be an important instrument of building the material structure of the Indian nation (i.e. territory), AFSPA proved ineffective as an instrument of building the ideational structure of the Indian nation (i.e. identity).

CONCLUSION

Nation-building has been one of the big governance challenges for independent India, like most other post-decolonization new states. The geographical referent of the post-Independent nation-building project in India has been the territory acquired as legacy of the British Empire *and* that acquired after the integration of the princely states. One of the biggest challenges to the Indian nation state has been the counter narrative of Naga national identity, which simultaneously challenged the physical as well as ideational structures of the Indian nation state. Armed forces (Special Powers) Act, 1956, was a response to this challenge. This Act securitized not only the issue of territorial integrity, but along with it also the issue of national identity. AFSPA has so far adequately addressed the former issue. But the securitization of the latter issue due to AFSPA has exposed the limits of state coercion in building a nation.

NOTES

1. The Conflict and Peace Research Institute of Copenhagen, where Barry Buzan, Ole Waever and Jaap de Wilde made their significant contribution to Security Studies, is known as the Copenhagen School.
2. See Ralph Emmerse, 'Securitization', in Allan Collins (ed.), *Contemporary Security Studies*, 3rd edn, Oxford: Oxford University Press, 2013
3. Ole Waever, 'Securitization and Desecuritization', in Ronnie Lipschutz (ed.), *On Security*, New York: Columbia University Press, 1995.
4. *Ibid.*
5. *Ibid.*
6. Matt McDonald 'Secutirization and the Construction of Security', *European Journal of International Relations*, vol. 14, no. 4, 2008.
7. *Ibid.*

8. To read more about Naga Memorandum to Simon Commission, see Vashum, Reishang, *Nagas' Right to Self-Determination,* New Delhi: Mittal Publication, 2005.
9. *Ibid.*
10. Namrata Goswami, *Indian National Security and Counter-insurgency: The Use of Force vs Non-violent Response,* Oxon and New York: Routledge, 2014.
11. 'THE ARMED FORCES (SPECIAL POWERS) ACT, 1958', see http://nagapol.gov.in/PDF/The%20Armed%20Forces%20Special%20Powers%20Act%201958.pdf
12 Hydari Agreement – Also known as 9 point accord – which was signed between the Governor of Assam Akbar Hydari and the representatives of the Naga National Council (NNC) on 26-8 June 1947.
13 The eleven administrative districts are – Kohima, Phek, Mokakchung, Wokha, Zunheboto, Tuensang, Mon, Simapur, Peren, Longleng and Kiphire. They are inhabited by 17 major tribes.
14. L.H.M. Ling et al., *India China: Rethinking Borders and Security,* Michigan: University of Michigan Press, 2016.
15 Rajeev Bhattacharyya, *Rendezvous with Rebels,* New Delhi: Harper Collins India, 2014.
16. 'No Solution Without Sovereignty and Integration', *The Morung Express,* 15 August 2015, see http://morungexpress.com/naga-sovereign-rights-affirmed/
17. 'Naga Issue is a Result of Unprovoked Military Aggression by India: NNC', *The Morung Express,* 26 November 2016, see http://morungexpress.com/naga-issue-result-unprovoked-military-aggression-india-nnc/
18. 'Any Agreement between GoI-NSCN(IM) would be Invalid: NNC/FGN', *nelive Web Portal,* 14 September 2015, see http://www.nelive.in/nagaland/news/any-agreement-between-goi-nscn-im-would-be-invalid-nncfgn

PART 4

GOVERNANCE IN SOUTH ASIA: CASE STUDIES

CHAPTER 9

Statecraft in Jammu & Kashmir

Collapse of Governance

Gopalji Malviya

INTRODUCTION

Jammu & Kashmir (J&K) has for long been a disturbed border state with 70 km of Actual Ground Position Line, 750 km of Line of Control and 210 km of international border. Persistent militancy, insurgency, cross-border terrorism and externally fostered internal security threats blended with a separatist mindset has raised the challenges for peace and security. With protracted low intensity conflict, the basket is full of turmoil, struggle, crises and unpredictable arson, violence and unrest in the state. Under these circumstances, addressing the problems of the common man, providing essential services and restoring peace and normalcy is an extremely difficult task and possess challenges for civilian administration at all levels of performance and evolving a delivery mechanism. The unprecedented wave of terror and violence which engulfed J&K in January 1990, has shattered the valley's peace and normalcy and caused human and economic losses to a large extent. Several lakh people, including virtually the entire Kashmiri Pandit community, were compelled to flee the state, leaving behind their heritage, homes and all that they possessed. The arising turbulence led to the breakdown of the democratic system and the imposition of a unitary regime which continued for a long period.

Good governance is an integral part of any effective government. It is the primary duty of administration to provide the basic amenities to the people under its care, create conducive condition for them to pursue their vocation, aspirations and dreams, as to enable them to lead a reasonable peaceful life. Vitiated political environment, weak pillars of governance and lack of direction have almost blocked the possible development of state. Narrow nationalism, sub-regional bias, little or no respect for the Indian Constitution, acrimonious relations of political rivals and lack of consensus among various stake holders, give very dim hope for improvement in near future. It is a saga of blood, sweat and tears, and also of constant danger of life and limb of innocent people and security forces.

There is hardly a village which does not have a story to tell and very few families that do not have a tale of woes to narrate. Then there are incidents of heroic actions, survival under trying circumstances, heart-warming incidents of help and succour to the needy and the very act of putting back, laboriously and painstakingly, the almost disjointed and disrupted structure of the civil and police administration. In this huge task and multifarious activities, a large number of citizens, political personalities, activists of different kinds, members of the civil society and civil servants from the lowest rung to the chief secretary and policemen from the rank of the constable to the director general of police, are involved.

The state of J&K has been struggling with the scourge of Pakistani-inspired, trained and aided militancy for almost three decades. This has caused untold miseries to the people of the state, and resulted in thousands losing lives, many more getting hurt and immense loss to public and private property. Apart from the fact that the normal day-to-day life has been seriously disrupted, the entire social fabric has been under very severe strain. The mass migration of the Kashmiri Pandits from the valley, under militant threats and acts of violence, has been extremely tragic. It is a matter of record, and also pride for the people of the state, that in spite of the many threats, communal killings and ghastly acts of violence perpetrated by the terrorists, the people have refused to abandon their traditions of amity, brotherhood and communal harmony. This region has also emerged as the crucible of social harmony and mutual fellowship, providing shelter, succour and solace to a large number of people belonging to different places, regions and faiths.

Two things stand out clearly: mischief from Pakistan's ISI continues and is unlikely to abate. Also a broad overview of the situation prevailing in different parts of the country clearly established that Pakistani designs are not limited to J&K only but target the entire country. India has had to deal with Pakistan as a difficult neighbour and a source of constant trouble, at times downright dangerous. Pakistan's involvement in the affairs of India, particularly in J&K, has serious implications not only to the national security and territorial integrity of this country but also hits at the very core of Indian nationhood, based on secularism, pluralism and liberal democratic values. The conflict is not just for an area or a section of population, it is much more fundamental, of cherished values and lofty ideals. India must garner all its national resources, much beyond the military prowess, to decisively defeat the Pakistani designs.

Restoration of peace and normalcy in J&K has often been attributed to security forces. The role of army and other security forces is certainly commendable for their supreme sacrifices and significant contribution. But one should also understand that no insurgency or internal disturbances can possibly be handled successfully by security forces alone. Security forces can aspire to create a secure and conducive atmosphere for political establishment; however, it is for the civil administrative structure to perform their legitimate functions and duties. Needless to say, all the actors – the civil servants and the police forces of J&K, central armed police forces and the army – deserve a salutation.

NEW WAR : A WAR WITHOUT FRONTS

Terms such as rebels, ultras, militants, insurgents, terrorists and 'jihadis' are in use rather loosely by various militant groups that are engaged in large-scale organized violence in different parts of J&K. Irrespective of their objectives, ideologies and doctrines, these groups adopt a crude methodology and new forms of war to paralyse the administration and disrupt the law and order machinery. They are also referred to as freedom fighters to justify the 'jihad'. Some intellectuals in the Islamic world consider this widespread indiscriminate violence as a struggle against aggression and oppression. They feel that wherever there is oppression, injustice, or Muslims are denied the freedom to worship, struggling to liberate them is 'jihad'. These intellectuals have devised this convenient explanation to justify the ongoing violence in J&K. Islam has nothing to do with this fight. In itself, it remains a great religion. It is these Islamic militants who have hijacked this great religion to push their agenda through indiscriminate violence. The concept of a new war for political assertion and domination has been designed and propagated by the Islamic fundamentalists and militants; they have also called it a pan-Islamic movement. Unfortunately, intellectuals and media in the Islamic and non-Islamic countries have fallen into the theological trap laid by the Muslim orthodoxy.

Low-intensity conflicts are sub-conventional/unconventional in nature and scope with devastating impact on the Trinitarian entity – the state, the people and military. It is a 'war without fronts'. The levels and frequencies of crisis in J&K has been varied, ranging from the routine border skirmishes, ambushes, artillery exchanges, border incursions, terrorism that featured killings, bomb blasts all are being actively prosecuted as protracted conflicts since 1990s. It has been initiated directly by a belligerent or rogue state bent on revenge and retaliation but also has been prosecuted by invisible and amorphous entities of terror networks. Their premium of action has been on strategic approach of devastating destruction perpetrating mass death and colossal destruction of property simulating a high frequency conventional war. Paradoxically, this war without fronts has all the ingredients of stunning surprise, stealthy manoeuvre, operational decisiveness, tactical brilliance couched in a coherent strategic framework that dares to utilize conventional utilities in an unprecedented manner of deployment. War has come to the heartland of nation states declared by the invisible adversary defying all conventional canons of contemporary strategy and technological innovation that hitherto had predicted military operations remote from the homeland.

This unconventional war confers the perpetrator, the psychological reassurance and fictitious honour of a martyr, armed with low technology tools having all the potential to defeat a high technology, highly secure and nearly invincible defendant nation state. This war without fronts is essentially a war between nation states grappling with a host of national security threats and transnational threats pitted against highly organized yet miniscule cells of terror networks. The terror networks are evident by their hydra-like characteristics providing them the advantage of shifting targets and shifting bases thus rendering any means of targeted retaliatory attacks futile. Aims and objectives of the new war without fronts is waged by the amorphous terror groups with the supporting structures of these state sponsors using mass terror perpetuating the retaliation as revenge for the previous attacks of the *status quo* powers. In this perpetuation of mass terror the aims of the terror networks perfectly coverage with their state sponsors. The argument that terror networks can sustain independently in their sustained terror campaign without substantial patronage, safe haven, financial, logistical and moral inspirational support of the states of concern is superfluous.

Currently, militancy in Kashmir has acquired more violent and brutal form in the name of Islamic Jihad. The three major organizations operating through foreign jihadi elements are (i) Harkat-ul Mujahideen (ii) Lakshar-e-Toiba and (iii) Jaish-e-Mohammad. Apart from these major groups, there are numerous smaller outfits that operate in the Kashmir Valley. This militancy has indigenous roots as well as control by a foreign face.

The mushrooming of Wahhabi *madrasas* in Kashmir in the recent years has helped LeT to garner sympathy and support from the local population. The group, in the guise of civil society groups, has also been instigating civilian protests across the valley on some pretext or the other, deepening the distrust between the people and the state. It is also suspected that LeT militants engage the security forces in open public places to cause civilian casualties which, in turn, helps the group's objective in keeping the pot boiling. The group has also been active in funding local recruits. Although it has not been successful in creating a large base in the valley, it has been steadily and slowly, gaining grounds in militancy-prone areas like Sopore, Pulwama, Budgaon, Shopian, Anantanag, Bandipura and Srinagar. With many youth influenced by the recent spate of stone pelting protests against the state and security forces, terrorist groups like LeT with sophisticated recruitment strategies are likely to attract increased number of new recruits to their cause. It is quite clear that operational capabilities to re-launch the proxy war in Kashmir do exist among the terrorist groups sheltered. What needs to be examined in Pakistan army's intent? There is no indication of the ISI giving up its Kashmir agenda or its policy of using terrorist groups like LeT and JeM as instruments of state policy. It appears that enemies are succeeding in its well cherished design slowly and subtly.

Since 2010 a new dimension has been added towards war without front, in the form of stone pelting brigade in J&K. The blueprint of this tactics conceived in Pakistan and was successfully launched in the valley under the leadership of Masrat Alam, currently in jail. To accomplish this task youth were indoctrinated, recruited and trained to attack identified military targets, hit and run and remain invisible. The geographical landscape of J&K provides vast resource of stones of all size and shape to suit the operational requirement. The terrain and topography of the valley offers excellent scope for camouflage and concealment to these offenders. This unconventional means of guerrilla type attack has now evolved as warfare. This type of war is economically cheaper, politically sound, psychologically a morale booster and strategically perfect. Easily available stones are collected, transported, stored and used by the new zealots of war against security forces at appropriate target and timing with guaranteed success.

Handsome money is paid to the members of the stone pelting brigade to keep their motivation alive. Anti-India slogans and hatred against security forces are the main components of training given to these youth. There was alarming rise in strength of stone pelters in 2015-16. The number of attacks in different parts of the valley has also increased. Initially this exercise was seen on Fridays but by April 2017 this movement has taken an ugly shape and this is being conducted almost everyday at different parts of the Kashmir Valley with increased number of young offenders. According to recent Home Ministry's report, stone pelting incidents have increased by 55 per cent. Various associations of stone throwers and stone pelters in J&K have sprouted. They are well funded, well-orchestrated and consistently given direction and command. These associations have full support of separatist outfits like the Hurriyat. Social media and networking has become a catalyst to enhance operational capabilities of the movement. Some of the tall political leaders by their irresponsible statements and utterances have further poisoned the mindset of these youth. It is unfortunate that top political leadership of the state ask for restraint from security forces, but does not have any word of advice to the misguided militants!

The pattern that is emerging is dangerous. The supporters and sympathisers of the insurgents in Kashmir are keeping the police and paramilitary forces occupied with continued protests and defiance. The sleeper cells have been activated and their members instructed to keep the struggle alive. Carried out under the banner of 'protest' the acts of selective indignation and civil disobedience are aimed at damaging property, disrupting transportation systems and government operations. Insurgents are able to move rapidly within and between these 'homegrown' cells. The general public is being kept in an agitated mode, with more attacks on security personnel and their families. Hiding behind the shield of agitators and protesters, insurgents feel free to operate with impunity. The latest strategy of militants is to involve young girls in the ongoing protests in the Kashmir Valley. This has further created headache for security forces to face this new challenge.

Thrown into confusion by the advent of this hybrid nature of insurgency, visibly clueless security practitioners in Kashmir are reacting indecisively. There is no indication that this changing pattern of insurgency is being considered seriously by decision makers in New Delhi. Rather, the security establishment in Kashmir seems to be reacting in a way that is not only ineffective at preventing the attacks that are regularly taking place but also dangerous both for the troops deployed and for those whom they are sent to protect. Further, no serious effort has been made to upgrade the operational and intelligence capabilities of the J&K police. There is severe shortage of policemen in J&K. This emerging reality should be well understood across the government agencies dealing with security issues in Kashmir. It seems there is a total lack of deterrent mechanism devised by the Indian security managers against the militants.

With a variety of limitations and inability of state administration, the army is involved in providing the much needed support to people residing in border areas and other pockets of the state. Humanitarian assistance like health, hygiene, education, food, shelter, transport and other infrastructural service is provided by the armed forces. Hence armed forces while facing the challenges from enemy at the border also provide assistance to civilian government for its governance at crucial period. A fragile social fabric, rusted state machinery and crippled bureaucracy with their limitations, are not in a position to take initiative for delivering the fruits of good governance in J&K. It is essential that the trust deficit among various stakeholders is addressed. It is clear with present indications that unless state and central government along with the people of J&K change their attitude and mindset, it is difficult to have any optimism of improvement in near future.

Recently, Pakistan handlers and jihadi outfits have launched Operation Tiger in Kashmir Valley which targets members of security forces and their families. The men in uniform are hustled into a local mosque and coerced. Physical assaults on police and CRPF men, and burning of school and office buildings are new tactics adopted by the militants. These young zealots have also been tasked to loot weapons from security forces and use them for terror strike. Rushing these stone pelting brigade to encounter zones, and help militants to escape in the ensuing confusion, are part of the new strategy adopted by Pakistan to raise the stakes in J&K. The main objective appears to prove that the uprising is domestic in nature!

CONCLUSION

The fact remains that political leadership at J&K and New Delhi along with mighty Indian army has become a mute spectator. They are watching this situation moving from bad to worse. Mere *bayan-baazi* at all levels, but no assertive decision or deterrent mechanism to minimize or contain the evil forces. It seems there is an attitude of ambivalence and approach avoidance syndrome prevailing in the minds of national security managers. The question thus arises whether New Delhi is aware of the demoralizing impact of the security forces? Whether top leadership is able to notice cracks in the security apparatus? There is no clarity in the minds of political masters, they are treating this issue with adhoc and incremental approach, which is not likely to work. Security forces have to review their rules of engagement in the light of the new emerging dynamics. Political leaders at the state and centre are yet to come up with the long-term, effective and flawless plan to deal with the current situation. In view of the various complex factors involved, most observers believe that there is no immediate prospect of a solution to the Kashmir problem, especially if sponsored terrorism continues to vitiate the atmosphere and Indian security establishments continue to be complacent.

CHAPTER 10

Representative Democracy, Identity Politics, and Participatory Governance

The Indian Experiment

Rajamanickam Srinivasan

INTRODUCTION

The makers of the Indian nation were quite conscious in selecting representative democracy as the cornerstone of governance, than federalist or republican democratic structures as found in Great Britain or the US. The reason was not merely guided by the huge influence of thinkers like John Rawls, Jean-Paul Sartre or John Stuart Mill on the founders of this country. Antony Copley[1] in his essay 'Is There a Gandhian Conception of Liberty?' explores the connections between Gandhian thought and Western libertarianism. Copley briefly compares Gandhian thought to such Western intellectuals as 'Isaiah Berlin, John Staurt Mill, John Rawls and Jean-Paul Sartre. An incomplete comparison is the natural result of space limitation, but his point clearly emerges. Gandhi did not identify with the aspirations of the Indian middle class, and this inevitably takes him away from a tradition of bourgeois liberalism.[2] The founders of Indian Independence identified themselves with the bulk of the population that actually lived in the pale of every government that had ruled India for centuries till then. Therefore, providing them merely independence from foreign rule would have changed nothing in their life since in any case they had been oppressed into oblivion. The great saint-philosopher of India Swami Vivekananda,[3] whose writings had a huge influence on B.G. Tilak, M.K. Gandhi, Jawaharlal Nehru, Sardar Patel, Subhas Bose and a host of national leaders of those times, was categorical when he described the conditions of the common citizens of the country:

> The peasant, the shoemaker, the sweeper, and such other low classes of India have much greater capacity for work and self-reliance than you. They have been silently working through long ages and producing the entire wealth of the land without a word of complaint. Never mind if they have not read a few books like you – if they have not acquired your tailor-made civilization. What do these matter? But they are the backbone of the nation in all countries. If these lower classes stop work, from where will you get your food and clothing?… And you regard them as low class people and vaunt your own culture?[4]

If India were to emerge from its shadows and shine as a truly democratic country, the makers of the nation realized that the masses that Vivekananda referred to have to be empowered to obtain their rightful place in the society. They have to be brought out of conditions that have marginalized them and erased their sense of identity as citizens with equal rights in a society that had usurped culture and religious practices to push them to the periphery of societal existence. In fact, Gandhi coined the famous phrase 'Harijan' to give the marginalized sections of Indian community their new identity. Under his guidance, leaders across the country led these masses to enter temples that were hitherto denied them their right to worship; to draw water from common ponds that were banned to them on threat of ostracization; to take up professions that were consider 'prohibited' to these people. The leaders, in doing so, did not attempt to break caste that has been held as the hereditary trade guild in India for millennia. They were merely attempting to break the social barriers that had denied millions of people social justice and equality. They realized that the root of all evils in India is the condition of the poor. They have been compelled to be merely hewers of wood and drawers of water for centuries, so much so, that they are made to believe that they are born as slaves, born as hewers of wood and drawers of water.[5]

OBJECTIVES OF GOVERNANCE: LAYING THE FOUNDATIONS

At the midnight on 14-15 August 1947 India had its 'tryst with destiny'. While the importance of independence from foreign rule was duly acknowledged, as the first Prime Minister of India, Jawaharlal Nehru, realized that merely freeing the masses from foreign rule was not an end by itself. He prophesied that the true meaning of independence would be realized only when social justice became a reality for the millions – safety, food, equality before law and equality of opportunity. His address (Nehru, 1947) to the Constituent Assembly at the hour of midnight when India walked into its freedom was:

> The service of India means the service of the millions who suffer. It means the ending of poverty and ignorance and disease and inequality of opportunity.... The future beckons to us. Whither do we go and what shall be our endeavour? To bring freedom and opportunity to the common man, to the peasants and workers of India; to fight and end poverty and ignorance and disease; to build up a prosperous, democratic and progressive nation, and to create social, economic and political institutions which will ensure justice and fullness of life to every man and woman.... All of us, to whatever religion we may belong, are equally the children of India with equal rights, privileges and obligations. We cannot encourage communalism or narrow-mindedness, for no nation can be great whose people are narrow in thought or in action.... To the nations and peoples of the world we send greetings and pledge ourselves to cooperate with them in furthering peace, freedom and democracy.[6]

Merely enshrining these words in a speech on a momentous occasion in history was not the end of endeavour of the makers of the nation. It was realized that these words have to be reinforced with the power of law and laid out as the foundations of democracy in India. The founders of the nation, therefore, drew up a constitution that specifically took care to address the issue of marginalization in the name of caste or community or religion. While declaring India its sovereignty, the Preamble of the Constitution proclaimed in clear terms:

WE, THE PEOPLE OF INDIA, having solemnly resolved to constitute India into a [SOVEREIGN SOCIALIST SECULAR DEMOCRATIC REPUBLIC] (GOI, 1977) and to secure to all its citizens:
JUSTICE, social, economic and political;
LIBERTY of thought, expression, belief, faith and worship;
EQUALITY of status and of opportunity;
and to promote among them all
FRATERNITY assuring the dignity of the individual and the [unity and integrity of the Nation] (GOI, 1977);
IN OUR CONSTITUENT ASSEMBLY this twenty-sixth day of November, 1949, do HEREBY ADOPT, ENACT AND GIVE TO OURSELVES THIS CONSTITUTION.

In the first three decades of Independence, the governance was focused on laying the foundations for the ideals set forth in the Constitution. The socialist objectives were set to be realized through robust public sector undertakings like BHEL, HAL, etc.; building of big dams like the Bhakra Nangal; setting up of huge steel factories like that in Bhilai; nationalization of coal mining and production; nationalization of banks and financial institutions; etc., which borrowed heavily on the Soviet Russian models (in many cases like Bhilai, built with Russian assistance). Even farming was encouraged on a massive scale like the communes in Soviet Russia with heavy subsidies to encourage the agricultural sector. These grandiose schemes in the early years relied on the Indian perception that the teachings of socialism suitably toned with democratic precepts of modern Indian thinkers would deliver economic justice to the large population that lived under poverty. This Nehruvian ideal was mammoth in imagination and commendable in its execution, considering that the newly-independent nation was 'poor' economically.

CASTE AND EMERGENCE OF IDENTITY POLITICS

The four wars of the first three decades (1948, 1962, 1965 and 1971), the resultant economic sluggishness as well as the continuing poverty of the masses, in the later years propelled late Prime Minister Indira Gandhi to coin the most direct call, *Garibi Hatao* (Remove Poverty), to address the core issue in India. It was also realized that proclaiming equality and legislating equal access to opportunity did not automatically result in the upliftment of the masses. Despite the other political upheavals (in fact, partly due to them like the late Prime Minister V.P. Singh's plank to political prominence – Mandal Commission agitations in India), the next two decades saw a series of amendments to the Constitution that addressed the issue of poverty from a different dimension – identity. It is important to note that in India, identity invariably means more of caste than the faith of individuals and communities. Swami Vivekananda put this across succinctly:

> What caste really is, not one in a million understands. There is no country in the world without caste. In India, from caste we reach to the point where there is no caste. Caste is based throughout on that principle. The plan in India is to make everybody a Brahmin, the Brahmin being the ideal of humanity.[7]

He further went on to emphasize that caste is a social custom and all our great preachers have tried to break it down. From Buddhism downwards, every sect has preached against caste and every time it has only riveted the chains. Caste is simply the outgrowth of the political institutions of India; it is a hereditary trade guild[8] and our castes and our institutions ... have been necessary to protect us as a nation, and when this necessity of self-preservation will no more exist, they will die a natural death, and further realizing that a system of structuring a society that had existed for millennia cannot be wished away; on the contrary, if social justice were to be achieved, he said, caste should not go; but should only be readjusted occasionally. Within the old structure is to be found life enough for the building of two hundred thousand new ones. It is sheer nonsense to desire for the abolition of caste. The new method is evolution of the old.[9]

The polity in India thought otherwise. The Constitution was amended eleven times over two decades from 1980. Each successive amendment either introduced a new provision or extended and expanded an existing provision to bring in the marginalized castes of India into mainstream politics and governance, while successfully 'marginalizing' the other so-called forward castes. The consequence of the constitutional amendments was the emergence of what may be termed as 'Identity Politics'. The first general election in India was held in the year 1951; just a year after the Constitution was adopted. Fourteen national and 39 regional parties contested in the election.[10]

A total of seven (All India Scheduled Caste Fedaration [SCF] at the national level and Chota Nagpur Santhal Parganas Janta Party [CNSPJP], Punjab Depressed Class League [DCL], Hill People Party [HPP], Khasi-Jaintia Durbar, Kuki National Association at Regional or State level) were the only parties that had 'identity' pronounced on their mascots and manifestos. The third general election held in 1962 saw the emergence of a new category of parties – Registered Unrecognized Parties [RUP],[11] which were patently reflective of the change that was taking place in the political landscape of the country. The emergence of sub-regional parties that had the aspirations of specific communities for political space at their core was witnessed. While this should be viewed as a mark of the vibrant democratic traditions that the founders of the country had hoped to instill, an interesting factor noticed during the period was the emergence of parties based on socialist ideologies as well as ethnic identities (We Tamil Party and Tamil Nationalist Party in the South on racial identity for example). At the national level at that time there were three parties even professing their own versions of communism – Communist Party of India, Praja Socialist Party and Socialist Party. The SCF that had championed the Scheduled Castes had by now merged into other parties within six years of its appearance on the electoral scene.

The year 1996 is a watershed year in Indian politics. The eleventh general election witnessed two phenomenons:

- The regional parties that had reduced to 20 in number by 1992, sprang their numbers to 30.
- The number of RUP that began at 10 in 1962 became 171.[12]

Among these, 17 of them had patently identity-based proclamations even in their names (10 per cent). The eleventh general election is also notable, for it saw the highest number of women contenders for the Lok Sabha, a record that is yet to be beaten. The national parties, regional parties, RUPs and independents together fielded 599 women candidates. Out of these only 40 candidates of the national and regional parties entered parliament. On the other hand, not a single one of the 424 independent candidates won a seat.

The 2009 general election saw seven national parties, 34 regional parties and 322 (the highest till now) RUPs enter the fray. Among these, six regional parties and 34 RUPs had either ethnic or communal identity as their manifest agenda, as pronounced in their name. In comparison with 1996, the identity based parties had doubled. Interestingly, number of seats in the parliament to represent the SC and ST communities, for whom the founders had the most noble of their concerns, had merely increased by 80 per cent for SC and 16 per cent for ST from 1951 to 2009, though the voting population had grown five times over, as can be seen from Figures (10.1 & 10.2):

The growth in number of political parties is represented in Figure 10.2.

Political parties are indispensable in a democracy. Thinkers like Mill opined that democracy is unimaginable without political parties. While it is true that democracy is founded on the principle of power to people (by the people, for the people, of the people – like Lincoln said in his famous Gettysburg address), the structure that is put in place cannot accommodate the whole population in decision-

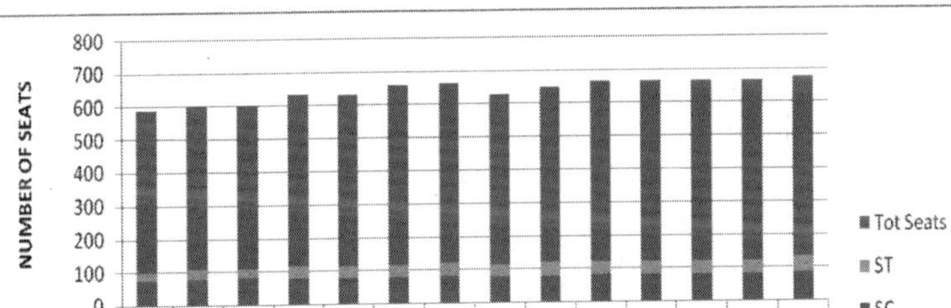

	1	2	3	4	5	6	7	8	9	10	11	12	13	14
Tot Seats	489	494	494	520	518	542	542	514	529	543	543	543	543	543
ST	28	31	30	37	36	38	41	38	39	41	41	41	41	47
SC	72	76	79	77	76	78	79	75	78	79	79	79	79	84

LOK SABHA ELECTIONS 1951-2009

Source: Compiled and tabulated with statistics collected from Election Commission of India, see http://eci.nic.in/eci_main1/ElectionStatistics.aspx

FIGURE 10.1: SC AND ST REPRESENTATION IN LOK SABHA SEATS

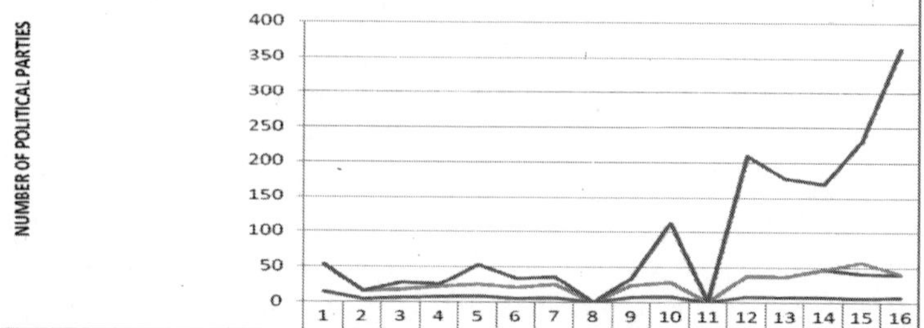

	1	2	3	4	5	6	7	8	9	10	11	12	13	14	15	16
REGISTERED UNRECOGNISED PARTIES	0	0	10	4	28	14	11	0	9	85	0	171	139	122	173	322
OTHER STATE PARTIES	0	0	0	0	0	0	0	0	0	0	0	0	0	0	15	0
REGIONAL/STATE PARTIES	39	11	11	14	17	15	19	0	17	20	0	30	30	40	36	34
NATIONAL PARTIES	14	4	6	7	8	5	6	0	7	8	0	8	7	7	6	7

LOK SABHA ELECTION (1951 TO 2009)

Source: Compiled and tabulated with statistics collected from Election Commission of India, see http://eci.nic.in/eci_main1/ElectionStatistics.aspx

FIGURE 10.2: GROWTH OF POLITICAL PARTIES IN THE YEARS 1951 TO 2009

making. Apart from this impracticality, governance requires domain expertise in its function which neither the numbers nor the commonsense of ordinary people can compensate. The obvious solution is to allow representatives of people and communities to carry the concern of the societies that they represent to the legislature for formulating policies and procedures. This is an outstanding innovation of the nineteenth century and aptly called representative democracy. It is in this domain of representation that political parties emerge. They are born of ideologies that appeal to certain segments of the society which believe that the leaders of such parties sharing their common ideology will become effective advocates for the society's concerns.

As the Indian nation progressed from independence, the faith that people of India placed in the national parties perhaps eroded. The reasons were many, mammoth parties like the Congress and the Communist Party of India that had grown out of the nationalistic and economic concerns of the bulk of the population found it difficult to truly incorporate the aspirations of people from remote corners of the country. The third general election of 1962 actually saw the emergence of Eastern Indian Tribal Union, Gorkha League, Haryana Lok Samiti, Nutan Maha Gujarat Janta Parishad, Tamil National Party and We Tamil parties, representing regional as well as localized concerns at the national level. It may not be out of context to recall the manner in which Naga uprising of 1957 was put down by the Government of India. The emergence of these parties indicates the alternative strategy by regional communities that felt estranged by the actions of central government – the strategy of entering mainstream national or regional politics to carve a niche for themselves and their people in the power structure.

The trend of regional parties based not only on ethnic or racial identity but on caste identities was first noticed in the ninth Lok Sabha elections of 1989 (Bahujan Samaj Party [BSP] and All India Dalit Muslim Minorities Suraksha Mahasangh [ADMMSM]) – both these parties came on the plank of social justice to Dalits or Harijans, a name Mahatma Gandhi christened the community with. By 2009, the number of such parties had grown to 6 at the RP level and 34 in the RUP level, as brought out in the Figures above.

It is also important to note the name adopted by ADMMSM. Islam is purportedly a casteless religion. The party came into being claiming its support base of 'Dalits' among Muslims. It also adopted the title 'Mahasangh' – like Hindu Mahasabha – conveying its secular credentials by adopting a Hinduized title. These are reflective of the loosely defined concepts of secularism in Indian polity as well as the need to appeal to identities for political purposes.

The growth in the number of RP/RUPs facilitates the following inferences:

- The ideologies of nationhood, democracy, liberty, equality, etc., that held sway at the time of independence had begun to lose their appeal as political ideologies. The cause was not merely political incapacity. The population had more than doubled and so had their aspirations. People aspired for deliverance than rhetoric. Figure 10.3 demonstrates the growth of the electorate from 1951 to 2009. It indicates that while the turnout percentile reflecting the actual number of people who participated in the democratic process by exercising their franchise grew just about

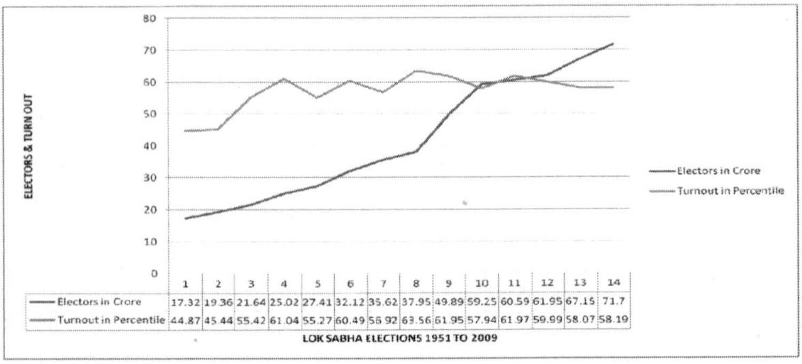

	1	2	3	4	5	6	7	8	9	10	11	12	13	14
Electors in Crore	17.32	19.36	21.64	25.02	27.41	32.12	35.62	37.95	49.89	59.25	60.59	61.95	67.15	71.7
Turnout in Percentile	44.87	45.44	55.42	61.04	55.27	60.49	56.92	63.56	61.95	57.94	61.97	59.99	58.07	58.19

Source: Compiled and tabulated with statistics collected from Election Commission of India, see http://eci.nic.in/eci_main1/ElectionStatistics.aspx

FIGURE 10.3: NUMBER OF ELECTORS AND TURNOUT IN GENERAL ELECTIONS: 1951 TO 2009

30 per cent (29.68 to be precise) in six decades, the eligible number of voters had grown over 300 per cent (313.97). We also find that at the average turnout of 57.23 per cent, 40 per cent of Indians, though otherwise eligible to exercise their 'voice' either chose not to or were unable to due to factors that would merit an independent analysis.

- The Nehruvian concept of secularism – a loose concept of denying religion a space in governance without affecting its influence in the private sphere had successfully negated the possibility of religious identities controlling political power. Deepa Ollapally notes that

> it was the recognition of the deep-seated religiosity of the Indians that prompted Nehru to work against the use of religions for political purposes, and avoid the dangers of communalism. The resulting construction was something that oscillated between a rather strict secularism and a looser version, reflecting the difficult environment that had been inherited. This flexibility has proved to be politically indispensable.[13]

While the partition of the sub-continent came on the basis of religious identity, the experiences of partition had taught a valuable lesson against political mobilization on the basis of religious identity. Ashis Nandy observes on how secularism came to be accepted as an essential 'rhetoric':

> As for secularism, by now it is obvious that the Indian concept of secularism has little to do with the concept as it was developed over the last four hundred years in the West. That secularism de-ethicizes public life and attempts to place politics upon the perceived secular trends in history. This secularism means, at worst, purely secular, political use of religious differences and, at best, equal respect for all faiths.[14]

Accordingly, 'secular' credentials became essential for political parties to project their popular image across communities. This indirectly prompted caste identity as the means for political mobilization even across religious identities since that would strengthen the 'secular' character of the party. The growth in the electorate also helped in this formulation since large populations, particularly as diverse in their socio-cultural identities, cannot be bound together on ideology alone.

- The emergence of caste as the plank for political mobilization also helped the political parties to project their concern for social justice – something that could be ascribed to historic origins; that had profound impact on peoples life; which guided their daily social interactions and beliefs – giving ample scope for them to play with the caste sentiments without affecting their 'secular' credentials. In fact, social analysts like Ashis Nandy summarize the 'talk' of political parties to just three rhetorics or catch phrases – democracy, secularism and socialism. While each of these terms have close links with the post seventeenth-century Western world-view but each have been Indianized to serve native purposes.[15] He further observes that political debates can take place around these concepts in modern India, as the concepts stand for a vague commitment to public good and morality.[16] Since all three concepts are essential to the posture of grand standing, however, varied in their implied or expressed meaning by every political party, caste became indispensable to project an individual party as the champion for social justice for a community. The emergence of BSP in Punjab originally but later with deep roots in Uttar Pradesh on the Dalit card is an outstanding example for the birth of caste-based identity. The appeal and success of BSP in UP actually signaled a new beginning in Indian politics – politics of identity.

- The SC and ST populations of the country who are at the heart of identity politics always received substantial political patronage – at least on paper. Right from the First General Election, constituencies were carved for both SC and ST in the belief that representation in power sharing will assist the communities to undo centuries of marginalization. In course of time, the number of seats assigned in Lok Sabha for SC and ST more than doubled. Figure 10.1 above illustrates the phenomenon.

Though other marginalized communities also deserved representation, specific assignment as done above was not adopted perhaps due to the size of the other communities and the fear that doing so would alienate other populations who were sympathetic to common cause than 'caste' politics. The abject poverty of majority of the population would also deprive the political parties their sources for funds if they expressly played the caste card. So, a balanced approach of espousing social justice to specific communities without antagonizing other communities was evolved with the twin objectives of popularity and survival. In fact, in the past UP elections, both BSP and SP wooed the Brahmin and Thakur communities, both of which, ironically, have been blamed for the oppression of Dalits historically. In the same manner, in Tamil Nadu, realizing the venomous campaign of anti-Brahmin and anti-upper castes approach of Dravidar Kazhagam (DK) coupled with 'rationalism' that slandered religions, as detrimental to electoral politics, Annadurai and Karunanidhi split from DK to establish Dravidar Munnertra Kazhagam (DMK) that professedly stood for Tamil racial identity across castes and religions. Though DMK continued to claim its umbilical connections to DK on matters of racial and rational identity, it has always been careful to avoid giving space to DK in power-sharing equations. Emergence of other parties in Tamil Nadu, aside AIADMK, like DMDK, VCK, MDMK, etc., also is indicative of the emergence of caste as the basis of political identity. Many of these parties have their support base exclusively in specific castes like the Nadars, Thevars, Koundars, etc. The Vallalars of Tamil Nadu, a powerful caste, even had their own Akila India Vallalar Peravai (AIVP)[17] in the electoral fray of 2009.

The BSP, a national party claiming to represent the Dalit cause pan-India, in 2009 general elections contested 500 seats out of 543; secured 21 seats;[18] lost deposit in 410 constituencies; polled 25728920 votes (in all 500 constituencies that it contested), which is 3.59 per cent of total electors in India and 6.17 per cent of votes polled. Ironically, the Indian National Congress party claiming pan-India, cross-communal and secular credentials polled 28.85 per cent of votes across India representing 16.65 per cent of the electors. A comparative table of national, regional and RUPs can be seen in Table 10.1. The comparative performance of a party that openly advocates caste identity (although flirting with upper castes) as against a proclaimed 'secular' 'nationalist' party is testimony to the sectarian or caste politics that Indian polity has pampered itself with during 1996-2009.

That this identity consideration has even influenced government in defining its highest institutions in terms of identity was visible when the UPA government showed enthusiasm to accommodate demands by BSP and SP to give representation to SC, ST, OBC communities in the Lokpal Committee that was being considered actively as the single-most contribution and demonstration of the will of the government to battle corruption. *The Times of India* reported on 19 December 2011:

> Brandishing the caste card is political stock-in-trade. And reservation is a tool of opportunistic electoral mobilisation. None of this is new. Even so, India's anti-corruption efforts being given a casteist twist qualifies for special flak. Outfits including SP and LJP recently demanded quotas for SCs, STs, OBCs and minorities in the proposed nine-member Lokpal and its selection committee. With UP polls round the corner, this was to be expected from regional satraps. But that the UPA nodded approvingly shows how strong the temptation is across the political board to indulge in competitive populism.[19]

TABLE 10.1: VOTE SHARE BY NATIONAL, REGIONAL AND RUP IN 2009

Sl. No.	*Party*	*Category*	*States contested*	*Total valid votes polled in state*	*Total valid voters in State*	*Seat won*	*Votes polled by the party*	*Vote Share*
1	BSP	National	Madhya Pradesh	1,94,84,608	3,80,85,179	1	11,40,044	5.85
		N	Uttar Pradesh	5,54,07,107	11,60,06,374	20	1,51,91,044	27.42
	BJP	N	Andaman & Nicobar Islands	1,70,103	2,65,108	1	75,211	44.21
		N	Assam	1,21,41,171	1,74,70,329	4	19,67,813	16.21
		N	Bihar	2,42,32,597	5,45,05,246	12	33,76,109	13.93
			Chhattisgarh	85,54,843	1,54,76,577	10	38,51,970	45.03
		N	Dadra & Nagar Haveli	1,10,363	1,50,704	1	51,242	46.43
		N	Daman & Diu	68,024	95,382	1	44,546	65.49
		N	Goa	5,64,255	10,20,794	1	2,52,694	44.78
		N	Gujarat	1,74,72,923	3,64,84,281	15	81,28,858	46.52
		N	Himachal Pradesh	26,90,290	4606674	3	13,33,774	49.58
		N	Jharkhand	91,35,818	1,79,34,095	8	25,15,265	27.53
		N	Karnataka	2,45,72,713	4,17,90,939	19	1,02,28,790	41.63
		N	Madhya Pradesh	1,94,84,608	3,80,85,179	16	84,65,524	43.45

N	Maharashtra	3,69,91,311	7,29,54,058	9	67,21,644	18.17
N	Punjab	1,18,29,304	1,69,58,380	1	11,90,144	10.06
N	Rajasthan	1,79,31,593	37060011	4	6557727	36.57
N	Uttar Pradesh	5,54,07,107	11,60,06,374	10	96,95,904	17.5
N	West Bengal	4,27,30,548	5,24,93,168	1	26,25,182	6.14

Source: Author. Compiled and tabulated with statistics collected from Election Commission of India, see http://eci.nic.in/eci_main1/ElectionStatistics.aspx

IDENTITY *VS.* DEVELOPMENT

The GDP in India grew phenomenally in the decade 2001-10, indicating the capacity for growth despite diverse issues on other fronts. While this growth was not even and the end beneficiaries were a small segment of the society, the growth propelled a middle class that expanded unlike the fifty years since Independence. The urbanization which was inevitable saw a huge influx of aspiring rural India moving to the cities. The urbanization of India has a huge impact on political thinking of the people. People who witnessed improving life styles of the urban class wanted proportional dissipation of that progress spread to villages. Communities hitherto looking for deliverance on identities started demanding their share of development too. While caste became the stock trade in politics with the advent of community-based political parties after 1996, the economic reform agenda that Narasimha Rao government launched in 1991 saw the emergence of market forces that began to touch peoples' lives differently. The midas touch of the IT industry propelled the mushrooming of technical education and the lure of Silicon Valley. Though not intended, this produced a great neutralizing effect on identity politics since it brought development as the agenda than identity and power sharing – reminding the famous quote from Eric Hobsbaum, 'Identity is all very well but what after identity?'

In the elections of 2009 and later for state assemblies, development overtook the concern of the common voter than the question of his identity. In the contemporary history of the world, 2011 is an important year. The breaking of the Berlin wall and the collapse of USSR signaled an important political message – that people are unimpressed with empty ideologies that appropriated power to the few and remained impassive to ordinary citizen's woes for livelihood. 'Whether it is Tahrir Square in downtown Cairo or Zuccotti Park in New York, the defining images of 2011 will be those of thousands of ordinary folks gathering to make their voices heard. From Athens to Madrid, from New Delhi to Moscow, people have been on the march and protests became the expression of choice against injustices, real or perceived.[20]

Polls for state Assemblies in Tamil Nadu, Kerala, West Bengal and Assam in 2011 again indicated the subtle change in the mentality of people asking for their share of daily bread than the share of power by their chosen representatives in the polity of the country on the basis of caste identity. National papers like *Times of India* reflected the sentiment of people in the following words: 'These are complex polls, involving sizeable areas, numbers and issues, some volatile. The states are familiar with the violence of identity politics. But in a positive sign for India, trendlines in these key states show the force of identity politics diminishing, with people concerned more with bread-and-butter issues such as development, jobs and price rise.[21]

That the ordinary citizen's disenchantment with identity politics, obviously due to its failure in deliverance, did not go unnoticed by the parties. The eroding support base in consecutive elections and the choices that people made have had their impact on polity. The RSS which is at the heart of all Hindutva forces in the political and social sphere as well as the national leaders of the next biggest population aside Hindus in India, Muslims, made huge appeals to the masses to cast away identity considerations in electing their representatives. *Times of India* reported:

> In a welcome, even path-breaking move, former RSS supremo K.S. Sudarshan and eminent Muslim cleric Maulana Kalbe Sadiq have issued a joint appeal to the electorate not to vote on religious lines. Instead they want voters to send honest representatives to assemblies and Parliament, regardless of their community of origin. That such a call should come from a prominent Hindutva leader and the vice-president of the All India Muslim Personal Law Board in unison is significant. By making a clear distinction between the politics of good governance and the over-leveraged rhetoric of identity based mobilisations, the two important community leaders have set the tenor for a new political discourse. [22]

Such sentiments did not arise from sudden awakening of people. The factors that lead to the change in peoples' attitude stems from their conditions based on ground realities. The founders of the nation and Constitution makers were not imperceptive about the estrangement of people from the considerations of the polity, executive and judiciary. In a huge country, connecting the government process to the people would remain a fundamental challenge. It was, therefore, essential to provide for a mechanism that would directly empower the bulk of 'marginalized' and poor people with governance. The father of the nation, Mahatma Gandhi had the most brilliant yet typically simple solution – revive village panchayats.

The term 'panchayat' stems from the age-old practice of self-governance that predates Christ. The Indus Valley Civilization as well as subsequent rulers like the Guptas, the Mauryas, and even to a fair extant the early Moguls at least up to Akbar, realized that the communities in rural India were bound by their common interests that spanned across caste lines. Caste actually acted like a trade guild allowing the people of the village not merely to co-exist but also resolve the issues that arose amidst them by a process that nominated five representatives to come together as the 'Panch' (meaning literally five in Hindustani) and vesting the power to resolve common, revenue, crime and communal issues through them. The village chose to abide by the Panch for its own identity, solidarity and security. As the lower most unit that the government had to deal with in imposing its will on people, the panchayat was not merely convenient but also minimized bureaucratic burden. The ancient rulers also found that mobilizing the peasantry in times of war was easier through panchayats than through direct regal decree. Empires like Kanishka, Chandragupta, Ashoka, Rajaraja Chola actually gave fillip to the strengthening of the institution of panchayats for the stated benefits.

Article 40 under the Directive Principles of State Policy (DPSP) called upon the states to take steps to organize village panchayats and provide them with necessary finances and authority to function as self-governments. The intent of the Constitution could not have been more eloquent in integrating citizens into governance, not merely as end-users but as decision makers. The spirit of Article 40 was unambiguous. However, with passing away of Nehru in 1964, the thrust for expanding the panchayati system through central monitoring, funding and encouragement almost disappeared. The states provided for cursory panchayati institution, mostly bereft of financial powers or authority to implement. But the biggest boost to the panchayati system came when Rajiv Gandhi assumed prime ministership in 1984. Realizing the need to reinforce panchayati raj institutions with constitutional authority, the L.M. Singhvi Committee suggested Amendment to the Constitution. The 73rd and 74th amendments to the Constitution in 1992 sought to bring freedom and sovereign power nearer to the people and make democracy more meaningful for the ordinary citizens at the grass roots. [23]

The new constitutional provisions of Part IX and IXA seek to change the structure of Indian polity by giving constitutional status to the three tier. Art 243 to 243ZG have the effect of reinforcing the basic constitutional value that in a democracy, power belongs to the people. They should be able to feel it in their hands and have the assurance of being able to exercise it themselves.[24] The amendments ensured that state finance corporations were mandated to work out the distribution of revenue between the state and panchayats. In order to bring the urban and semi-urban poor also within the ambit of self-government, municipalities were brought within the ambit of panchayati raj institutions (PRI). The PRIs were empowered to impose certain taxes, collect revenue and undertake planning activities on both the dimensions of life in rural areas – economic development and social justice.

The policy perspective, thus, had unambiguous aim – make ordinary citizens not mere beneficiaries of government schemes but give them the power to make their own destinies. While the aim was clear, the government had also realized practical difficulties in empowering citizens. Considering the huge backward castes and sizeable populations of SC and ST communities, it was also envisaged that the proportional representation of these communities in panchayats would be ensured to meet the ends of social justice. It was

TABLE 10.2: IDENTITY-BASED REPRESENTATION IN PANCHAYATI RAJ INSTITUTIONS

No. of Panchyats	*Category Wise Elected Members in Panchayats*							
	General	*SC*	*%*	*ST*	*%*	*Total*	*Women*	
							Number	*%*
2,39,582	19,04,419	5,14,284	18.25	3,17,425	11.26	28,18,018	10,38,045	36.84

Source: Government of India, Ministry of Panchayati Raj, Annual Report 2007-8. The data is as on 31 March 2008.

perhaps hoped that the empowered segments of the 'marginalized' people would be only too willing to transform their lives.

India has 6,40,867 villages (Census of India, 2011).[25] There are 2,39,582 panchayats with 28,18,018 elected representatives as on 2008. Among these 18.25 per cent are SC, 11.26 per cent are ST and 36.84 per cent are women. The representation of marginalized communities thus is proportional to the population. This is an indication of the strength of national will to accord empowerment to the oppressed classes. However, while noble ideals may find their expression in constitutional and policy provisions, their real success would always be in translating these ideals into realities on the ground in terms of livelihood of people. The polity as well as the planners was also aware of challenges in the functioning of panchayats. The Annual Report (MoPR, 2012) of the Ministry of Panchayati Raj stated:

> Gram Sabha is central to local self-governance and transparent and accountable functioning of the Gram Panchayat. This is a forum that ensures direct and participative democracy. It offers equal opportunity to all the citizens.
>
> It is well recognised that many elected representatives of the PRIs may not have the leadership qualities and attitude or sufficiently be literate and may have low awareness about development programmes, planning, systems and procedure. They require training to undertake the tasks expected of them as people's representatives. Further, a large number of Panchayats do not have their own office space or adequate staff to look after the functions assigned to them.[26]

Before an analysis on the subject of delivery on all these intents is taken, the policy paradigms are to be completed. Table 10.3 gives the grants by central government for strengthening PRIs.

Table 10.3 indicates that over a period of three financial years, the government of India allocated Rs. 2,000 crores towards the development of PRIs and processes. States like Andhra Pradesh, Bihar, Madhya Pradesh, Uttar Pradesh, Maharashtra and West Bengal received substantial portions of these grants, while other states had just nominal allocations. The state governments, therefore, found it convenient to blame it on the centre for not providing adequate grants for furthering PRIs. A look at the grants for training and infrastructure for PRI staff in Table 10.4 further confirms that the

TABLE 10.3: RELEASE OF GRANTS OF 12TH FINANCE COMMISSION FOR PANCHAYATI RAJ INSTITUTIONS

(Rs. in lakh)

Total Allocation	*Amount of one instalment (Six Monthly)*	*2005-6*		*2006-7*		*2007-8*	
		Amount released		*Amount released*		*Amount released*	
		1st Installment	*2nd Installment*	*1st Installment*	*2nd Installment*	*1st Installment*	*2nd Installment*
20,00,000	2,00,000	1,93,884	1,92,324	1,92,324	1,84,879	1,00,230	1,79,130

Source: Ministry of Panchayati Raj Documents, see http://panchayat.gov.in

TABLE 10.4: SUMMARY OF RELEASE DURING 2011-12 UNDER RGSY[27]

(*Rs. in lakh*)

Component	*BE*			*Actual Expenditure**		
	Non-NE	*NE*	*Total*	*Non-NE*	*NE*	*Total*
Training & capacity building	5,250	750	6,000	2,803	649	3,452
Infrastructure development	2,100	300	2,400	1,983	0	1,983
Total	7,350	1,050	8,400	4,786	649	5,435

Note: * Till 29 February 2012.
Source: Annual Report of the Ministry of Panchayati Raj, 2011-12, see http://panchayat.gov.in

intentions for promoting participative governance were actually not translated into actions.

While the actions were not commensurate to the intentions, we may summarize the merits of the PRI initiatives in following words:

- Direct citizen participation in governance was perceived as essential in delivering the fruits of growth to the marginalized sections of the society.
- It was also understood that the hitherto oppressed and exploited sections of the society will need earmarked representation in local governance, if their concerns were to be registered and acted upon.
- It is not possible for the mass of people living in poverty and in conditions of illiteracy and societal exploitation to find their voice automatically. They need to be trained, protected and empowered to discharge their functions in local governance.

In keeping with the above three realizations, the government had drawn upon the RGSY and Backward Regions Grant Fund (BGRF), Rajiv Gandhi Panchayat Sashaktikari Abhiyan (RGPSA) and various other schemes to provide for the strengthening of this grassroot democratic institution. The grants from central and state governments were primarily meant to train the functionaries in panchayats and to provide for infrastructure needed for official functions. Thus, through the institutionalization of panchayati system and providing for the efficiency of the PRIs, India, perhaps, is a unique model for developing countries by having functioning mechanisms for representative democracy at the national-cum-state level and participatory democracy at the grassroot level. The intention and spirit of such provisions are truly ambitious. The commendable feature of both the institutional structures was the identity-based representation for obtaining social justice and progress.

IDENTITY POLITICS AND DELIVERY IN GOVERNANCE

The 20th Anniversary Report of the Expert Committee on Leveraging Panchayats for Efficient Delivery of Public Goods and Services, Government of India, observed in April 2013: 'Though more than fourteen years have gone by since the Constitutional mandate was brought into effect, there has been little progress except in a very few states.'[28] Alas, nine more years later there has still been little progress except in a very few States.

Further, the report stated in para 2.17 of its observations that

> The above conclusion of sharply worsening income inequality is based on the NCAER finding that the lowest income earners, that is, those comprising at least 60 per cent India's population, secure only 19.6 per cent of India's national income while the richest 5 per cent secure nearly a quarter of the country's national income, 23.8 per cent. The share going to the highest income and wealth percentile is probably much higher since NCAER's reported income survey figures are able to capture only 54 per cent of national income, the remaining 46 per cent not being admitted to, a figure which closely resembles the estimate by Global Financial Integrity that over the period of economic reforms, the unaccounted share of the Indian economy has risen to 43 per cent from 27 per cent.[29]

It added in para 2.18 that

> The other deeply disturbing NCAER finding is that the poorer an Indian is, the more entrapped in personal debt he is likely to be. Thus, the poorest 5 per cent, earning less than Rs. 8 a day, consume Rs. 3590 a year against an income of Rs. 2145 a year: their ratio of expenditure to income is 167 per

cent of income. As one goes up the scale, income approximates to expenditure only at 15 per cent. It remains as high as 79 per cent for the best of 5 per cent segment of 50 per cent of our population and does not significantly taper off till we have reached three-quarters of our population. It is only the richest five per cent of our population whose percentile savings at 37 per cent approximates the national savings rate. It is this high level of personal indebtedness of the poor, combined with easy access to corporate debt for the rich, that necessitates our regarding not only the utterly destitute as poor but also the vulnerable as poor.[30]

The reality of the gap between identity, institutions and actual performance was summed up by *Financial Express* in the following terms: 'The problem is not that the rich have got richer but that those at the bottom have not been provided the wherewithal to improve their earning capability … over time, the benefits of near double digit growth should have percolated to the economically disadvantaged sections of society, which has not happened.'[31]

THE IMBROGLIO

Though the representative character of polity and government are seen to be favourable to the identity-based demographic distribution of the Indian society, there appear to be huge gaps in delivery. This brings to the fore some fundamental questions: does the identity driven political environment need re-orientation for better governance? Do political parties need to understand that the participative model envisaged in the PRIs with appropriate representation of marginalized communities need more strengthening than being preoccupied with identity politics for its own ends? The answer appears to be in the affirmative. While observing the preparations for polls in Tamil Nadu, Karnataka, West Bengal and Assam, *Times of India* reported that 'These are complex polls, involving sizeable areas, numbers and issues, some volatile. The states are familiar with the violence of identity politics. But in a positive sign for India, trend lines in these key states show the force of identity politics diminishing, with people concerned more with bread-and-butter issues such as development, jobs and price rise.'[32] And again in 2012, after the stunning defeat of BSP in the state assembly polls, the newspapers highlighted two lessons that political parties advocating identity politics must learn: the first takeaway for the political class is that identity politics has its limits. The second lesson is that, beyond a point, *aam admi* (common people) will not rest content with vicarious consumption of the fruits of growth and development. They want the real thing. For, people across the country increasingly want a governance style that brings about tangible improvements in their material conditions of living. There's just no getting away from the need for broad-based, secular governance agendas that treat citizens as individuals to be empowered rather than supplicants for patronage. Uttar Pradesh is the most caste ridden society in India. In a state where the upper caste domination was successfully countered by BSP on Dalit plank for nearly two decades, the lessons in 2012 elections are hard hitting. However, as *Times of India* pertinently asked, 'Will the winners in these state elections deliver? It's in their interest to do so, given voters are punishing business-as-usual – developmental shortfalls, poor services delivery, administrative apathy, corruption, vote-bank politicking – repeatedly.'[33]

While a panoramic view of the Indian polity, identity politics, and representative democracy in action tends to give a perception that the challenges in India that have existed for centuries have only been compounded by the mess that the combine of representative democracy-identity politics have created. This view is not only myopic but is also quite alienated from reality. The emergence of identity politics propelled a greater integration of the society, over three decades, for developmental agenda. Presuming that the Indian economy bubble had managed to touch people's lives even in the remote corners of the country in some pronounceable manner, it would probably have led to the cementing of the fragmentations of the society on casteist lines. The rapid urbanization and sudden but acute disparity between urban-rural lifestyle has led to the breaking down of the hold of caste on the society. This may be a bit more pronounced in the urban areas but its far reaching effect will eventually mitigate the rigidity of mindsets that one may still experience in caste-bastions like Uttar Pradesh.

The media has played a huge role in highlighting identity politics and its negative ramifications. While constantly linking the 'dole' culture of successive governments to pacify segments of the society through populist schemes and subsidies, and by linking such exuberance of the polity to the caste moorings in party ideologies, media has inadvertently helped in creating an aversion in public mind for identity politics. Another huge development that has attained dynamic proportions in the dilution of identity politics is the exposure of 'scams'. The constant media hype on scams has actually discouraged politicians from dispensing in largesse to particular segments of their vote banks, directly or covertly.

Although the government of the day may be either praised or condemned, two single most developments in India, two acts, have also had a huge impact in diluting identity politics: The Protection of Human Rights Act 1995 and the Right to Information Act 2005. Coming as they did in a gap of a decade, both the acts and the Human Rights Commissions and Information Commissioners that these acts brought into public life have contributed to the growing awareness amongst people across caste lines about their social and economic rights.

Judicial activism, particularly the jurisprudence on public interest litigation, is a game changer in creating mass awareness. While through the last decade or so people have also come to realize that law alone cannot make the government deliver, the trend has actually created an acute demand amongst the people asking the government to deliver on court verdicts.

Civil society movements, particularly those that originated on social, environmental and economic issues have made near-indelible mark on the society and in turn propelled forces among hitherto voiceless populations to demand delivery. The Chipko Movement, Narmada Bachao Andolan, and NGO/Public Activist groups like PUCL deserve specific mention as they created awareness among people as much as they demonstrated the 'unassailability' of government decisions as a myth. These movements in this sense truly empowered people.

Last but not the least, the credit for making people demand that development is their 'birth right' must be given to the polity. While the unscrupulous amongst them brought in an aversion in people's mind of the unashamed nature of political class, the principled and visionary amongst them, however, they may otherwise have faulted, were (and are) responsible for truly understanding the needs of the people and translating them into systems through inspired legislative process. But for those few, people would never be able to realize their dreams for development in a truly democratic environment.

THAMASOMA JYOTHIR GAMAYA:[34] FROM DARKNESS TO LIGHT

The most unique factor about India rests in the domain of its spirit. The intellectual tradition of its society and the robustness of its mind have stood the test of millennia. This may appear to be self-glorification in one sense. Therefore, it is essential to look at certain historical precedence. European, African, American and history of the West as well as Southeast Asian history tells us that every other society that was influenced either by centuries of foreign rule or an external religion eventually changed at its core and accepted the external factor as its own identity. Even England that came to rule the rest of the world at one point of time changed its core with the arrival of the Anglo-Saxons. The Christian traditions or Islamic culture that the West and most of the East now claim as their own actually came from West Asia. Over millennia they have become so ingrained in their social conscious that it is not even possible to believe that the world has become 'Asianized' in its faith, while India and China have retained their original social conscious in spite of huge impressions gained through their centuries of interaction with Western societies. The sociological dimension of this resilience in the Indian society is an important factor if changes in governance are to be brought about.

Representative nature has been accepted as the soul of democracy. In societies that have near homogeneous population interconnected by uniform cultural traditions, representative form of democracy has the strength to truly reflect the aspirations of all segments of society. In countries such as India, the challenges to effective representation stem from various factors:

- *Language* – India speaks 22 official languages, 415 recognized languages and over 1,600 tongues that are spoken by populations ranging from 100 to 10,000. The difficulty to understand any concept in one single perspective can easily be judged by this variety.

- The literacy rate, which in India is generally taken as the ability of an individual to write his name (which is the case mostly, as acknowledged by Census 2011 report) makes it a challenge to communicate ideas to even a reasonable size of the population.
- The poverty and subnormal living conditions of majority of the population preoccupy them with concerns of daily life. This can easily be inferred from the fact that only 50 per cent of the 2/3 eligible voters actually vote to elect their representatives. Understandably, even 50 per cent of the electors voting on a day do so under the sway of temporal offerings from local candidates.
- The elected representatives have huge constituencies with as much variety of issues as would some countries in the Sub-Saharan Africa or the Pacific have. Physically connecting with the populations of a constituency therefore remains a challenge. The official engagements of the legislators also occupy their prime time along with the pressures of their public office. Thus an elected representative of over millions of people in a constituency (the average works out to 22 million populations per member of Lok Sabha) actually gets to reflect the sentiments and concerns of the most vociferous segments of his constituency than the majority of his constituency in his legislative sphere.

The importance of participatory governance through PRI gains tremendous significance when seen from this perspective. As against 543 members of parliament and 4,120 members of Legislative Assembly in state legislatures (not adding the Rajya Sabha seats since some of the members of Rajya Sabha are nominated), there are 28,18,018 elected panchayat representatives in India. That panchayats function in the immediate communities whose reps are drawn from it gives the PRIs actually better connectivity to the concerns of the community.

From independence till now, four high power committees[35] have examined various aspects of functioning of the Panchayati Raj system. Each of these regretted the lack of commitment in implementing the Panchayati Raj system in the spirit in which constitutional provisions envisaged it. The sentiments reflected by the Ashok Mehta Committee continue to be of relevance:[36]

2. … The dis-association of the growing and complex programme of development with PRIs which were considered inadequate, the inability of the bureaucracy to be attuned to execute the programme through elected bodies, the lack of political will to foster these institutions, several internal deficiencies in the functioning of PRIs and, above all, the lack of clarity about the concept itself have weakened the entire system.
3. Part of the disappointment arises from the syndrome that they have not been assigned significant functions and tried continuously and with zest. The development programmes were not channeled through them. Some of the comments like the emergence of oligarchic tendencies are inherent in the social milieu, and some others are common to other tiers of the polity also. PRIs should not be singled out for these comments. It has many achievements to its credit in introducing a process of democratic seed-drilling in the Indian soil, in breaking the gulf between the bureaucratic elite and the people and in generating a new leadership not merely relatively young in age but pro-social change in outlook.
4. Panchayati raj, like democracy at the national and state levels, is both an end and a means. As an end, it is an inevitable extension of democracy; as a means, it would continue to be responsible for discharging obligations entrusted to it by the national and state governments in spheres not yet transferred to its exclusive jurisdiction. Altogether, both as an end and a means, Panchayati raj should contribute to the philosophy as well as practice of a rich, rewarding life in rural India.
5. The establishment of democratic bodies below the state level is an imperative from the political and socio-developmental perspectives. Democratic institutions with periodic elections at all levels will provide a forum for the assertion of their strength in large number by the weaker sections. With the people and political parties having adequate opportunities to exercise power at various levels, national energy in political recrimination will yield to constructive competition and mutual co-operation in developmental activities among political parties.

The L.M. Singhvi Committee Report suggested the following measures to strengthen grassroot governance through citizen participation:

- Financial allocation by government at the centre as well as state
- Training of elected representatives
- Provision of infrastructure for effective discharge of their functions.

The Government of India, grasping the importance of these recommendations, has put in initiatives to translate these lessons into reality. Another important initiative of the government has been the introduction of Gram Nyayalaya Bill 2008,[37] bringing the power of courts to the domain of people. Though the legal fraternity in India has expressed reservations on the issue,[38] it is to be seen as yet another step in the direction of bringing people closer to rule of law process which remains the most crucial foundation of democracy.

CONCLUSION

It is impossible to lay down a precise path for democracies to adopt by which they could fulfil the aspirations of its population. The world has always been driven by innovation in thinking, ideological conflicts, aspirations for development and conflict of interests in various proportions while debating governance. Should we refine the representative character of democracy? Should we revert back to the city-state like participatory models? Is there a via-media that would help us to draw a balance between the two approaches? Will we ever find the most ideal path? These questions would continue to haunt political thinkers as much as would affect people. The most probable answer would perhaps remain elusive, since the changing dynamics in every society across the world creates newer aspirations and demands in the hearts of people and no system has the flexibility to change as fast.

The Indian experiment in embedding both representative and participatory democracy in the unassailable foundations of constitutional provisions has one important lesson to students, advocates and practitioners of democracy everywhere – people are at the heart of governance. The political environment in India, the economic swings, internal and external security challenges and the much-to-be-desired maturity in political class of India notwithstanding, the Constitution reflecting the people at its heart will prevail. America which is 250 years old as a democracy is given to intense political and public debate on the quality of its governance many a times. India is just 70 years young as a democracy. Given the short span but commendable stability of Indian political institutions and the emerging consciousness amongst its populations for good governance, there is every hope that it would find its due place in the annals of history as a nation of its people, than of empty premises and promises.

Strengthening its participative roots through PRI (grassroot village level governance) will remain a crucial challenge for India as the PRIs reflect the will and aspirations of over two-thirds of the population. Not being content with committees and commissions, setting aside the ideological differences on other spheres, political parties across the spectrum need to work in conjunction with the PRIs in order to fulfil their role as intermediaries between the people and governance. Politicization of the process on identity or other such differentials needs to be meticulously avoided since politicization at such grassroot level would actually splinter the unity of the fabric of Indian society despite all its diversities.

The political parties need to keep in mind that identities are an effective medium for mobilization. However, politicizing identities excessively for electoral purposes eventually divides the society, bringing a sense of bitterness and alienation amongst communities. In the northern parts of India, a distinct murmur against politicization of identities through 'khap' panchayats (caste-based local bodies wielding power over people) is already gaining decibels.[39] Such exploitation will render the most unique Indian experiment of balancing representation and participation through a legitimate constitutional mechanism ineffective and the aspirations of millions of illiterate yet good citizens of the country far from realization.

NOTES

1. Anthony J. Parel (ed.), *Gandhi, Freedom, and Self-Rule*, New York and Oxford: Lexington Books, 2000, p. 42.
2. *Ibid.*
3. Swami Vivekananda, *Rebuild India*, Kolkata: Advaita Ashrama, 2006, pp. 2-3.

4. *Ibid.*
5. *Ibid.*
6. Jawaharlal Nehru, in his speech 'A Tryst with Destiny', on the night of 14-15 August 1947, in the Constituent Assembly of India, see http://parliamentofindia.nic.in/ls/debates/vol5p1.htm
7. Vivekananda, n. 3, p. 7.
8. *Ibid.*, p. 8.
9. *Ibid.*, p. 9.
10. Statistical Report on General Elections, 1951, to The First Lok Sabha, vol.1 (National and State Abstracts & Detailed Results), Election Commission of India, see http://eci.nic.in/eci_main1/ElectionStatistics.aspx
11. Eastern Indian Tribal Union (EIT), Gorkha League (GL), Haryana Lok Samiti (HLS), Lok Sewak Sangh (LSS), Nutan Maha Gujarat Janta Parishad (NJP), Revolutionary Socialist Party (RCP), Revolutionary Socialist Party (RSP), Socialist Labour (SL), Tamil National Party (TNP), We Tamil (WT).
12. Statistical Report on General Elections, 1996, to the Twelfth Lok Sabha, vol. 1 (National and State Abstracts & Detailed Results), Election Commission of India, see http://eci.nic.in/eci_main1/ElectionStatistics.aspx
13. Deepa M. Ollapally, *The Politics of Extremism in South Asia*, New Delhi: Cambridge University Press, 2009, p. 48.
14. Ponna Wignaraja and Akmal Hussain, *The Challenge in South Asia: Development, Democracy and Regional Cooperation*, New Delhi: Sage, 1989, pp. 316-17.
15. Ashis Nandy, 'The Fate of the Ideology of the State in India', in Ponna Wignaraja and Akmal Hussain (eds), *The Challenge in South Asia: Development, Democracy and Regional Cooperation*, New Delhi: Sage, 1989, p. 316.
16. Ibid., p. 317.
17. See http://eci.nic.in/eci_main/archiveofge2009/Stats/VOLI/02_ListOfPoliticalPartiesParticipated.pdf
18. One seat in Madhya Pradesh and 20 in Uttar Pradesh, though it fielded 500 candidates across Rajasthan, Haryana, Himachal Pradesh, Chattisgarh, Delhi, Punjab, Bihar, Madhya Pradesh, Maharashtra and Uttarakhand.
19. 'Caste it Away', Editorial page, *Times of India*, 19 December 2011.
20. 'Year of Protests', Editorial page, *Times of India*, 23 December 2011.
21. 'Identity Politics', Editorial page, *Times of India*, 13 April 2011.

22. 'A Positive Appeal', Editorial page, *Times of India*, 11 November 2011.
23. Subhash C. Kashyap, *Citizens and the Constitution*, New Delhi: Publication Division, Ministry of I&B, Government of India, 2nd edn., 2002, p. 209.
24. *Ibid.*
25. See http://censusindia.gov.in/2011-prov-results/paper2/data_files/india/Rural_Urban_2011.pdf p 13.
26. Annual Report of the Ministry of Panchayati Raj, 2011-12, para 1.17, see http://panchayat.gov.in
27. *Ibid.*, p. 12.
28. *Towards Holistic Panchayat Raj: Twentieth Anniversary Report of the Expert Committee on Leveraging Panchayats For Efficient Delivery of Public Goods and Services*, vol. 1, New Delhi: Ministry of Panchayat Raj, 20 April 2013, p. 18.
29. *Ibid.*, p. 42.
30. *Ibid.*
31. *Financial Express*, 15 January 2011.
32. 'Caste it Away', Editorial page, *Times of India*, 19 December 2011.
33. 'Years of Protest', Editorial page, *Times of India*, 23 December 2011.
34. The ancient texts, the Vedas, have a prayer for daily life: *asato dma sa gamaya; thamaso ma jyotir gamaya; mrityorma amritam gamaya; om, shanti, shanti, shanti hi* (Let there be truth in place of untruth; let there be light in place of darkness; let death be conquered by eternal life; My Lord, let there be peace, peace and peace in the world).
35. Balvant G. Ray Committee, 1957; Ashok Mehta Committee, 1978; G.V.K. Rao Committee 1985; L.M. Singhvi Committee, 1986. Full text reports are available at the Ministry of Panchayati Raj website, Documents section, http://panchayat.gov.in
36. Ministry of Rural Development, Government of India, Committee on Panchayati Raj Institutions, 1978, paras 2-5, p. 3. Full report available at Documents section of the Ministry's website http://panchayat.gov.in
37. The Gram Nyayalaya as a different court was proposed by the 114th Law Commission way back in 1986. The report recommended the concept of the Gram Nyayalaya with two objectives: to address the pendency in the subordinate courts; to introduce a participatory forum of justice that would cater for expediency and local sensitivity. See lawcommissionofindia.nic.in
38. The Gram Nyayalayas Act, 2008 moves Indian citizens with small claims, who live in rural areas, out of the adversarial system with its procedural guarantees. As a statute with limited procedural guarantees

to adjudicate allegedly small claims, including those that implicate a plethora of social welfare legislations, this act compromises the promises of the Constitution. Menaka Guruswamy and Aditya Singh, 'Accessing Injustice: The Gram Nyayalayas Act, 2008', *Economic & Political Weekly*, vol. 45, no. 43, 23 October 2010, pp. 16-19.

39. Chander Suta Dogra, 'Retrograde Avatar of Repressive Traditions', *The Hindu*, 11 February 2014.

CHAPTER 11

Politics of Performance

A Comparative Study of Governance Models in India

Abhishek M. Chaudhari

INTRODUCTION

The role of political parties is of prime importance in any democratic set-up. In representative form of government, parties function as a link between the government and the people. Primary objective of any political party is to contest elections and to capture the seat of power. After coming to power, they convert their agenda into policies and programmes, and thereby try to work for maximization of people's welfare.

India is a multi-party democracy. In the post-Independence period, India has experienced rise of several parties at the union as well as state level. The political parties in India are spread across political spectrum. The oldest party in India is the Indian National Congress (popularly known as the Congress), which emerged from India's struggle for independence. Bharatiya Janata Party (BJP) is the right-wing party, with philosophical undercurrents of *Antyodaya* (uplifting of the weakest section of the society). At the same time, there are leftist parties like the Communist Party of India (CPI) and the Communist Party of India (Marxist) (CPM). Several parties have come up at the regional level also, which are largely confined to their respective states. They include parties like All India Anna Dravida Munnetra Kazhagam (AIADMK), Dravida Munnetra Kazhagam (DMK), Telugu Desam, Shiv Sena, Akali Dal, Bahujan Samaj Party,

Trinamool Congress, and so on. All these parties have positively contributed to the development of Indian polity.

Evolution of the party system in India is a fascinating example of modern multi-party democracy. Rajni Kothari in his book *Politics in India* argues that the party system in India evolved from an identifiable political centre, which was carved during the nationalist movement. The Congress party was the institutional manifestation of this political centre. Hence, the party system during the first two decades after Independence was termed as the *Single Dominant Party System*, as the Congress party occupied the central space of electoral politics.

The changing socio-economic and demographic profile of India changed the nature of the party system during 1960s. This era also witnessed the rise of proprietary peasant class in rural India due to the land reforms. This was the beginning of the decline of the dominant party system. The change in the nature of party system was initially visible at the state level where a number of non-Congress governments were formed. By 1970s, the land owning socially dominant sections, mainly belonging to the backward castes, attained sufficient economic strength to demand a share in political power. This led to the formation of parties reflecting the interests of these newly-mobilized classes. This era witnessed the emergence of a multi-party system in the true sense. The BJP slowly emerged as other pole of the political system. Presence of multiple parties, coupled with the compulsions of electoral arithmetic, led to politics of coalitions and alliances, which was prevalent for more than two decades.

The 2014 general elections marked a significant shift in the party system of India. After almost three decades, a majority government was formed in the centre. Another striking development was that for the first time a majority government was formed by any party other than the Congress. The contemporary era is witnessing a shift from instability to stable governments both at the centre and state.

PARTY SYSTEM AT THE STATE LEVEL

The Indian Constitution has adopted a federal set-up. Therefore, political system at the state level is equally significant. Party system at state level is intrinsically linked to national politics. Despite few similarities, each state has its own peculiarities. In some states, there is alternation of power between at least two parties. In many other states, politics is not clearly divided between the two parties; and there is the presence of multiple parties.

National parties like the Congress, BJP and the Left have strong presence in most of the states. However, presence of the regional parties mostly confined to their respective states is a peculiar feature of the Indian party system. Many regional parties have come up either through anti-Congress agitations or as a result of regional movements. Regional parties have marked strong presence in states like Tamil Nadu, West Bengal, Assam, Punjab, Kerala, Jammu & Kashmir, Uttar Pradesh, Bihar, Maharashtra, Karnataka, Andhra Pradesh and Odisha. These parties have played a vital role in politics at the state as well as national level.

GOVERNANCE: A CONCEPTUAL FRAMEWORK

Governance generally relates to the process of making decisions and implementing them. In the context of the government, governance implies establishing the policies and continuous monitoring of their proper implementation by members of the government. In fact, government policies and decisions reach the people through what is called governance. Till date, a number of academic experts as well as practitioners have come up with several definitions of governance. However, definition given by the UNDP is used as the basic framework in this chapter.

The United Nations Development Programme (UNDP), in its 1997 policy paper, defined governance as 'the exercise of economic, political and administrative authority to manage a country's affairs at all levels. It comprises the mechanisms, processes and institutions through which citizens and groups articulate their interests, exercise their legal rights, meet their obligations and mediate their differences.'[1]

In order to understand governance in the Indian context, one can refer to the definition developed by the Tenth Five Year Plan. It states, 'Governance relates to the management of all such processes that, in any society, define the environment which permits and enables individuals to raise their capability levels, on one hand, and provide opportunities to realize their potential and enlarge the set of available choices, on the other.'[2]

The Eleventh Five Year Plan outlined six benchmarks of democratic governance:

- Free, fair and timely elections in all spheres of political authority;
- Transparency and accountability of all institutions of the state to its citizens;
- Efficient and effective delivery of socio-economic public services;
- Effective devolution of authority, resources and capabilities to PRIs and municipalities;
- Rule of law, where legal rights are clear and understood, and legal compliance and enforcements of those rights is time-bound and swift; and
- Needs and interests of hitherto excluded sections of society are privileged and included, with dignity.

In the democratic set-up, government's performance is continuously monitored by opposition parties, political analysts and the media. In addition to this, common people also keep an eye on government moves. In this age of globalization and information revolution, people have started to express their likes and dislikes for government acts on the social media. In the contemporary political set-up, evaluation of governance can be an important tool to verify if governments are actually delivering what they had promised during elections. Governance has become a keyword in Indian political thinking in recent years. It has redefined the relationship between the government, bureaucracy, political parties and the people.

POLITICAL DISCOURSE IN INDIA

As discussed earlier, political parties contest elections, gain power and try to maximize people's welfare. During the course of elections, parties tend to offer certain promises, which they try to fulfil after achieving power. In the new parlance of terminology, their delivery of promises and attempts to enhance people's welfare is called governance. Performance of any government can be measured through their delivery of governance.

In India's political discourse, political parties and the ideologies guiding them have always occupied prime space. The discussion on the political parties of India generally revolves around ideas rather than performance. Besides, the electoral discourse too revolves around notional ideas like socialism, secularism, liberalism, freedom of speech, non-violence, role of state, *swadeshi*, etc. Thus, it can be said that Indian analysts have overrated ideological discourse over the outcome-oriented analysis.

While the political leadership, observers and analysts rate political parties on ideological scale, their governance track record and outcome is seldom taken into consideration. Analysts fail to study and rate the performance of the parties through their governance track records. Nonetheless, as prime objective of any political party is delivery of governance, it is required to study governance records of various parties.

FOUR GOVERNANCE MODELS IN INDIA

In any political set-up, there emerge distinct governance models. These models are derived from various factors like historical experiences, socio-economic conditions, overall political culture, political party system, evolution of parties and their ideologies, and the government-people relationship. Number of governance models generally reflects country's party system. For example, in the one-party system like China, there is a single governance model of the Communist Party. In bi-party democracy like the US, two governance models of the Republicans and the Democrats are prevalent.

Governance models developed in India since Independence can be classified under four major categories, viz., governance models of the Congress, BJP, the Left Front and the regional parties. Governance model of the Congress party has, by and large, been characterized by socialism, populism and the rights-based approach. On the other hand, BJP's governance is guided by the philosophy of *antyodaya*, applied through market-friendly economic policies. The Left Front follows the Marxist ideology that places the state at the commanding heights of the economy, focusing on rights and equality. Governance models developed by various regional parties generally share the socialist ideology, and govern in response to socio-economic set-up of their states. These parties seek to find local and immediate solutions to contemporary regional problems. To analyse and compare the aforementioned four governance models in India is the focus of this chapter.

RESEARCH METHODOLOGY

The performances of the four governance models are compared on the basis of various performance indicators and the socio-economic outcomes. In this chapter, the indicators such as rule of law, delivery of basic needs and infrastructure, transparency, ease of doing business and so on are taken into consideration. This chapter uses both qualitative and quantitative research methods. The research is mainly empirical in nature.

Data used in this study was collected from a variety of sources, including the census, planning commission reports, international indices (such as the World Bank's Worldwide Governance Indicators) and national indices (such as CRISIL's Financial Inclusion Index). Attempt was made to collect data from both the state and the centre. The socio-economic outcomes across these four models for the period of 1991-2013 have been selected for comparison.

The performance of a political party is analysed in the light of the data from the years, in which it was in power in the centre or any particular state. For instance, BJP ruled Rajasthan from 1993-8 and 2003-8, while Congress ruled it from 1998-2003 and 2008-13. Hence, all variables and indicators for Rajasthan for the years 1993-8 and 2003-8 are taken to be the outcomes of BJP rule, whereas, those for the years 1998-2003 and 2008-13 are taken to be the outcomes of Congress rule. On the basis of this, averages are calculated for each indicator for all the years in which particular party was in rule. Hence, difference in quality of governance between the governments of BJP, Congress, regional parties and the Left Front in various states and the centre is analysed.

LIST OF INDICATORS

This chapter is based on the comparison between the four governance models, based on certain indicators, which are carefully chosen across the sectors. These indicators can be categorized as below (see Table 11.1).

GOVERNANCE INDICATORS

The governance indicators used for the study include:

- Rule of law, levels of corruption, quality of regulations/law and levels of populism, which measure 'predictable, open and enlightened policy making', a 'bureaucracy imbued with a professional ethos' and 'transparency and accountability'.
- Infrastructure and e-governance, which lead to 'efficient and effective delivery of socio-economic public services'.

For comparing performance on count of rule of law, the primary data used was the *Economic Freedom of Indian States Report*, published by the Cato Institute,[3] which measured 'Legal Structure and Security' in 20 states of India during 2005-13. Under BJP-rule, the average score was 0.41, under regional parties and Congress-rule, the average was 0.37, under Left-rule, the average was 0.2625. Amongst these Madhya Pradesh, under BJP-rule, was the highest ranked state

TABLE 11.1: GOVERNANCE, SOCIAL AND ECONOMIC INDICATORS

Governance Indicators	*Social Indicators*	*Economic Indicators*
Rule of Law	Health Indicators	Growth: Sector-wise growth rate of GSDP
Corruption	Basic Amenities: Access to safe drinking water	Unemployment Rate
Ease of Doing Business	Education: Public expenditure levels	Financial Inclusion
Electricity		
Subsidies		

Source: Table developed by the author.

TABLE 11.2: SUMMARY OF AVERAGES TAKEN ON GOVERNANCE INDICATORS, PARTY-WISE OVERTIME

Indicator	*Source*	*BJP ruled states*	*INC ruled States*	*Regional Parties ruled states*	*Left Front ruled states*
Rule of Law Index	*Cato Institute, 2005-13*	0.41	0.37	0.37	0.26
Corruption Perceptions	*Transparency International, 2008*	2.29	2.40	2.67	1.33
Ease of doing Business: Regulation of labour & business	*Cato Institute, 2005-13*	0.39	0.34	0.32	0.28
Infrastructure: 1. %age of Households using electricity as primary source of lighting	Census of India, 2001 & 2011	71.61	69.45	66.61	61.13
2. Increase in installed electrical capacity	*World Bank, 2008-12*	59.86	36.81	22.28	12.25
e-governance: 1. Average no. of e-transactions per person	*e-Taal (Deity), 2013-14*	5.41	2.39	1.77	1.30
2. Average no of service available for e-transactions		142.33	101	149.5	135.5
Populism: Per capita subsidy on power (in Rs.)	*Indiastat, 2007-8 to 2012-13*	209.62	285.65	438.70	289.72

Source: Table developed by the author.

in this regard with a score of 0.62 and Tamil Nadu, under regional party rule, was the second highest ranked with a score of 0.55.

On corruption count, 'India Corruption Study', conducted by *Transparency International*[4] in 2008 to measure state-wise corruption in India, is used. Regional party-ruled states were found to be the most corrupt with an average score of 2.67, followed by Congress with an average of 2.4. The BJP-ruled states had an average score of

2.28 and Left-ruled states were the least corrupt with a score of 1.33. Hence Left Front states lead on this indicator.

For comparing state-level quality of regulations and ease of doing business in states, the primary data used was the *Economic Freedom of States of India Report,*[5] which measured the 'Regulation of Labour and Business' in 20 states of India during 2005-13. The average State-wise score in this regard was 0.39 for BJP-ruled states, 0.34 under Congress, 0.32 under regional parties and 0.275 under Left. Gujarat was the leading state in this regard, with a score of 0.87, followed by Tamil Nadu in distant second, with a score of 0.51.

To analyse the performance of political parties on infrastructure, 'percentage of household using electricity as primary source of lighting' and 'increase in total installed electrical capacity' data points are used. Census data of 2001[6] and 2011[7] and World Bank data of 2008[8] and 2011[9] are used. The percentage of households using electricity as the primary source of lighting was 72 per cent in BJP-ruled states, 69 per cent under Congress-rule, 67 per cent under regional party rule and 61 per cent under Left-rule. From World Bank data, the percentage increase in total installed electrical capacity in the state sector from 2008 to 2011 was calculated. It was found that BJP-ruled states showed the largest increase with an average increase of 60 per cent, Congress of 37 per cent, regional parties of 22 per cent and Left of 12 per cent. The largest increase occurred in Himachal Pradesh (169 per cent) and Gujarat (105 per cent).

The e-governance data are primarily sourced from *eTaal,*[10] as available from January 2013 to December 2014 (Department of Electronics & Information Technology). The average per capita number of e-transactions in BJP-ruled states (calculated by dividing by total population of states) was 5.4. It was 2.4 under Congress, 1.8 under regional parties and 1.3 under Left. Gujarat, a BJP-ruled state, had the highest percapita number of transactions at seventeen, followed by Andhra Pradesh, a regional party-ruled state at eleven. Similarly, average number of services available for e-transactions was highest in states ruled by regional party at 150, followed by BJP at 142, and Left at 135, and Congress at 101. Andhra Pradesh, a regional party ruled-state, provides the highest number of services for e-transaction at 593, while Gujarat, a BJP-ruled state, is a distant second at 257. In this regard, the average for regional party ruled-states is skewed by Andhra Pradesh, which offers almost four times the number of services offered by the second-ranked RP-ruled state, Uttar Pradesh.

For analysing populism, it is approximated with subsidies doled out by the respective governments in power. Data for power/electricity subsidy given to domestic consumers from 2007-8 to 2012-13 across states in India was considered, sourced from *Indiastat.*[11] On comparing the averages it was observed that states under BJP-rule gave the minimum per capita subsidies, leading to less electricity theft and fewer power-cuts for their citizens, while regional party ruled states doled out the highest per capita subsidies hence leading to unreliable power distribution in their states.

SOCIAL INDICATORS

Governance when carried out in an ordered and accountable manner helps create a favourable social and economic environment. After observing the performance of the four models of political parties that have ruled across states in India on the basis of governance indicators in the previous section, further it is attempted to observe the performance of these four models on social indicators. Therefore, the social indicators under health, education and basic amenities are considered, in the following matrix (see Table 11.3):

- Health: Maternal Mortality Rate (MMR) and Infant Mortality Rate (IMR).
- Basic Amenities: Access to Safe Drinking Water.
- Education: Public Expenditure on Education (as percentage of total expenditure).

The data for MMR across states obtained from Sample Registration System (SRS) and Central Bureau of Health Intelligence (CBHI)[12] was averaged based on which party was in power in each state during 1999-2013. It was found that all parties have managed to bring down the MMR over time. The Congress and regional parties have reduced MMR from an average 335.75 in 1999-2001 to 185.2 in 2010-12

TABLE 11.3: SUMMARY OF AVERAGES TAKEN ON SOCIAL INDICATORS, PARTY-WISE OVERTIME

Indicator	*Timeline*	*BJP-ruled states*	*INC-ruled states*	*RP-ruled states*	*Left Front-ruled states*
HEALTH:	1999-2001	370.5	335.75	256.33	218
1. MMR	2001-3	172	262.2	244	194
(SRS, CBHI. 1999-2013)	2010-12	165.33	185.2	198.2	91.5
2. IMR	2005	62.2	41	44.56	34.5
(Databook, 2005-2012)	2008	53.29	38.1	46.4	27
	2010	45.5	23.67	40.67	23.67
	2012	36.71	28	34.56	28
BASIC AMENITIES:	1991	71.38	51.74	51.96	82
Access to safe drinking water	2001	76.65	77.35	69.17	54.8
(Economic Survey, Census 1991-2011)	2011	87.77	70.27	85.31	67.5
EDUCATION:	2006-7	14.3	13.2	13.3	16.1
Public expenditure on education as %age of total expenditure	2007-8	14.3	13.2	13.3	15.4
	2008-9	14.9	14.1	13.1	14.7
(RBI, PRS. 2006-2011)	2009-10	15.9	14.9	14.2	16.9
	2010-11	17.4	16	15.6	17.1

Source: Table was prepared by the author.

and 256.33 in 1999-2001 to 198.2 in 2010-12, respectively. The Left Front has reduced average MMR from 218 in 1999-2001 to 91.5 in 2010-12. This steep reduction owes to the Left Front being in power in Kerala in 2010-12 and not in their usual other states, which skews the average in their favour. In the BJP-ruled states, average MMR was brought down from 370.5 in 1999-2001 to 165.33 in 2010-12.

The data for Infant Mortality Rate (IMR) obtained from Planning Commission Databook, 2014,[13] for the time period from 2005-12. The figures are average IMR in each state during a given time period. Again it was found that all parties have managed to bring down the IMR over time. Congress and the Left have reduced IMR from average of 41 in 2005 to 34.17 in 2012 and 34.5 in 2005 to 28 in 2012, respectively. Regional parties have been inconsistent in controlling the IMR over years. The average IMR in regional party ruled states went from 44.56 in 2005 to 46.4 in 2008 and finally 34.56 in 2012. The BJP-ruled states have brought the figures down from average of 62.2 in 2005 to 36.71 in 2012.

The data on access to safe drinking water was obtained from *Economic Survey of India*[14] *and Census.*[15] The Left Front had the best figure for access in 1991 with an average 82 per cent of households having access to safe drinking water. However this came down to the average of 67.5 per cent by 2011, owing to poor conditions in West Bengal. On the other hand, regional party-ruled states have shown consistent growth in the provision of safe drinking water, with the figure rising from 51.96 per cent in 1991 to 85.31 per cent in 2011. Congress-ruled states showed inconsistent figures, with average 51.74 per cent in 1991 rising to an average of 77 per cent in 2001, and again dropping to 70.27 per cent. The BJP-ruled states have shown consistent growth from an average of 71.38 per cent in 1991 to 76.65 per cent in 2001, and 87.77 per cent in 2011.

The party-wise trend in expenditure of state governments on education (as a percentage of total expenditure) was analysed based on the data obtained from Reserve Bank of India Reports during 2006-11.[16] The regional parties-ruled states have shown slow, but consistent, increase in expenditure on education. It was increased from 13.34 in 2006-7 to 15.62 in 2010-11. The Left-ruled states declined from 16.07 in 2006-7 to 14.73 in 2008-9 and again rose to 17.1 in 2010-11. The Congress-ruled states grew slowly from 13.12 in 2006-7 to 15.96 in 2010-11. The BJP-ruled states showed increase from 14.28 in 2006-7 to 17.36 in 2010-11.

Economic Indicators

At last, performance of the four models of political parties governing across states in India was analysed on the certain economic indicators mentioned in the following matrix (see Table 11.4).

- Growth: Percentage Growth rate of Gross State Domestic Product

(GSDP), Agriculture & allied sector growth rate, Growth rate of GSDP in Manufacturing (at constant prices 2004-5).

- Inclusive Growth: Unemployment rates, Financial Inclusion Index.

Party-wise trend in percentage growth of GSDP based on the data obtained from Central Statistics Office and Directorate of Economics & Statistics for 2006-14,[17] were averaged based on which party was in power in each state at the given time period. Left and regional parties-ruled states have shown a declining percentage of growth. The Left Front has gone down from 7.99 in 2006-7 to 6.63 in 2008-9 (data for 2013-14 NA). The regional parties have

TABLE 11.4: SUMMARY OF AVERAGES TAKEN ON ECONOMIC INDICATORS, PARTY-WISE OVERTIME

Indicator	*Timeline*	*BJP-ruled states*	*INC-ruled states*	*RP-ruled states*	*Left Front-ruled states*
GROWTH: **1. %age growth of GSDP** *(CSO, DoES, 2006-14)*	2006-7	10.1	9.3	9.5	8
	2008-9	9.1	7.6	8.5	6.6
	2013-14	9.1	6.9	6.6	0.0
2. Agriculture & allied sector growth *(Planning Commission. 2005-14)*	2005-6	9.37	4.59	2.15	2.72
	2008-9	13.73	8.21	6.46	0.99
	2013-14	8.71	5.76	2.66	0.0
3. GSDP growth rate in Manufacturing sector (at constant prices 2004-5) *(Planning Commission, 2006-13)*	2006-7	18.15	12.29	19.13	7.15
	2008-9	8.24	4.13	-0.74	2.1
	2011-12	5.32	4.59	6.65	4.34
	2012-13	4.01	3.77	4.57	0.0
INCLUSIVE GROWTH **1. Unemployment Rates** *(Labour Bureau, 2004-13)*	2004-5	3.47	4.77	3.26	12.50
	2009-10	1.95	4.19	4.18	7.83
	2012-13	3.17	4.33	5.36	8.55
Financial Inclusion *(CRISIL Inclusix, 2011*	2011	41.16	39.0	36.80	45.40

Source: Table was developed by the author.

gone from 9.51 in 2006-7 to 8.55 in 2008-9 and 6.62 in 2013-14. Congress-ruled states have also shown a consistent fall in growth dipping from 9.3 in 2006-7 to 7.56 in 2008-9 and 6.9 in 2013-14. The BJP follows the same trend of declining growth percentage, but stood relatively at higher growth than other party-ruled states. The figures have gone from 10.05 in 2006-7 to 9.3 in 2008-9 and finally to 9.07 in 2013-14.

Agriculture and allied sector growth rate data is obtained from Planning Commission Databook 2014[18] for 2005-14. The Congress and regional parties-ruled states have shown an inconsistent growth rate in the agriculture and allied sector, from the average growth rate of 4.59 in 2005-6 to -0.79 in 2008-9 to 5.76 in 2013-14, and 2.15 in 2005-6 to 2.66 in 2013-14, respectively. The growth rates in Left Front-ruled states have gone down tremendously. The BJP-ruled states have been consistently showing higher growth rates as compared to the other states.

The trends of growth rate of GSDP in manufacturing (at constant prices 2004-5) state-wise under different party-rules, based on the data derived from the *Planning Commission Databook,* 2014.[19] The figures were arrived by calculating the average of growth rates of GSDP in manufacturing sector based on which party was in rule during a particular time-period (*Note*: The data excludes the north-east states).

The Congress and Left Front ruled-states have seen a decline from 12.29 in 2006-7 to 3.78 in 2012-13 and 7.15 in 2006-7 to 4.34 in 2011-12, respectively. The regional parties ruled-states have shown better contribution from the manufacturing sector, but have inconsistent growth rates. The growth rates under regional parties ruled-states went from 19.13 in 2006-7 to -0.74 in 2008-9 to 4.57 in 2012-13. In 2006-7 states like Karnataka added to its credit for a short period of time. The BJP ruled-states can be broadly seen second to the regional parties ruled-states in this context. Their average growth rates went from 18.15 in 2006-7 to 4.01 in 2012-13.

Labour Bureau, 2004-13 data[20] has been used to compare unemployment rates. Averages of unemployment rates state-wise based on which party was in power for a given time period is taken here for analysis. The Left Front ruled-states have the highest rates of unemployment with the figures at 12.5 in 2004-5, 7.8 in 2009-10 and 8.55 in 2012-13. The regional parties ruled-states are seen to have performed better than the Left Front, with lower unemployment, but the rates have been rising steadily since 2004. It was 3.26 in 2004-5, 4.18 in 2009-10 and 5.37 in 2012-13. Congress ruled-states have had least impacted unemployment levels, 4.77 in 2004-5, 4.19 in 2009-10 and 4.33 in 2012-13. The BJP ruled-states have been seen to lower rates of unemployment, from an average of 3.47 in 2004-5 to 1.99 in 2009-10 and was at 3.17 in 2012-13.

The data for financial inclusion has been taken from CRISIL's Inclusix[21] (financial inclusion index) for states. For analysis, averages of the financial inclusion index for states from 2009-11 based on which party was in power during that period has been taken. The Left Front has a higher financial inclusion index due to the State of Kerala where the numbers have always been positive with greater branch, deposit and credit penetration as compared to all other states in India. On the other hand, the BJP ruled-states have consistent financial inclusion figures with states like Karnataka, Himachal Pradesh and Uttarakhand doing relatively well. The figures in Karnataka were 51.5 in 2009 and 57.7 in 2011, in Himachal Pradesh they were 51.7 in 2009 and 58.5 in 2011 and in Uttarakhand they were 45.6 in 2009 and 50.5 in 2011. The regional parties ruled-states and the Congress ruled-states have shown lower financial inclusion averages at 39 and 36.80 in 2011, respectively.

CONCLUSION

The comparative study of four governance models of political parties ruling across India, based on different indicators, certain social and economic outcomes, is indicative. Keeping in mind the ideologies behind these four models of political parties, and their delivery of governance, following conclusions can be made:

1. The model BJP is trying to establish can be described as least populist, technology friendly, high on infrastructure with improvements in terms of basic amenities such as power, drinking water, rural roads and other rural infrastructure.

2. Congress is the oldest party amongst the four groups of parties taken for the analysis. Therefore, the model developed by the Congress can be described as conventional, with focus on improving social indicators through populism; moderate economic growth and less focus on infrastructure.
3. The regional parties tend to be most populist responding to particular needs of the times. They perform worst on counts of corruption perceptions, however, providing number of services through e-governance and ensuring better access to safe drinking water. The regional parties grouping is heterogeneous to establish any model. However, broadly speaking, this model can be summarized as populist with serving immediate needs of the state.
4. In case of the model propounded by the Left Front, it tends to score high on social indicators but very poorly on service delivery, e-governance and infrastructure. However, high count on social indicators is paradoxically attributed to the performance of Kerala that has primarily contributed to this high performance.

NOTES

1. Governance Indicators: A User's Guide, UNDP, see http://www.undp.org/content/undp/en/home/librarypage/democraticWgovernance/oslo_governance_centre/governance_assessments/governanceWindicatorsW2ndWedition.html
2. *Tenth Five Year Plan, Planning Commission*, New Delhi: Government of India, 2008.
3. Reports by Sample Registration System (SRS) and Central Bureau of Health Intelligence (CBHI), 1999 to 2013.
4. Transparency International, 'India Corruption Study', 2008, see http://www.transparencyindia.org/resource/survey_study/India%20Corruptino%20Study%202008.pdf
5. Bibek Debroy, Laveesh Bhandari and Swaminathan S. Anklesaria Aiyar, *Economic Freedom of States of India Report, 2013*, New Delhi: Academic Foundation, 2014.
6. *Census of India, Housing Listing and Housing Census Data*, New Delhi: Ministry of Home Affairs, Government of India, 2001.
7. *Ibid.*

8. World Bank, 'India and World Bank Group in a Time of Transformation', New Delhi: The World Bank Group, 2008.
9. *Ibid.*, 2011.
10. *State-wise Reports: Electronic Transaction Aggregation and Analysis layer (e-Taal)*, New Delhi: Department of Electronics & Information Technology (DeitY), Government of India, 2013-14.
11. Report on Electricity Subsidy, India State, 2007-8 to 2012-13, see http://www.indiastat.com
12. Reports by Sample Registration System (SRS) and Central Bureau of Health Intelligence (CBHI), 1999 to 2013.
13. *Planning Commission Databook, 2014,* New Delhi: Planning Commission, Government of India, 2014.
14. *Economic Survey of India, 1991, 2001, 2011*, New Delhi: Ministry of Finance, Government of India.
15. *Census of India, 1991, 2001, 2011*, New Delhi: Ministry of Home Affairs, Government of India.
16. *Social Sector Expenditure: Trend Analysis*, New Delhi: Reserve Bank of India, 20011.
17. Central Statistics Office and Directorate of Economics & Statistics for 2006-14.
18. *Planning Commission Databook,* 2014, n. 13.
19. Ibid.
20. *Labour Bureau Data*, 2004 to 2013, New Delhi: Ministry of Labour & Employment, Government of India.
21. CRISIL, CRISIL Inclusix, June 2013, see http://www.crisil.com/pdf/corporate/CRISIL-Inclusix.pdf

CHAPTER 12

Wildlife and Governance in India

Shaurabh Anand and Nishant Srinivasaiah

INTRODUCTION

Governance of wildlife in India has typically been concerned with two main tasks: conservation of legally protected wildlife species and management of wildlife in general. Conservation of protected species in India has largely followed a protected area (PA) approach. A protected area is a 'clearly defined geographical space, recognized, dedicated and managed, through legal means in order to achieve long term conservation of nature with associated ecosystem services and cultural values'.[1] Enjoying a certain degree of protection from human activities, wildlife is expected to not venture out from such earmarked areas. However, a number of rare and common species are known to occur in close proximity of human habitations. This presents an extremely complex management challenge, one that involves keeping both the animal and people out of harm's way. In the case of a rare and protected species, the prevalent approach has largely been to prevent destruction of their forest habitats and to curb actions that directly impact animal populations negatively, for example, poaching. The other extreme of wildlife governance in India concerns the management of so-called 'common' species. These species have had a long history of co-existence with humans. However, when such species cause large-scale damage to resources valued by humans, their management simply involves getting rid of the 'problem', with very little concern for their ecology. These differences exist not only with respect to the preferred method, but also with respect to aims of management. Hence, an overall picture of governance practices with respect to wildlife conservation and management is intricate and is often typified by extremes.

THE CURRENT CONSERVATION AND MANAGEMENT APPROACH

The task of species conservation, that wildlife governance institutions in India currently deal with, has its roots in historical events. The pre-Independence, British-era witnessed large-scale persecution of charismatic carnivores during royal game hunts or *shikar*. During this time, mega-carnivores were viewed as vermins and coordinated efforts along with financial incentives were put in place to systematically eliminate them from a number of locations in India.[2] This severely constricted the viable wild populations of a number of large carnivores such as tiger, leopard and wolf. During the same time, large herbivores such as elephants were hunted for their valuable body parts such as tusk, etc., for trade. These developments not only reduced the overall number of species but also isolated them to certain pockets of the country's landmass. In post-Independence era, the situation of dwindling wildlife population was further exacerbated by large-scale poaching and anthropogenic modification of natural habitats. A series of environmental awareness campaigns in the late twentieth century drew attention of the government toward this problem. This resulted in the implementation of a series of legal instruments such as Wildlife Protection Act (1972), Forest Conservation Act (1980), and Environmental Protection Act (1986) that focussed on nature and species conservation. Although, these measures varied in their scope, at the core of it was the process of setting aside a parcel of land dedicated to wildlife. This gave rise to the Protected Areas (PA) model of species conservation leading to the creation of Wildlife Sanctuary, National Park, Conservation and Community Reserves. Currently, there are total of 764 PAs in India,[3] covering approximately 5 per cent of the country geographical area.[4] Ever since its initiation, the establishment and successful running of PAs continued to be a top priority for wildlife governance in India.

However, long-ranging species often move great distances in search of required resources. While doing so, they often venture out of the protected area, coming in close proximity with human habitations. In certain cases, this leads to conflict between wildlife species and humans. The incidences of conflict involving elephants are typical examples of such situations. Mitigation of such incidences of conflict and management of wild species outside protected areas present a complex challenge for authorities. This is primarily due to the divergence in the stakeholders' view about most suitable management intervention.

Apart from the challenge of conservation of protected species, another important challenge that governance of wildlife in India deal with concern the so-called 'common' species. These species are presumably abundant in number, thrives in human modified environment and have a long history of co-existence with humans. Although the management of these common species has not been the primary tasks of wildlife management in India, it has gained significant importance in recent years due to their increasing conflict with humans. Widespread incidences of conflict involving these species have necessitated the active management by state authorities. Hence, in the case of common species, the management authorities focus exclusively on conflict management and not on conservation. When compared with approaches of mitigation of conflict involving protected species, we see that there is a stark difference in choice of management interventions and their method of implementation.

This chapter discusses the prevalent approaches to governance of wildlife in India by taking two contrasting examples of protected species (the Asian elephant) and a common species, the rhesus macaque. This chapter provides a brief background of the need for management in each of these cases and describes the approaches through which existing issues have been addressed. The chapter concludes with the discussion on the scope, methods, effectiveness and challenges of governance of wildlife in India.

GOVERNANCE OF PROTECTED SPECIES

The Asian Elephant

Twentieth-century Asia has been witness to the large-scale persecution of elephants for their ivory and for their use as beasts of burden.[5] Recognizing the need to protect and conserve the last remaining population of elephants, the Asian elephant was listed under Appendix I of the Conventional on International Trade in Endangered Species of Wild Fauna and Flora (CITES) and under the Endangered category-A2c; ver 3.1 of the International Union for Conservation of Nature (IUCN) Red List.[6]

Asian elephants today are found in the wild in 13 countries across Southeast Asia. Their number in the wild is estimated to be about 44,000-56,000. Owing to the large-scale poaching of the elephant for its tusk (ivory) and rapid reduction of its habitat, it was declared a Schedule I species under the Wildlife Protection Act 1972 of India, providing it with the highest level of protection. 'Project Elephant', a government of India scheme, was also launched in 1992 providing impetus towards its protection and to mitigate human-elephant conflict. The elephants today occur in the southern, north, east-central and north-eastern regions of India. India today holds more than 50 per cent of Asia's wild elephant population.

At the dawn of the twenty-first century, however, with Asian elephant populations being stable at least in some of its range countries, a new threat has emerged – that of increasingly antagonistic interactions with humans. Termed as human-elephant conflict (HEC), this mutually detrimental aspect of their relationship has now reached epic proportions, with nearly 500 people and 250 elephants succumbing to it annually across the Indian subcontinent[7] and around 200 elephants and 70 people in Sri Lanka,[8] the two largest Asian elephant-range countries. Such sustained conflict and a failure to mitigate it effectively have resulted in aggravated animosity of people towards elephants across their increasingly shared habitats and a consequent loss of conservation support for the threatened species.

Conservation and Management Initiatives

A number of short-term and long-term measures have been put in place to conserve the remaining viable population of the Asian elephant and minimize the conflict with humans. Conservation initiatives have focussed on providing the safe habitat and prevent the unnatural causes of death. Conflict mitigation initiatives have aimed at increasing the physical separation between the species and human habitation and ensuring the proper support to affected communities. The following section describes these initiatives.

1. *Securing and Expanding Elephant Habitats*

   The elephant reserves in India with an area of 1,50,000 km^2 encompassed the regions in north, north-east, east central and southern. The elephant reserves, thus, create a large network of reserves for the conservation of elephants. Besides this, in the past few years, action has been taken to provide habitat connectivity to the PA network within the state either through expansion of existing PA, notifying certain ecologically important areas as PA. Such efforts of linking of PA will not only ensure the meeting of long-term objectives of elephant conservation but also other species found in these areas. For instance, since 2012, the Karnataka state has declared nearly 2600 km^2 area of forests as protected, thus linking a series of national parks, tiger reserves, and sanctuaries.[9]

2. *Protecting Elephants from Unnatural Deaths*

   The average annual natural mortality of elephants is around 2 per cent, calculated over a five-year period (2009-13), which is also the expected mortality rate in most elephant populations in the wild. Poaching for ivory and electrocution or gunshot injuries as anti-depredation measure are the generally most important causes of unnatural deaths of elephants. Largely due to a number of mitigation measures implemented by the forest department including the strengthening of physical barriers along the elephant habitat, strengthening the network of Anti-Poaching Camps (APC) and creating awareness among people, the unnatural deaths of elephants in the wild has decreased. One of the important steps in this regard has been the establishment of APC in sensitive areas and the creation of service roads along the boundaries of the protected areas for efficient and timely response to threats.

3. *Mitigating Human-Elephant Conflict:*

   As stated earlier, changes in the land use through changing cropping patterns, activities such as quarrying, mining, unchecked ecotourism, construction of dams, high-tension wires, roadways and railway lines cutting across or close to elephant habitats have resulted in large-scale fragmentation and degradation of the elephant habitat resulting in increased human-elephant conflict over time. Further, with the implementation of the Forest Rights Act, land use changes have come up in elephant habitats resulting in increased anthropogenic activities such as cattle grazing and cultivation of crops. A five-year data (2009-13) from Karnataka forest department records on conflict indicate that on an average 30 people succumb to this conflict annually and Rs. 931 lakh is paid as ex-gratia for crop and loss of lives.

(a) *Creation and Maintenance of Barriers:* One of the ways to mitigate conflict is to prevent elephants from entering agricultural land at the same time reducing direct human and elephant encounters both within and outside the elephant habitats, especially with cattle grazers. Such a separation has been brought by construction and maintenance of elephant proof barriers such as elephant proof trench, solar fence and rubble wall along the forest boundary. Considerable effort has been invested by the department in excavation and maintenance of these barriers. Whenever possible the maintenance of such barriers is carried out by involving the eco-development committees.

(b) *Formation of Anti-depredation Squads for Active Conflict Mitigation:* Mobile squads consisting of forest staff equipped with torches, crackers and guns (to scare the elephants by firing in the air) have been created in the sensitive areas. These squads act as the second line of defence, in case the passive barrier fails to contain the elephant. As a rapid response team, the squad moves in jeeps as soon as it gets information of crop raid by elephants and drives the elephants back into the forest while assisting the villagers in guarding their crops.

(c) *Ex-gratia Payment towards Loss of Life and Property:* The elephant range states have taken steps to streamline/speed up the disbursal of ex-gratia payment towards crop, property and loss of life in order to provide relief to people. Timely payment of the ex-gratia is an important step to provide relief to the victim's family in the case of loss of life. In the case of damage to crops or property, ex-gratia is paid as per the government order. Ex-gratia is also paid towards the injury, permanent disability and cattle deaths.

(d) *Capacity Building:* Eco-Development Committees have been formed to build capacity and awareness among the local communities towards elephant conservation and to involve the locals in conservation activities such as barrier maintenance. Training in the use of geographic information systems and legal aspects in wildlife protection act for elephant protection has been conducted at the circle level.

(e) *Habitat Management:* In order to reverse the impact of harmful anthropogenic activities on elephant habitat, a number of works such as removal of invasive weed species to allow elephant fodder species to grow, desilting of waterholes/tanks to provide sufficient water to the animals, especially in the dry season, dibbling of bamboo seeds since most of the bamboo in high density elephant habitat has flowered, and controlling instances of fire that will prevent the regeneration of bamboo and other plant species is being carried out.

Governance of 'Common' Wildlife Species

Governance of common wildlife species in India (such as rhesus macaques, wild boar, and blue bull) follows a different approach than that of legally protected species (such as Asian elephant, tiger and leopard). This difference in the governance stems from the certain prevailing characteristics of these common species that span across taxa. The characteristics that set these species apart include, but are not limited to, increasing or stable population size, ability to survive in the human-modified environment and generalist feeding behaviour. These traits enable these species to flourish in highly human-modified ecosystems without any external support and hence they are often devoid of any active protection. Hence, unlike protected species where governance deals with both species conservation and conflict management, governance in the case of common species focus exclusively on conflict management.

However, effective management of the conflict involving common species is required not only for the reduction of the damage but also to ensure the long-term survival of the species. This is particularly important because the survival of a number of common species in the human-modified environment depends on the people tolerance toward their presence. Hence, effective management is required to ensure that conflict does not exceed the tolerance level of communities and people do not restore to reactive, lethal measures for conflict mitigation.

Here, a case study of rhesus macaque has been used to elaborate on the governance of common species in India. Through this exercise, this chapter describes the various methods of management, their relative effectiveness and associated challenges.

THE RHESUS MACAQUE

The rhesus macaque is one of the most commonly found macaque species in India with a wide distribution across north and north-eastern India. It has a long history of co-existence with humans with a historical presence in the human-modified environment. Rhesus macaque is also part of the religious and cultural symbolism of different communities and is often venerated as God in many parts of the country.[10] However, in the recent decades, the interactions between humans and rhesus macaques are increasingly being seen through the lens of conflict. The increase in human population, expansion of developmental activities in natural areas and reduction in natural food resources have resulted in various forms of human-rhesus macaque conflict in both rural and urban areas. The conflict between human and rhesus macaques occurs in three broad contexts of crop depredation, house raiding and nuisance value which include activities such as food snatching and attacks on humans.[11] In rural areas, crop-raiding by rhesus macaques is the most prevalent form of conflict. Although, primate crop-raiding is not a new phenomenon in India, the frequency and intensity of crop depredation has increased significantly in recent years. Conflict due to crop-raiding by rhesus macaques is a much discussed problem across northern India, with its impacts being particularly severe in the twin hill states of Himachal Pradesh and Uttarakhand.[12] Crop damage and resultant financial loss do not only pose threats to the sustainable livelihood of the farmers but also has the potential to threaten the long-term survival of the species which is highly adapted to live in human-dominated landscapes. In urban areas, the conflict between humans and rhesus macaques has been termed as 'monkey menace', where monkeys damage properties and attack humans that occasionally turn fatal. The demand for active management of various forms of conflict started from the beginning of last decade. This resulted in the implementation of a number of interventions by a different state. The management interventions that have been used to deal with various forms of human-rhesus macaque conflict in rural and urban areas is discussed below.

Management of Human-Rhesus Macaque Conflict

(a) *Translocation:* Translocation is capture and removal of problem individuals or groups from one location (source) to another location (destination) to mitigate the conflict at the source. Despite having a number of undesirable effects such as capture-related stress, injuries, and mortalities, shifting of the problem from one location to another and its ineffectiveness in controlling conflict at the source location, translocation is often preferred as a management method due to its nonlethal nature. In India, translocation has been used extensively for the mitigation of conflict involving species such as leopard, elephant and tiger. In the case of human-rhesus macaque conflict, it has been in practice for long. The earliest use of rhesus macaque translocation goes as early to 1984 when Southwick and colleagues carried out translocation of monkeys in Aligarh district. A similar drive was carried out again in 1988 in Aligarh. This was followed by translocation of troops in Delhi from urban areas to rural areas in 1989 and 1995. In recent years, cases of rhesus macaque translocation have occurred in Uttar Pradesh, Delhi and Himachal Pradesh. In Uttar Pradesh, a mass translocation of 600 monkeys from Vrindaban area of Mathura district was carried out in 1997.[13] In Delhi, rhesus macaque troops were captured and translocated from highly populated urban areas to Pilibhut and Kano National Park in 2004 and to Asola Bhatti Wildlife Sanctuary since beginning of 2007.[14] In Himachal Pradesh, a translocation drive was carried out in Shimla urban areas in early 2006 to mitigate the conflict.[15] Translocation as a management intervention to reduce the human-rhesus macaque conflict has largely drawn negative reactions from different stakeholders. In the cases mentioned above, while the translocation drive in Vrindaban is considered to be successful in reducing conflict, the more recent examples from both Delhi and Himachal Pradesh have drawn severe criticism. In both of these cases, translocation has not only failed to reduce conflict at the original location, but also exacerbated the conflict intensity at the released location. At present, the use of translocation as a management intervention of human-rhesus macaque conflict is seen with a high degree of skepticism. However, it is still preferred by some stakeholders in the place of lethal methods such as culling.

(b) *Sterilization:* Sterilization is increasingly being considered as the humane way to mitigate human-animal conflict. It is one of the fertility control methods, which inhibits the reproductive power of individual through surgical procedures. Surgical sterilization techniques have been used widely to control the population of both domesticated and wild animals across the globe. In India, this was first applied in the case of rhesus macaques in the state of Himachal Pradesh. Rhesus macaque sterilization programme in Himachal Pradesh is one of its kind programme in the country to use fertility control method to control the population of wild animals. It was started in 2007 with the establishment of the first Monkey Sterilization Center (MCS) in Shimla. In ten years since its initiation, Himachal Pradesh Forest Department has established eight MSCs spread across seven districts in the state. Spread across MSCs, a total of 1,15,269 rhesus macaque individuals have been sterilized till mid-December 2016.

(c) *Classification as a Vermin Species:* The classification of rhesus macaques as a vermin species is a particularly drastic measure that has been used twice for the management of human-rhesus macaque conflict in the state of Himachal Pradesh. Farmer organizations have been persistent about their demand to declare rhesus macaques as vermin in order to allow farmers to cull rhesus on their field. In order to address their concern, the state government of Himachal Pradesh declared the species as vermin (permitting lay citizens to cull individuals at will) twice; once in 2010[16] and more recently in 2016.[17]

CONCLUSION

The population management and conflict mitigation of the Asian elephant and the rhesus macaque present a rather complex and intricate challenge in India. This complexity is not only compounded by the ecology and behaviour of the species, but also by the varied opinions people have about the species and its management. Diversity of viewpoints makes the decision-making process extremely difficult. It is important to take these viewpoints into account before implementing any state-wide management intervention in place.

With an aim to conserve the last populations of the wild Asian elephant in India, it is important to recognize, preserve and bring to the forefront a deep understanding and knowledge of elephant keepers, biologists and managers of elephants and their habitats. The conservation and management strategy of the state forest departments is to ensure the long-term survival of viable populations of elephants in large forested elephant habitats with minimal conflict through improved farm-based management practices, strengthening of barriers, habitat improvement, protection and consolidation. The survival of elephant populations within these protected areas is to reduce conflict in human-dominated areas by adopting adaptive management strategies to deal with individual elephants on a case to case basis striving to keep these elephants as part of the wild population based on sound scientific practices.

State authorities have adapted both short-term and long-term measures for conflict mitigation with respect to rhesus macaque.

However, short-term measures have not been very effective in addressing this issue. The state of Himachal Pradesh is the pioneer state in the country to initiate a long-term population management programme (sterilization) for management of rhesus macaque population. The result of this programme is likely to be observable in coming years. However, population management programmes such as sterilization should not be seen as short-term conflict mitigation strategy.

For an endangered species such as the elephant, the management practices that are sought after are mostly targeted at increasing their numbers while trying to minimize conflict and providing space. While for the rhesus the measures in place seem to be more intrusive and targeted at the species than at buffering people for their loss and building conservation support. However, recent developments suggest that authorities are willing to explore measures beyond their traditional domain for effective management. Proposed immunocontraception programme for the elephants is one of such examples. In the case of rhesus macaque, too, authorities are moving from their exclusive species focus approach toward habitat management (increased plantation efforts of fruit-bearing species to increase the food resource base). These examples are rather encouraging and indicate that both parties will be benefited from such exchanges.

Another confounding factor that makes the governance of wildlife in India a complex challenge is the cultural and religious symbolism of the species in question. A number of both rare and common species in India have cultural and religious symbolism and long-held perception of species often hid people from making a rational, informed choice for management of these species. The impact of symbolism on the management is well-pronounced for both of the species in the case study. It is worth noting that we need to take into account these perceptions, as they have potential to affect the outcomes of any proposed management measure. Additionally, the implementation of these measures has proved to be a difficult task as people have different viewpoints toward rhesus macaques.

Along with targeting the population management of the two species, there is a need to address human cultural practices in order to reduce the conflict with humans, such as food provisioning with rhesus. We also need to understand the people perceptions of the conflict and its underlying causes so that it can be addressed properly. While population management will ensure that we maintain a sustainable population size, addressing the underlying causes of conflict will ensure that affected communities do not demand for or covertly practice the reactive, lethal mitigation options. These combined efforts may ensure the long-term survival of species in the region.

NOTES

1. N. Dudley (ed.), *Guidelines for Appling Protected Areas Management Categories*, Gland, Switzerland: IUCN, 2008.
2. M. Rangrajan, 'The Raj and the Natural World: The War against "Dangerous Beast" in Colonial India', in J. Knight (ed.), *Wildlife in Asia: Cultural perspectives*, New York: Taylor and Fancis, 2005, pp. 207-32.
3. Wildlife Sanctuaries: 543; National Park: 103; Conservation Reserves: 73; Community Reserves: 45.
4. ENVIS Centre on Wildlife & Protected Areas, *Protected Areas-Subject Area: Wildlife Institute of India, Ministry of Environment & Forests,* 2017, see http://www.wiienvis.nic.in/Database/Protected_Area_854.aspx
5. R. Sukumar, *The Living Elephants: Evolutionary Ecology, Behavior and Conservation*, New York: Oxford University Press, 2003.
6. A. Choudhury et al., *Elephas maximus,* 2008, see www.iucnredlist.org.
7. M. Rangarajan et al., *Gajah: Securing the Future for Elephants in India*, New Delhi: Ministry of Environment and Forests, 2010.
8. P. Fernando, personal communication
9. S. Gubbi, K. Mukherjee, M.H. Swaminath and H.C. Poornesha, 'Providing More Protected Space for Tigers Panthera Tigris: A Landscape Conservation Approach in the Western Ghats, Southern India', *Oryx*, vol. 50, no. 2, April 2016, pp. 336-43.
10. S. Radhakrishna, 'Songs of Monkeys: Representation of Macaques in Classical Tamil Poetry', in S. Radhakrishna, M.A. Huffman and A. Sinha (eds.), *The Macaque Connection: Cooperation and Conflict between Humans and Macaques*, New York: Springer Science+Business Media, 2013, pp. 53-68.
11. N.E.C. Priston and M.R. McLennan, 'Managing Humans, Managing

Macaques: Human–Macaque Conflict in Asia and Africa', in Radhakrishna, Huffman and Sinha (eds.), ibid., pp. 225-50.

12. V. Jardhari, P. Rao and A. Choudhary, *Crop Damage by Wildlife in a Garhwal Himalayan Village*, Technical Report, Pune: Kalpavriksh, 2008; R. Saraswat, A. Sinha and S. Radhakrishna, 'A God becomes a Pest? Human-Rhesus Macaque Interactions in Himachal Pradesh, Northern India', *European Journal of Wildlife Research*, vol. 61, no. 3, 2015, pp. 435-43.
13. E. Imam, H.S.A. Yahya and I. Malik, 'A Successful Mass Translocation of Commensal Rhesus Monkeys Macaca Mulatta in Vrindaban, India', *Oryx*, vol. 36, no. 1, January 2002, pp. 87-93.
14. J. Lenin, 'The Business of Monkey Control', *Reintro Redeux,* no. 3, 2008, pp. 14-15.
15. Imam, Yahya and Malik, n. 13.
16. *Ibid.*
17. Ministry of Environment Forest and Climate Change, Gazette Notification No. S.O. 1922 (E), dated 26 May 2016 regarding listing of Rhesus Macaque in Schedule-V of the Wild Life (Protection) Act, 1972 in the State of Himachal Pradesh, 2016, see http://www.moef.nic.in/sites/default/files/HIMACHAL PRADESH-RHESUS MACAQUE-2.pdf

CHAPTER 13

Revisiting Indus Water Treaty

Vaibhavi Palsule

INTRODUCTION

After the Partition of British India into India and Pakistan, Kashmir became the bone of contention between the two nations. Kashmir issue is primarily understood and analysed as the territorial conflict, the disagreement between India and Pakistan over the control of disputed territory of Kashmir. The issue is one of borders and Pakistan has tried to alter the borders by using military instruments which resulted in actual wars and several low intensity conflicts in recent years. For India and Pakistan, issue of Kashmir is the core national interest and conflict over Kashmir is a national crisis. Due to India's military dominance, New Delhi features prominently in Pakistan's security concerns and the latter's aggressive policy designs make it a major security threat for India. It is, thus, the most important duty of governments of India and Pakistan to protect the nation and its citizens by using 'power' in all its forms. Political, economic, diplomatic and military power is used to resolve Kashmir conflict. Thus, conflict over Kashmir falls in the category of traditional security threat.

Though, Kashmir conflict is a conventional/traditional security threats, it has a potential to act as a non traditional security threat for Pakistan. Non-traditional security threats are those which challenge the survival and well-being of people and state and which arise primarily out of non-military sources and can be dealt with non-military means. Kashmir issue is associated with sharing of river water resources between India and Pakistan and water issues are the non-traditional security threats.

The Indus River and its tributaries that supply water to Pakistan originate in India flow through Kashmir. These rivers satisfy Pakistan's need for food, water and power. Pakistan's existence is entirely dependent on Indus system and subsequently on Kashmir. Because of India's control over Kashmir, Pakistan fears that India is in a position to control the flow of water to Pakistan. It can be argued that, rather than religious demography of Kashmir, Pakistan's claim over Kashmir is linked to its water requirements. So, at the heart of the Kashmir conflict lies the water insecurity of Pakistan. Once this non-traditional security threat perspective is accepted, then the need is to go beyond the traditional perspective of state and military security and understand Kashmir conflict in the light of sharing and control of water resources between India and Pakistan.

THE PROBLEM OF WATER DISTRIBUTION BETWEEN INDIA AND PAKISTAN

The Indus basin water dispute had its basis in the Partition of India and Pakistan. The line of partition of the Indian subcontinent cuts across the Indus River system. In the united India, a cohesive and unitary network of canals existed in Punjab for irrigation. But the Partition disrupted the well-established irrigation system. At the time of Partition, when territorial borders between India and Pakistan were demarcated, the decision was not taken in dividing the water resources of the Indus River system between the two nations.

INDUS RIVER SYSTEM

Indus, Jhelum, Chenab, Ravi, Beas and Sutlej form what is called as Indus River system. The Indus River originates in Chinese-controlled Tibet and flows through Jammu & Kashmir. The Chenab originates in India's Himachal Pradesh state, travels through Jammu & Kashmir. The Jhelum rises in Jammu & Kashmir and flows into Pakistan, finally joining Chenab. The Sutlej originates in Tibet, flows through Himachal Pradesh and Punjab before joining the Chenab. The Beas and the Ravi originate in Himachal Pradesh state and flow into Pakistan, emptying into the Chenab. Taking into account the flow of the rivers, the importance of the Chenab and the Indus becomes clear. The Chenab is the key tributary, as it carries the waters of the rest four rivers the Jhelum, the Sutlej, the Beas and the Ravi, to form a single water system which then joins the Indus in Pakistan. Glaciers and snow melt of Himalaya and Hindukush is major source of water of Indus River System. Water from Indus River is the principal source of drinking water in Pakistan. The water is also used for agriculture, industry, thus making economic development of Pakistan dependent on Indus River. Indus River is rightly called as the life-line of Pakistan.

In 1947, Pakistan came into being and province of Punjab was divided into two parts between India and Pakistan. The immediate result of Partition was the Indus basin division and conflict arose between both countries. Moreover, the head works at Madhupur on Ravi and at Ferozpur on the Sutlej were in India but many of the canals taken off from them were irrigating the agricultural land of the Punjab. The division of Punjab, thus created major problems for irrigation in Pakistan. To resolve this problem, the irrigation system of Punjab was divided between East and West Punjab, by the standstill agreement.[1] According to this agreement, both the countries agreed to continue with the then existing water sharing agreement for one year. This agreement expired on 31 March 1948. By that time war had already started in Kashmir. After the standstill agreement expired, the Indian Punjab cut the water flows to Pakistan.[2] It affected crops in Pakistan. As Pakistan's three-fourths of agricultural output came from the Indus basin, it felt its livelihood was threatened. Pakistan realized that it is vulnerable and a weak state because of India. This was considered as a major threat to the newly-established Pakistan. Thus, Kashmir and water conflict overlapped creating more insecurity for Pakistan.

TOWARDS INDUS WATER TREATY

To resolve the issue of legal rights to the waters of Indus basin, the governments of India and Pakistan signed the Inter-Dominion Agreement on 4 May 1948.[3] It was a temporary solution to meet the immediate needs of West Punjab. According to this agreement, India was to release sufficient water to the Pakistani regions of the basin in return for annual payments from the government of Pakistan. The negotiations continued for a more permanent solution. As the issue was bilateral, India refused Pakistan's suggestion to take the issue to the International Court of Justice.[4] Pakistan's insecurity increased as Pakistan's position was dismal and India could do whatever it wanted.

The deadlock over the distribution of Indus water system continued with several rounds of negotiations. David Lilienthal, formerly the chairman of the Tennessee Valley Authority and of the US Atomic Energy Commission, visited the region. He proposed that India and Pakistan work out a programme jointly to develop and jointly to operate the Indus Basin river system, upon which both nations were dependent for irrigation water. With new dams and irrigation canals, the Indus and its tributaries could be made to yield the additional water each country needed for increased food production.[5] However, there was no agreement between India and Pakistan over the allocation of Indus river water. The Indus river system was vital for India's Punjab, Haryana and Rajasthan – which were water deficient areas and whereas for Pakistan it was extremely important for Pakistan's sustenance, as the agricultural activity was totally dependent on Indus system.[6] Hence resolving the issue of water distribution was crucial for both the countries.

Finally, in 1954, World Bank offered its own proposal. There were prolonged talks between the two governments and the World Bank and finally the Indus Water Treaty was signed. Indus Water Treaty partitioned the water resources between India and Pakistan allotting three western rivers Indus, Jhelum and Chenab to Pakistan and three eastern rivers to India – Ravi, Beas and Sutlej. Indus Water Treaty of 1960 aimed to resolve the existing and potential conflict over the Indus River system.

Under the treaty, India can use up to 20 per cent of the water of Indus, Jhelum and Chenab for agriculture, transport and power generation. India is not allowed to build storage dams on the rivers allocated to Pakistan except to a very limited extent.[7] India can construct water storage facilities on the three western rivers that can hold 3.6 MAF.[8] The countries agreed to exchange data and cooperate in matters related to the treaty. The treaty creates the Permanent Indus Commission, with a commissioner appointed by each country.

There were provisions for the resolution of the differences that might arise.

- Questions if any arose were to be resolved within the commission;
- If agreement could not be reached at the commission level, the matter was to be referred to the two governments;
- If it fails, the question would become difference to be referred to a neutral expert and his findings would be final and binding; and
- If neutral expert decides that the matter is a dispute, it would go to a court of arbitration.

The treaty deliberately avoids any mention of the competing claims of India and Pakistan over the territory of Kashmir thereby separating Kashmir from the issue of distribution of water. In spite of major wars between them, the treaty has not been abrogated even ones. The treaty has survived for the past 57 years and both the countries have tried to resolve the conflicts regarding various projects on Indus River system within the framework of the treaty. Till today both the countries have not tried to alter the status quo. So Indus Water Treaty is regarded as a successful model of conflict resolution or the best example of dealing with the non-traditional security threats between the two intractable neighbours.

REEMERGENCE OF WATER ISSUES BETWEEN INDIA AND PAKISTAN

Though Indus Water Treaty distributed water resources to both the countries in 1960, water allocation which was made is no more sufficient to meet the needs of growing population and the agricultural and development needs of India and Pakistan. The pressure on the Indus water system is consistently growing due to increase of population in both the countries. As the people in both the countries face the problem of water scarcity, the natural consequence is to blame the other country for water shortage. As a result, there are extreme views expressed in both the countries about 'War over Water'. Those who justify military rule in Pakistan, link territorial issue of Kashmir with religion and with water conveniently. The fundamentalist organizations that are operative in Kashmir justify their Jihad as Water Jihad, a strategy against India which can use water as a weapon of war.

WATER: CORE PROBLEM WITHIN PAKISTAN

After Partition, Pakistan further expanded its irrigation system by linking the waters of the Indus and Jhelum rivers. The hydel projects constructed on Jhelum supply most of the electricity to the valley. Dams built on Jhelum – Mangla Dam and on Indus – Tarbela Dam and the Kotri barrage on Indus River near Hyderabad, Sind, provide additional supplies for Karachi and provide for the need of irrigation and electricity. Chenab provides for the water needs of Sindh and other provinces. The extensive linking of tributaries with the Indus has also helped spread water resources to the valley of Peshawar, in the Khyber Pakhtunkhwa. These irrigation and dam projects provide the basis for Pakistan's large production of crops such as cotton, sugar cane and wheat. The dams also generate electricity for heavy industries and urban centres. Pakistan depends on the Indus for its sustenance and survival.[9]

In spite of building several dams and barrages for the past several years, Pakistan has been facing serious problems of water scarcity. When Pakistan suffered a drought during 1998 to 2001, there were violent riots in Karachi. There was a severe crisis of load shedding as a result of power-shortage in the country. People in a number of cities like Karachi, Lahore, Multan, Faisalabad, etc., lodged violent protests against the load shedding, culminating into loss of property and life.[10] The problem of water scarcity in Pakistan is the result of growing population and climatic changes on the one hand and poor water management on the other.

WATER DISTRIBUTION AND PROVINCIAL DISHARMONY IN PAKISTAN

The provinces of Pakistan especially Punjab and Sindh have serious differences over water sharing. Punjab, the most dominant province in Pakistan, gets maximum water from Indus and Jhelum. Chenab-Jhelum combine, a tributary of Indus also provides the water requirements of Punjab. Sindh and Punjab's eastern part is dependent on Indus basin for irrigation and Pakistan's food crops are grown in these parts. Punjab, which is the upper riparian province and Sindh being lower riparian, in case of water sharing of Indus, Punjab has a natural advantage. As a result, Sindh, an agriculturally important province in the country and also other provinces that depend totally on water from Chenab are facing water shortage leading to disputes among provinces. Sindh claims that Punjab province gets the larger share of water and is responsible for desertification of Sindh as well as shortage of electricity.

Water from Mangla and Tarbela dams is used for electricity generation required by Punjab province. But this results in restricting water for Sindh province. Various irrigation projects built up by Punjab also results in deprivation of water for Sindh province. These big dams create a large storage of water which is used by Punjab at the cost of water needs of other provinces. As the gap between water requirement and the water availability grows, it leads to provincial discord and provincial disharmony. It is a vicious circle of depleting resources, unemployment and terrorism.

The electricity shortage, the food shortage and the resultant violent conflicts and the conflicts over water sharing among different provinces of Pakistan especially Punjab and Sindh, prove the failure of the military or democratic governments of Pakistan to manage the water resources available to Pakistan. It becomes a necessity for Pakistan's government to blame India for the water shortage in Pakistan.

PAKISTAN'S OBJECTIONS TO INDIA'S PROJECTS

In 1999, India began constructing a hydroelectric power project on the Chenab River in the Doda district of Jammu & Kashmir – Baglihar Dam. Pakistan took objection regarding the architecture of the project that includes gates as spillways that are used to flush out silts. This is, in fact, the normal architecture of any dam. But Pakistan argued that such gates could be used either to flood Pakistan or to restrict water to Pakistan. Since the Chenab is the key tributary of the Indus, Pakistani policy makers, religious and political parties and political commentators feared that India could exert control over the waters. Such control could affect Pakistani economy and livestock, or could be used to cause floods in Pakistan by release of water during times of war.

Pakistani commentators, pressure groups and religious leaders created a fear that by building run of the river projects on Indus, Chenab and Jhelum rivers that pass through India's Jammu & Kashmir state, India is controlling the river waters to strangulate Pakistani agriculture, which could affect Pakistani exports and increase its dependency on food imports.

Kishanganga Dam and Tulbul project are also under dispute. Kishanganga hydroelectric project that is designed to divert water from Kishanganga River to a power plant in Jhelum river basin. Pakistan is worried that the project will have adverse impact on the flow of Neelam River (Kishanganga called Neelam in Pakistan) which meets Jhelum. Pakistan is constructing the Neelam–Jhelum hydropower plant downstream of the Kishanganga. Pakistan fears that Kishanganga project will reduce power generation in the Neelam-Jhelum plant.

Wullar Barrage or Tulbul navigation project is a barrage on the River Jhelum, at the mouth of Wullar Lake, India's largest fresh water lake, in Kashmir Valley. The Indian argument has been that the dam will help maintain better water levels in a nearby lake and regulate the flow of flood waters and the barrage would make the river navigable in summer. Pakistan protested claiming that the purpose, for which the barrage needs construction, is first, not permissible under the treaty and second, it is hardly relevant as several improved communication links, serving as better alternatives to river navigation, have come up in that area. The major contention is the Indian occupation of Kashmir that allows its access to the source of the rivers. Pakistan fears that India intends to control the flow of the rivers and to use water as a geo-strategic weapon. Due to this the river water distribution between Pakistan and India acquires a larger political dimension.

RE-LINKING KASHMIR CONFLICT AND WATER

Though Indus Water Treaty treats Kashmir and water as separate issue, Pakistan links Kashmir with the problem of water scarcity. For Pakistan, India's control over Kashmir is a serious problem, as all these rivers flow through Kashmir, where India is the upper riparian state and Pakistan, the lower riparian. Naturally India is in the advantageous position and can make use of this advantage in the conflicting situations. Pakistan, therefore, argues that unless Kashmir issue is resolved, the problem of water sharing cannot be resolved. According to Pakistan, political and territorial solution to the problem of Kashmir would also resolve the issues of distribution of water between India and Pakistan.

One of the solutions to the Kashmir issue is making line of control (LOC) the permanent border. But Pakistan is not very keen on accepting present LOC as the permanent border. If LOC is to be turned into a permanent border, India will permanently become the upper riparian state and Pakistan the lower riparian. LOC will allot valley to Pakistan but Jammu province and Ladakh remain under India, Pakistan would then have complete control over only the Indus, Jhelum, and some of their tributaries. The Chenab, Ravi, Beas and Sutlej rivers would fall under India's jurisdiction which will deprive Pakistan of its major water resource.

In the late 1990s, during Musharraf regime, Pakistan started advocating Chenab formula. This formula is based on the 'Dixon Plan', proposed in 1950 by Sir Owen Dixon, who came as a United Nation's representative for India and Pakistan.[11]

CHENAB FORMULA

According to this formula, the state of Jammu & Kashmir would be divided on the lines of Chenab River. The north side of the river will go to Pakistan and the south side will come to India. This proposal assigned Ladakh to India, the Gilgit-Baltistan and Pakistan occupied Kashmir to Pakistan, suggested splitting of Jammu between the two and envisaged a plebiscite in the Kashmir Valley where the Hindus and Muslim population is balanced. Plebiscite should not be for the entire Jammu & Kashmir as it will again create the problem of refugees. According to this formula the city of Jammu and some districts of Jammu province would come to India on the ground that it would coincide with religious demography disputed part. The control of the city of Srinagar, most parts of the Kashmir Valley, as well as parts of Jammu region (majority Muslim areas) would be transferred to Pakistan. Thus India will lose almost 80 per cent of its controlled land. Initially Pakistan opposed this formula on the ground that plebiscite has to be for entire Jammu & Kashmir and not only in Kashmir Valley. But later it agreed when it realized that with this formula all the rivers important to it, Indus, Jhelum and Chenab would come under Pakistan's jurisdiction and it could get the opportunity to tap rivers in the present Indian Kashmir.

India has a strong opposition to this formula for two important reasons: (1) India argues that this formula advocates religious division of Kashmir – again a two nation theory; (2) 'Chenab Formula' of dividing Kashmir is not acceptable for security reasons. The division of Kashmir on the lines of Chenab River gives control of Akhnoor to Pakistan. Akhnoor area in Jammu is the only all-weather route available to India. During the Indo-Pak wars of 1965 and 1971, Pakistan had launched attacks to capture Akhnoor and the strategic bridge across the Chenab, the Akhnoor bridge is currently India's sole link to Poonch valley. Besides, the area around Akhnoor is of primary strategic importance as it provides the best terrain for inter-border movement and is most conducive for large-scale operations.[12] Thus, India's opposition to Chenab formula is based on military considerations as well.

Though Pakistan links the control of Kashmir to its water security, Pakistan does not want to make Kashmir another federating unit of Pakistan. If Kashmir is made a federating unit, then Pakistan would also have to ensure that the water requirements of the Kashmir region are satisfied. Diverting water to irrigate the land of Kashmir would mean reducing flows to Punjab and Sindh, which will never be acceptable to the two leading provinces of the country. Moreover, Sindh, which is already suffering the consequences of reduced water flows, will witness a further decline and erosion of its economy. If Kashmir becomes a federating unit of Pakistan, it will create new problems of provincial disharmony as there is a possibility that Punjab and Sindh can join hands to resist Kashmir. Water dispute in Pakistan would become graver.

This probability explains Pakistan's strategy regarding Kashmir. In recent years, Pakistan has always supported the movement of independence of Kashmir and has never claimed that Kashmir would become the integral part of Pakistan. It is then clear that for Pakistan, Kashmir is an instrument for the development of its provinces, especially Punjab. Kashmir is needed for access to water and develop hydropower projects that will ensure reliable supply to the provinces in Pakistan. As a result, for the past several years, Pakistan has adopted the strategy of supporting self-determination of Kashmir and also the Jihadi elements in Kashmir valley calling them 'freedom fighters'.

NEED FOR REVISION OF INDUS WATER TREATY

The Indus Water Treaty is not a water sharing agreement but it is the partitioning of water. When the agreement was reached in 1960, the purpose was merely dividing the water resources without much of future projection about increasing need of water by both the countries due to increasing population. Increased population has stressed the water resources required for agriculture, for personal consumption as well as for electricity generation. The Indus Water Treaty partitioning water granted autonomy to India and Pakistan as to the management of water resources for irrigation, hydroelectric use, and development thereby tried to avoid conflict over water. Dividing the water was seen as a solution to the conflict over water but the environmental considerations were not taken into account at the time of preparing the treaty. The treaty has become stagnant as it does not adapt to the future changes and challenges.

- When the treaty was made, the impact of climate change on the Indus system was not the issue under consideration. Glacier melt contribute to a great extent in the Indus basin. The increasing temperature leads to increase in speed of melting of glaciers, which increase the flow of water, thus flooding the Indus basin. In future when glaciers will melt entirely, the major water source of

Indus basin will cease to exist decreasing water flows in the Indus tributaries which will lead to scarcity of water.

- Climate change also affects the rainfall resulting in either droughts or flood. Further, the period of rainfall may decrease but there may be extreme rainfall for few days or vice versa, rainy season may be extended with a scanty rain. In both the cases the effect will be on availability of fresh water. The climate change is irreversible and both India and Pakistan will be facing the similar problems and the solution is the optimum and judicious use of water resources of Indus basin. However, what is optimum and judicious is different for both the nations, leading to non-acceptance of the claims causing conflict between the two. The treaty does not provide for such a type of conflict resolution.
- Climate change results in water scarcity and decreased agricultural productivity, disturbed rainfall and quality of soil. The treaty needs to be modified to reflect these effects of climate change. Environmental scarcities interact with other factors generating violence and given the disturbed relationship between India and Pakistan and the conflict prone Kashmir, it becomes the potential cause of conflict between the two. Even if the political and territorial solution to Kashmir is sought, climate change will make the treaty redundant and the treaty will turn 360 degrees from a successful model of conflict resolution to a pertinent cause of conflict between the two countries bringing Kashmir back to the centre stage. Conflict over water will become the highest concern in the near future. It has the potential for war between them.
- The concerns of Kashmir – water is the main natural resource of Jammu & Kashmir and is essential for the economic development, for its agrarian needs as well as for the production of hydroelectricity. The Indus Water Treaty divided rivers between India and Pakistan. Pakistan got the exclusive rights to use western rivers and the restrictions were imposed on India to build any projects on western rivers. India got the exclusive right to use eastern rivers and India agreed to that as those rivers are important to satisfy the needs of eastern Punjab and Rajasthan – the water deficient areas. Jammu & Kashmir argues that when the treaty was

made, the interests of the state were not taken into consideration. The western rivers allotted to Pakistan flow from Jammu & Kashmir and therefore belongs to Jammu & Kashmir. Because of the restrictions imposed on India as to the use of western rivers, Jhelum and Chenab, Jammu & Kashmir is deprived of the benefits of rivers in irrigation, electricity generation or navigation. Due to this Jammu & Kashmir has to face millions of dollars of economic loss. Due to scarcity of water and uncertain rainfall, even the agricultural pattern of Kashmir is changed and Kashmiri agriculture has shifted from paddy fields to horticulture activities. It has obviously hampered economic development of Jammu & Kashmir. There is increasing demand for scrapping of the treaty from the activists and the people from the state. This feeling is expressed more strongly after cross border terrorism began and Kashmir became the hub of Pakistan sponsored terrorist activities. Since then, various views have been expressed for abrogation or renegotiation of the treaty.

PROBLEM AREAS

- After signing of the Indus Water Agreement, India never accepted the need to renegotiate over the treaty or has accepted that Kashmir and water are the two sides of the same coin and, therefore, even after the composite dialogue process has been started, water issue has not been considered as point of discussion. In fact, India's stand that Kashmir will not be the central issue shows that India treats Kashmir and water as separate and distinct issues. Composite dialogue does not include the revision or rethinking of water agreement.
- Pakistan links territorial issue of Kashmir with religion and with water conveniently. Even though India has not violated the Indus Agreement even once, they link water security to their control over Kashmir. The fundamentalist organizations that are operative in Kashmir justify their Jihad as Water Jihad, a strategy against India which can use water as a weapon of war. In this manner Pakistan is trying to internationalize the water issue with the

argument that a hostile neighbour with a natural advantage of being upper riparian state is trying to manipulate water that judiciously belongs to Pakistan.

- Currently, territorial control of Kashmir is the most significant cause of conflict between India and Pakistan. Conflict over water is often treated as the subsidiary of the Kashmir conflict. What is unique about the water conflict is that it will grow serious with the climatic and environmental changes. Climate change and the resultant challenges have brought the different countries of the world together to have some common solutions, but in case of India and Pakistan the case is different. As there is no apparent and direct conflict over water, there are no signs of cooperation over the issue of water. Kashmir issue surpasses the threat of climatic change and the resultant conflict over water sharing and the situation may worsen when the conflict will be finally addressed. Shortage of water is a critical problem for both the countries. It is the need of an hour that both cooperate to combine their resources and find mutually beneficial solutions.

CONCLUSION

India currently is not making optimum use of water which is permitted under the treaty. For making that optimum use, India needs an infrastructure of storage dams and a canal network, which does not figure in India's plans in the near future. If in reality water flowing to Pakistan is to be stopped to punish it, it would be most irrational as without the required infrastructure which is not even permitted under the treaty it may also violate environmental consideration, Kashmir would be flooded and it would lead to disastrous consequences.

India's relations with its neighbours would also be affected, as India also has water treaties with Nepal and Bangladesh. And India is the lower riparian state in case of sharing water of Brahmaputra with China. India is aware of the implications of abrogation of the treaty. Therefore, despite growing protests from the Kashmiri people, no policy maker in New Delhi is ever likely to even contemplate this move. The act of abrogation on the part of India could cause insecurity among the other countries that are lower riparian to India.

India and Pakistan share a common water resource – Indus basin – which is one unit but perceived as independent resource and, therefore, have independent policies of development. This is where the problem lies. If it is a common resource and even climate change will have similar impact for both India and Pakistan, then the development of Indus basin should be a joint venture of both the countries. But due to the mistrust between the two, any joint effort is not possible. There is absence of a common vision of a problem. The Indus Water Treaty then needs to be revised to make it a trans-boundary water sharing agreement that would treat Indus basin as a single unit and would help in reaching a more realistic water sharing agreement based on environmental considerations and the needs of the people of both India and Pakistan and not on the basis of political considerations.

NOTES

1. Shaheen Akhtar, 'Emerging Challenges to Indus Waters Treaty', *Regional Studies*, vol. 28, no. 4, 2010, pp. 3-66.
2. See http://thediplomat.com/2016/06/kashmir-a-water-war-in-the-making/
3. *Inter-Dominion Agreement, between the Government of India and The Government of Pakistan, on the Canal Water Dispute between East and West Punjab*, New Delhi, see http://mea.gov.in/bilateral
4. Frank Caso, *Freshwater Supply*, New York: Infobase Publishing, 2010, p. 92.
5. Indus Basin Dispute – Press Clippings – Correspondence 01 Folder ID: 1805183 Dates: 8/1/1951 – 12/1/1953 Fonds: Records of the South Asia Regional Office (WB IBRD/IDA SAR).
6. See http://www.aljazeera.com/indepth/spotlight/kashmirtheforgotten conflict/2011/07/2011781215447899 2.html
7. Abdul Rauf Iqbal, 'Water Shortage in Pakistan: A Crisis Around the Corner', see ndu.edu.pk/issra/issra.../01-Water-Shortage-in-Pakistan-Abdul-Rauf-Iqbal.pdf.
8. IDSA Task Force, 'Water security for India: The external dynamics', *Institute for Defence Studies and Analyses*, September 2010, p. 36.

9. Mohan Guruswamy, 'Indus Waters Treaty: Turning off the Taps to Pakistan', see http://www.dailyo.in/politics/visited 19/4/17.
10. Sajjad Shaukat, 'India's Water Aggression Against Pakistan', see http://readersupportednews.org/pm-section/86-86/28740-indias-water-aggression-against-pakistan.
11. A.G. Noorani, 'The Dixon Plan', *Frontline*, vol. 19, no. 21, 12-25 October 2002, see http://www.frontline.in/static/html/fl1921/stories/20021025002508200.htm
12. 'Unwelcome Interventions', *Indian Defence Forum*, see defenceforumindia.com.

CHAPTER 14

Governance and Geopolitics in South Asia

Som P. Pudasaini

INTRODUCTION

The South Asian Association for Regional Cooperation (SAARC) has been in trouble from its inception in 1985. Its performance in the field of trade, connectivity, fostering understanding among member states, anti-terrorism initiatives or poverty reduction have all been far from satisfactory. It has not even been able to hold its annual summit regularly; with only 18 summits held in 32 years. Among a number of factors responsible for the poor performance of this South Asian regional organization, the never-ending conflict between India and Pakistan, two of the most important member states, stands out as the most detrimental.

Consequently, SAARC has been written off by some as an irrelevant entity. Some consider it to be a 'life support system' needing a major push, particularly from India and Pakistan, if it is to be a more meaningful and effective regional set-up in the future. However, many professionals across the SAARC countries and people and politicians from the smaller member states seem to be of the view that it continues to be relevant even if its performance has been unsatisfactory and must be revitalized with all necessary effort to promote regional cooperation and collective progress. Given the troubled status of the South Asian cooperation organization, this chapter aims to look at two key issues: governance and geopolitics.

First, it looks at the governance issue conceptually, including how it has been defined by different organizations. Then, try to come up with a broadly accepted and useful meaning or definition that could be used by a range of professionals and policy makers in SAARC. Presentation of a quick overview of the status of governance and key factors responsible for poor governance in SAARC, including some country specific examples of corruption, then follows.

Second, the emerging geopolitics in SAARC, which has a strong implication for its survival and effectiveness, is then dealt with in more detail. The focus of geopolitical discussion will be largely on two aspects: views of SAARC professionals and Belt and Road Initiative (BRI). First, it briefly reviews the perceptions and views of professionals in SAARC countries concerning its non-performance and its relevance. Second, it looks at China-India dynamics in South Asia with focus on China's flagship mega-project known as the BRI, which is also called the One Belt One Road (OBOR) Initiative. It is considered an important aspect to be viewed as China has emerged as a critical player in SAARC and BRI is one of the important instruments China is using to strengthen its presence in the region and beyond.

Also, it is important to look at the initiative in terms of its implication in South Asia as Pakistan is a strong supporter of BRI. India is opposed to it; while rest of the member countries (except Bhutan) want to benefit from it to enhance their infrastructure and development. Consequently, it is a dilemma for other smaller countries – Bangladesh, Maldives, Nepal and Sri Lanka – how to benefit from BRI and plenty of cash China has to enhance their much needed infrastructure and pace of economic development without unduly alienating or alarming India. The Indo-Chinese Doklam standoff and Nepal's difficulty in balancing relations between its two big and critical neighbours is also briefly discussed in the context of the geopolitics in SAARC.

SOUTH ASIAN GOVERNANCE

Good governance is a much talked about and widely desired goal across the continents, particularly in developing nations, including in South Asia. It has been occupying a predominant space in national, regional and international imagination and debates for over the past three decades. However, it remains an almost utopian dream yet to be achieved to the desired extent. Clearly, governance is a multi-dimensional aspiration pertaining to political, judicial, social and developmental concerns. Achieving good governance is a challenge that demands sound vision, strong commitment and prompt implementation at multiple fronts. There are two critical challenges confronting good governance in South Asia and beyond.

First, it continues to be indeterminate conceptually. In other words, it is interpreted to mean different things by different countries and organizations to suit their interests and politico-economic milieu. A lack of clear and broadly agreed definition of the concept adds confusion and complication to both the design and implementation. Second, the South Asian nations are quite varied in terms of size, population, political system and stability and transparency. Thus, they differ in terms of understanding of what good governance means and status of governance to be able to clearly generalize it at the SAARC level. The effort here is to unearth broadly acceptable concept of good governance. And then to highlight governance challenges confronting SAARC nations and the South Asian region in broad terms, including by citing some country specific governance problems or scandals.

According to UNESCAP, governance is 'the process of decision-making and the process by which decisions are implemented' or not implemented.[1] It is participatory, consensus oriented, accountable, transparent, responsive, effective and efficient, equitable and inclusive and follows the rule of law. Good governance, thus, concerns with the fairness and effectiveness with which public institutions conduct public affairs. Managing public resources and people's welfare efficiently, inclusively and equitably being responsive to both the present and the future needs of a society must be at the heart of the governance process. Clearly, state, private sector and civil society all have an important role in promoting and sustaining good governance.

For IMF, governance 'encompasses all aspects of the way a country, corporation, or other entity is governed.... Relevant questions with regard to those policies are: their effectiveness; their transparency, and thus the accountability of policy makers; and the extent to which they meet internationally accepted standards and good practices.'[2] The responsibilities and capabilities of government and government bodies to meet the needs of masses as opposed to select groups, are central to good governance. And ensuring the rule of law, improving the efficiency and accountability of the public sector, and tackling corruption within which economies can prosper are essential elements. Strategic vision and honesty of political and developmental apparatus is, thus, critical for good governance. Also, respect for human rights, fair trial and justice, elimination of poverty and livelihood for all are increasingly stressed as crucial ingredients of good governance in recent decades.

A well respected thinker Al-Rodhan[3] lists 'eight minimum criteria' for good governance: participation, equity and inclusiveness; rule of law; separation of powers; free, independent and responsible media; government legitimacy; accountability; transparency and limiting the distorting effect of money in politics. While there may be some variation in criteria adopted by the UN, the World Bank, IMF and others, Al-Rodhan's eight criteria largely encompass ingredients of good governance to form a broadly acceptable definition.

TROUBLED SAARC GOVERNANCE

Afghanistan, Bangladesh, Bhutan, India, Maldives, Nepal, Pakistan and Sri Lanka, which constitute SAARC, are quite varied. SAARC is troubled by poor governance and is also confronting massive existential crisis as a regional organization. There are vast differences in geography, size and growth of economy, population, and political stability, extent of internal conflict and level of media freedom among the member states. India constitutes almost 70 to 80 per cent of SAARC regardless of the variable chosen. Pakistan and then Bangladesh each account for about 5 to 10 per cent of the economic, geographic and demographic key variables of the block. What is left of the remaining five countries – Afghanistan, Bhutan, Maldives, Nepal, Sri Lanka – is miniscule.

Given the wide variability, the eight SAARC nations also differ significantly in effectiveness of governance and meeting the needs and expectation of the masses. However, all of them are characterized by high politico-bureaucratic corruption, ethnic or socio-political conflicts and widespread poverty. Private and corporate sector's honesty and inclusiveness is far from satisfactory. Civil society expected to play an effective role of a watchdog are largely politicized and with poor accountability. Many non-governmental organizations (NGO) and international non-governmental organizations (INGO) funded by external agencies or vested interests are questioned widely for their transparency, accountability and capacity to deliver to the marginalized in an unbiased manner. Organizations such as the police, judiciary, land administration, forestry, tax and customs are among the more corrupt and hinder more than help.

Big and widening income inequalities between urban and rural area as well as the rich and the poor are the other important characteristics common to all. Poor service quality and delivery, unemployment and inadequate safety nets affect poor masses across the region. Poor response of the politicians to citizen needs after being elected and enforcement of the rule of law against the powerful is a big problem. Inadequate representation of dalits, women and marginalized groups in formal economy, decision-making and politics affects governance too.

Politics is heavily influenced by money and muscle power. The decline of ideology-based politics and the increasing use of hoodlums and thugs in elections makes governance more precarious. The election and nomination of criminals and black-money holders to high political and parliamentary positions continue to be an important issue of concern. Increased politics-business nexus and their unhealthy deals are institutionalizing corruption in South Asia. Factionalism, confrontational politics and expensive electoral competition contribute significantly to governance dilemma. Nepotism, political interference in administration, corrupt civil servants and poor parliamentary oversight constitute other governance challenges. The separation of power among executive, judiciary and legislative branches necessary for check and balance is rather inadequate in all most all South Asian countries.

Pakistan's Supreme Court disqualified its Prime Minister Nawaz Sharif from political office for ten years over corruption charges in July 2017 and his family members are embroiled on corruption allegations unleashed by the 2016 Panama Paper Leaks. The Janata

Tower corruption scandal led to the conviction of former military dictator H.M. Ershad in Bangladesh in 1990s. The former Maldivian Vice-President Ahmed Adeeb sits in prison in a 2014 corruption case for transferring millions of dollars to his private accounts from a government tourism company; the Maldives Marketing and Public Relations Corporation. In India, the Bofors scandal of late 1980s, Colgate scandal of 2012 and pending criminal cases against 31 per cent (2012) of parliamentarians and members of legislative assemblies offer striking examples of corruption and governance problem in the country. India is also struggling with religious and caste tensions affecting its governance. Examples of corruption and criminalized politics are not uncommon in other SAARC states, including in Nepal and Afghanistan. If the biggest member of SAARC, India, with a stable democracy and politics, is in such imbroglio, the governance challenges confronting other SAARC nations with political instability and at different stage of democratic governance is obvious.

Afghanistan's governance is complicated by internal strife, corruption and external interferences. Terrorism taking deadly toll almost daily, even in capital Kabul, needs no emphasis. Religious fundamentalism, terrorism, ethnic conflict, corruption, interferences from army and intelligence agencies over civilian affairs continues to be large governance issues in Pakistan. Sensitive Baluchistan and other tribal areas, tense Afghan and Indian border, make governance a huge problem in Pakistan. Unhealthy tussle between the two prominent political parties, fundamentalism and corruption continues to haunt Bangladesh; while a half cooked democracy and monarchy controlled Bhutan has its share of corruption, inclusiveness, transparency and human rights issues colouring good governance. Political instability, corruption and nepotism in Nepal affect governance seriously. Sri Lanka, a post-conflict state, struggling to attain ethnic balance and the Maldives with a troubled democracy and power transfer confront their own type of governance challenges.

Clearly, good governance faces myriads of challenges in South Asia. However, increasing education, youthful population and public awareness about their political and economic rights offers hope towards promoting good governance. Also, increasing effort to democratize polity, enhance transparency through rights to information acts and enhanced access to social and other media represent encouraging developments. Over-politicization and commercialization of media and lack of effective use of right to information continue to drag transparency and good governance initiatives. Emergence of some good public and civil society watchdogs, proactive supreme courts and strengthening parliamentary oversight also offer better hope to enhance good governance. Anti-corruption movements, such as by Anna Hazare in India to establish powerful anti-corruption agency (Lokpal) and establishment of powerful constitutional anticorruption agency, such as the Commission for Investigation of Abuse of Authority (CIAA) in Nepal, can help strengthen good governance if properly utilized.

SAARC GEOPOLITICS

SAARC, which was established in 1985 to boost regional economic growth and promote cooperation and mutual trust, 'has largely failed to achieve its objective. Its agenda related to poverty reduction, connectivity, economic development and trust-building among member states is still a long way to go to be considered satisfactory and successful'.[4] In its 32 years of its existence, only 18 summits have been held. The postponement of the nineteenth summit scheduled for Islamabad in November 2016 due to tensions between India and Pakistan over Uri terrorist attacks has further undermined the SAARC process.

India's foreign ministry said in a statement: 'Increasing cross-border terrorist attacks in the region and growing interference in the internal affairs of Member States by one country have created an environment that is not conducive to the successful holding of the 19th SAARC Summit.' While all member states are responsible for the lethargic past predicament of SAARC, the never-ending Indo Pak conflict continues to be the biggest drag on its progress. With the two most important members of the block constantly at loggerheads, is there a viable future for SAARC? There are three conflicting views: SAARC is dead, it is on life-support and that it continues to be relevant in spite of slow progress. In this context, two important points may be noted.

First, the conflict between the two SAARC titans has been encouraging the idea of a 'Greater South Asia' under which India and Pakistan want to bypass each other to a maximum possible extent and build allies beyond the SAARC region. India has sought the Bay of Bengal Initiative for Multi-Sectoral Technical and Economic Cooperation (BIMSTEC) with Bangladesh, India, Myanmar, Sri Lanka, Thailand, Bhutan and Nepal as its members and the Bangladesh-China-India-Myanmar Forum for Regional Cooperation (BCIM) as alternatives. Pakistan has tried to be close to China, Iran and the Central Asia to counter India. India has also been trying to cozy up to Iran and Central Asia, with some success. So the promotion of Iranian port of Chabahar by India and Afghanistan, while China and Pakistan advance their own China Pakistan Economic Corridor (CPEC) and Gwadar port (in Pakistan) are notable. Also, India's initiative to establish and strengthen sub-regional Bhutan-Bangladesh-India-Nepal (BBIN) grouping is an interesting development.

Second, China has emerged as a crucial competitor in South Asia and is reinforcing its power through trade, investment and geopolitics, including its ambitious mega-project BRI/OBOR. India, the most important SAARC player, aims to contain China while expanding its own role in the region and beyond. Washington is pursuing strategic partnership with New Delhi to stabilize Asia-Pacific, with deeper cooperation on defense and security, driven by a shared mistrust of China. On the other hand, China and Russia are increasingly building a sort of an axis with Pakistan to challenge US power in the region, which is likely to cap Indian influence too. Given these twin realities, how do we view the SAARC's future?

EXPERTS AND POLITICAL VIEWS

Indian intellectuals[5] emphasizes that the 'SAARC offers hope for the better future of South Asia. It should not be allowed to die.' Also, former national security advisor to the former Indian Prime Minister Manmohan Singh, observes that SAARC has been on 'life-support'. But to dilute SAARC due to the ongoing conflict between India and Pakistan may well be an instance of 'throwing the baby out with the bathwater'. India's stakes in SAARC are high, he says, and 'propping up bodies such as BIMSTEC and BCIM in place of SAARC is hardly the answer, and could even prove counterproductive'.[6]

A Pakistani expert believes even the slow pace of SAARC is preferable to there being no regional framework. As 'India behaves like a hegemon and Pakistan as obstructionist', SAARC may atrophy into 'smaller sub-regional groupings' that would be much less beneficial to the region. To dismantle or dilute SAARC for the convenience of the two countries may prove 'costly'.[7] An editorial in *The Dawn* speaks about a geographic bloc with great cultural and language convergences and which can be an engine of growth and regional stability. But the Pakistan-India rivalry and India's aspirations to 'dominate the bloc' and deal Pakistan a 'diplomatic blow' have led to a SAARC that is moribund and ineffectual.

Pakistani Prime Minister Nawaz Sharif's message on the 31st anniversary of SAARC said 'I take this opportunity to reaffirm Pakistan's commitment to the objectives of SAARC and our journey together towards achieving our shared objectives under its umbrella'.[8] He stressed Pakistan believes in the 'viability of SAARC' and 'stands steadfastly' by the principles of the SAARC Charter. He regretted that while it had 'survived' but did not 'triumph' as had been envisaged to 'achieve progress and prosperity for the common people'. The Pakistani view stresses to the point that only by adhering to the principles of sovereign equality and mutual respect among member states could SAARC countries achieve the cherished goal of shared progress and peace. They emphasize that India does not believe in sovereign equality of all members and wants to use the platform to dictate its terms and establish its political and economic monopoly.

Bangladeshi Prime Minister Sheikh Hasina, for her part, said on the sidelines of the World Economic Forum that 'there's a lot to work on it . . . SAARC is very much alive.'[9] A former Nepali Ambassador says we must show our 'wisdom, diplomatic skill and friendship to hold the SAARC summit on time'. But he stressed that the general perception in Nepal is even though the 'summits have been postponed half the times, mainly due to Indo-Pak tensions, 'the death of SAARC, however, may be exaggerated'.[10]

In the views of a Sri Lankan expert, SAARC has reached its nadir.

With Brexit shaking up the European Union and nationalism rising the world over, it is not surprising that the 'least economically integrated region of the world is breaking apart'.[11] South Asian cooperation cannot flourish in the midst of two acrimonious neighbours and thus 'sub-regional cooperation' among SAARC countries may better achieve the goals of development and poverty reduction. The trouble with SAARC lies in the fact that 'geopolitics has taken over geo-economics in most cases and even when the countries concerned know the clear economic gains, they are reluctant to let down barriers to trade and investment for geopolitical reasons'. Another Sri Lankan expert notes that it may be easy to cancel annual SAARC summit because of the Indo-Pak tensions, but it is 'precisely such tensions and the threat of regional devastation that make the holding of regional meetings imperative'[12] to put pressure on the antagonists to calm down, divert from political flashpoints and focus on potential for cooperation and mutual benefit.

It is generally perceived that, in Nepal, India wants to maintain its clout given its proximity and multifaceted relations while China also wants to increase its sway. A balanced relation with India and China is critical for Nepal's security and development. A Nepali expert stresses that 'Nepal had long been forced to maintain a delicate diplomatic balance between its two neighbours. The Indian influence far exceeded the Chinese, and various Nepali leaders had dreamed – and continue to dream today – of using Chinese support as a counterweight to Indian attempts at domination. But their efforts are rarely successful. The tenor of Nepal's foreign policy has been marked by great caution, and its primary concern is to 'avoid offending either neighbor'.[13] He adds 'Nepali communists had always tended to denounce India with exaggerated fervor'. Even the Maoists 'vociferously opposed India's meddling' during the ten-year long violent conflict they sustained in Nepal 'sought to cultivate the Indian establishment in order to strengthen their position within the domestic sphere' upon entering mainstream politics. A 'Vigorous diplomacy is noticeable in the range and quality of Chinese involvement in Nepal', according to another expert.[14] Further, 'China continues to enjoy wide-support at the political and the popular levels' unlike 'India's image as the big brother'. While Colombo turned to Pakistan and

China for arms and logistical support to defeat LTTE, its relations with New Delhi have warmed under the new government. China and Japan are competing in Bangladesh for developing its deep sea port, while the former is already a key investor there.

India sees China's growing influence in Sri Lanka, Bangladesh, the Maldives and Nepal as a part of China's larger strategy to encircle it in South Asia. But China believes India is overprotective of its sphere of traditional influence, denying China a well-deserved status as the second most important country in the world. While the relation between India and Afghanistan has improved, that of Afghanistan and Pakistan has deteriorated. Afghanistan is also trapped in conflict of interest among China, Russia, the US, Pakistan and India, with strong repercussions for regional peace and security.

In sum, it is true that SAARC has been sluggish for most of its existence, but it is still very much relevant. Smaller nations of South Asia still pin big hope on it so that they can benefit from the collective wisdom. Neither India nor Pakistan will gain in the long run from its death or even by keeping it perennially on life support. In this context, sub-regional initiatives such as BBIN as well as the 'Greater South Asian' idea should be used to complement SAARC rather than to unduly weaken it.

CHINA'S BELT AND ROAD INITIATIVE

The OBOR concept was floated by Chinese President Xi Jinping in 2013. In Boao Asia Forum 2015, he clarified that 'the building of the Belt and Road shall adhere to the principles of joint consultation, joint building and joint sharing, since it is open and inclusive rather than closed; it will not be a solo of China by itself, but it will be a chorus participated in by many countries along the Belt and Road'.

The OBOR includes a maze of roads and port projects. The China-Pakistan Economic Corridor (CPEC) is highlighted as a 'flagship project'. It also included BCIM Economic Corridor, New Eurasian Land Bridge, China-Mongolia-Russia Economic Corridor, China-Indochina Peninsula Economic Corridor and Twenty First century Maritime Silk Road. To further its initiative China organized the Belt and Road Forum (BRF) in Beijing on 14-15 May 2017, which was attended by 29 heads of state and government besides representatives of over 100 countries and international organizations including UN Secretary-General Antonio Guterres, World Bank President Jim Yong Kim, and International Monetary Fund Director Christine Lagarde.

The Chinese President Xi Jinping stressed that 'This is indeed a gathering of great minds' and called BRI 'a project of the century' in a 'world fraught with challenges'. He said it represents a 'road for peace' and 'isolation results in backwardness'.[15] He also cautioned that 'all countries should respect each other's sovereignty and territorial integrity'. In the Chinese view, the BRI has emerged as a forward looking platform signed by 68 countries and international organizations. They stress BRI complements the development programmes of other countries and international organizations to ensure coordinated development. The Chinese officials also stressed that the BRI is an open and inclusive platform for win-win cooperation that is not based on ideological grounds or a political agenda or exclusive arrangements.

India skipped the Forum following sovereignty concerns over the CPEC. MEA spokesperson Gopal Bagley on 13 May 2017 said 'no country can accept a project that ignores its core concerns on sovereignty and territorial integrity'. According to an Indian specialist, the CPEC will cement 'Pakistan's status as China's economic and security client – has become a convenient cover for Beijing to include major strategic projects, stretching from Gilgit-Baltistan to Pakistan's Chinese-built Gwadar Port. The Bunji and Bhasha dams are also claimed to be part of CPEC, which, by linking the maritime and overland 'Silk Roads' that China is creating, will gravely impinge on India's security. A grateful Pakistan has given China exclusive rights to run Gwadar Port for the next 40 years' he adds.[16]

Pakistani Prime Minster Sharif, possibly keeping in mind the Indian reaction, said during the BRF inaugural that 'Let me make it very clear that CPEC is an economic undertaking open to all countries in the region. It has no geographical boundaries. It must not be politicized.'[17] It is time we 'transcend our differences, resolve conflicts through dialogue and diplomacy, and leave a legacy of peace for future generations', he added. In his view, geo-economics must take precedence ov geo-politics and the centre of gravity should shift from conflict to cooperation for overcoming terrorism and extremism.

Given the close relations that Nepal has with India, it was very difficult for the former to decide on formally joining the OBOR given the latter's opposition to the Chinese initiative. However, it took the decision to join it only a day before the Beijing BRF. Talking to the *Times of India*, Nepal's envoy to India Deep Kumar Upadhyaya said 'we are aware of India's reservations about CPEC'. Nepal is not 'taking any position on the issue by joining OBOR' but it cannot remain 'indifferent to a big economic power like China as it seeks more foreign investment and development'. He added we would like the two countries to resolve 'their differences amicably' as Nepal's position is 'neutral' on any security-related issue between China and India.[18]

As India's strategy to partially offset OBOR, the Indian prime minister Narendra Modi made the 'pitch for developing an Asia-Africa Growth Corridor (AAGC), with support from Japan',[19] during the annual general meeting of the African Development Bank (AfDB) in Gandhinagar, Gujarat, on 23 May 2017. The Indian and Japanese governments presented a vision document which proposes to propel

> growth and investment in Africa, by curtailing the ever-increasing presence of the Chinese on the continent.... Under the AAGC, there is a plan to connect ports in Jamnagar (Gujarat) with Djibouti in the Gulf of Eden. Similarly, ports of Mombasa and Zanzibar will be connected to ports near Madurai; Kolkata will be linked to Sittwe port in Myanmar.[20]

Japan is to contribute technology and build infrastructure, while India is to bring in its 'expertise of working in Africa'. Unlike land corridor based OBOR, AAGC will essentially be a sea corridor linking Africa with India and other countries of Southeast Asia and Oceania, 'more consultative' and private sector funded rather than government funded (unlike OBOR) it is claimed.[21]

OBOR is a debt-based infrastructure project rather than free foreign aid initiative or simply a network of trade activities. Skeptics see OBOR as 'largely a ruse to boost China's own economy by shifting excess industrial capacity to less developed nations' and EU wanted guarantees that projects would be 'economically and environmentally sustainable and subject to fair tendering processes'.[22] China is also criticized by some by saying it plans to build ports, roads and railways in under-developed Eurasia and Africa mainly out of political motivation rather than real demand for infrastructure. They also emphasize that OBOR is a way to extend Chinese influence at the expense of the US and a smart move by China to establish itself as a world-leading economy and to spread its power. The critic also suspect OBOR is China's strategy to establish hegemony, particularly in the South Asian region, leading to India's encirclement and eventual isolation.

In another expert's view 'China put on an impressive diplomatic show, but had little new to say about its flagship project'.[23] He further adds 'geopolitical worries' kept India from sending any official representative to the summit; the United States only announced at the last minute that it would send a government delegation. In spite of Xi's keynote speech to assuage concerns by saying 'We are ready to share practices of development with other countries, but we have no intention to interfere in other countries' internal affairs, export our own social system and model of development, or impose our own will on others', the BRF was more a celebration of the project and China's diplomatic clout in getting it accepted by as many countries as possible than an expansion of its parameters or a serious consideration of the challenges that face the Belt and Road. He stresses the BRF was 'all about optics – the sheer number of attendees and agreements signed – rather than substance'. Regardless, he agrees China was 'clearly pleased' with those results and a second BRF will be hosted in 2019.

NEPAL'S BRI/OBOR PARTICIPATION

In case of Nepal, it delayed the decision to sign the OBOR framework agreement till a day before the BRF in Beijing on 14-15 May 2017. There was not much doubt Nepal would ultimately sign the agreement and participate in the high-profile conference given that it was proposed by one of Nepal's close and powerful neighbours and had components that are potentially beneficial for Nepal's development and for its international image. Additionally, Nepal had already inked a preliminary OBOR agreement in 2014. But there should have been more preparation on specifics of the initiative between 2014 and 2017. The goal should have been to maximize benefits for the Nepali people, who have not been able to enhance the quality of their lives even though they live in the middle of two of the fastest growing economies in the world. The Nepali general perception then was they, therefore, have to use their collective wisdom to fully benefit from OBOR in line with the dictum 'better late than never'.

In this context, the author of this chapter feels 'five issues are of great importance from Nepal's perspective'.[24] First is securing rail link and access to suitable ports in China and within the OBOR network across Asia, Europe and Africa. Second, getting China's formal commitment against 'free trade', given minuscule Nepali trade and economy compared to the gigantic Chinese one. Third, getting China to agree to invest in US dollar and Nepali currency rather than the Chinese Yuan is important. Fourth, developing and strengthening the vision, the underlying projects, the institutions and the requisite human resources to fully benefit from the mega initiative. Fifth, paying adequate attention to geopolitics and advice of regional and global powers on OBOR is important. But Nepal must act on the desirability of joining it and specific project under it that will be beneficial to it must be promptly decided by itself.

While government ministers and officials have disclosed some details on the status of negotiations on connectivity, banking, currency, trade, etc., they must be more open so that professionals, experts and even common folks may pitch in their inputs to make OBOR beneficial to Nepal, China and other participants. Nepal has reportedly told China that it can't sustain custom and duty-free access to thousands of Chinese goods and that investment in Nepali rupees or US dollar is important. Additionally, access to Chinese ports, including one near Iran, and rail and road links will be negotiated with China later. However, promptly arranging for rail link with China is a must to promote Nepali exports and minimize ever-increasing trade deficit as a part of OBOR.

Interestingly, while the government was sluggish in its preparation, the first OBOR-Nepal Conference (2017)[25] that saw the participation of Chinese and Nepali professionals and officials had given eight suggestions through its declaration on 19 January 2017: (1) proactively establish people-to-people communication to develop Nepal as a bridge between China and South Asia, (2) get China and India to agree to trilateral cooperation, (3) better integrate South Asian countries, (4) develop Nepal-China Economic Corridor, (5) forge strategic partnership through private sectors, (6) activate public diplomacy and knowledge partners/institutions to better connect peoples, (7) use Buddhism/Lumbini to enhance Nepal-China tourism and understanding, and finally, (8) make OBOR-Nepal Conference an annual event to remind authorities of such declarations. However, the so-called experts from Nepal and China failed to include critical issues such as free trade, currency for investment and rail link in the declaration.

India's objection to OBOR is likely to affect Nepal's benefits and engagement. It is in Nepal's best interest to have realistically balanced relations with both India and China, including matters related to trade, investment, geo-politics and OBOR. 'While OBOR offers opportunities for Nepal to attract Chinese investment in infrastructure, the benefits may not be as great and achieved as fast as our politicians and media would have us believe, unless proper planning and implementation of OBOR-funded projects is undertaken wisely.'[26]

The Tibetan Autonomous Region (TRA) acts only as a 'bridge' to South Asia, i.e. the OBOR Initiative passes through Tibet only to trade with neighbouring countries. The TRA accounted for over '90 per cent of China's foreign trade with Nepal since the opening of the Xining-Lhasa railway in 2006, implying that the railway facilitated the transportation of goods from coastal China to the TRA and on to Nepal.'[27] The BCIM positions 'Yunnan as the Chinese hub' for exchanges with India, but the Yunnan route 'only connects to Northeast India and the BCIM is currently in a state of uncertainty'. What sort of cross-border trade will take place through all the 'infrastructure construction underway in the TRA'? Will the road and rail network inside TRA merely facilitate transport of commodities from coastal China to Nepal-India, thereby 'accentuating the trade imbalance', or will goods flow both ways? Bhutia stresses that 'China is not likely to allow the free passage of Tibetan people in and out of Tibet into South Asia', primarily to India. So 'what are the rails and roads are good for?'[28]

OBOR, a mega global initiative, has been promoted primarily to raise China's global profile and boost its slowing economic growth. But it can also benefit participating countries, which are encouraged to devise their own strategic plans to expand trade for their economic development. But Nepal has not been proactive in analysing the pros and cons of OBOR and in negotiating projects under it accordingly. Answers to the following questions may determine how beneficial Nepal's involvement in OBOR will be: Which infrastructure – rail, road, metro, airport, hydro-power, hotels – under OBOR will bring most benefit to Nepal? Which part of Nepal will or should be covered by OBOR? Will Nepal be only a bridge to ferry goods between China and South Asia, or will its exports also be facilitated substantially, and on preferential basis? Is the $50 billion that China is reportedly willing to invest in infrastructure in each country of this region within our need and capacity to handle? Additionally, the China-Nepal Economic Corridor floated by China may be more beneficial if converted into China-Nepal-India trilateral cooperation. But this is unlikely given India's reservations on OBOR as well as to any trilateral initiative.

TURNING POINT IN NEPAL-CHINA TIES

A new chapter in age-old Nepal-China ties opened in 1955 when Nepal established diplomatic relations with the People's Republic of China and recognized Tibet as being part of it. Over the years, Nepal's relation with China has undergone a big change and 'three important developments have further deepened and widened these bonds'[29] according to a Nepali expert. The first is the recent economic blockade imposed by India. The second is the OBOR Initiative undertaken by China. The third is China's rise as the second-most important economic, military and political power.

The Indian embargo, imposed in alliance with some belligerent Madheshi leaders, lasted from September 2015 to February 2016 and caused tremendous hardship to the common Nepalis as cooking gas, fuel, medicine and other essential supplies became scarce. The embargo resulted from India's reluctance to welcome (it was just 'Noted' by India) Nepal's New Constitution formulated Constituent Assembly (CA) and endorsed on 20 September 2015 by over 90 per cent members of the elected members of CA based on reservation of some Madhesi leaders. This led to an almost immediate understanding between Kathmandu and Beijing that Nepal should not depend completely on India for transit and essential supplies, particularly petroleum products; this understanding gained wide political and public support. In March 2016, Nepal and China signed ten agreements and memorandums of understanding on, among other things, using China's sea ports, building a regional international airport in Pokhara, exploring the possibility of signing a bilateral free trade agreement and exploring oil and gas reserves in Nepal. While a lot of work is yet to be done to operationalize these pacts, this was a turning point in Nepal-China relations. Two other points are worth stressing in the context of a paradigm shift in China-Nepal ties. One, China used to follow a hands-off policy regarding Nepal's internal political issues, while India has been consistently involved in Nepali politics mostly by design and some by default. This changed in July 2016 when China tried to save the K.P. Oli administration, seen as being more pro-China, from being replaced by Pushpa Kamal Dahal, who is seen as being more pro-India. Two, the Chinese People's Liberation Army (PLA) and the Nepalese Army held a first ever joint military drill for ten days in Kathmandu in April 2017 even though such joint army exercise with India and few other countries, including US, have been going on regularly. The exercise had been planned to last longer and cover wider aspects, but it was scaled down due to Indian lobbying. Nevertheless, the message it gave to the southern neighbour and the West was clear.

China has also been deepening its engagement in Nepal in the social and economic sectors. Nepali politicians, professionals, military leaders, business persons, journalists and youths are increasingly being invited to China for seminars, consultation and pleasure visits. A similar flow of Chinese visitors to Nepal has visibly increased. More and more Nepalis are learning Mandarin and going to China for higher studies. China is Nepal's second largest tourist source market after India. China seems to be determined to deploy its 'hard' and 'soft' power to strengthen its influence in Nepal. Naturally, a section of the Indian establishment and media resent Nepal's widening ties with China. They believe that Nepal has gone a bit too far and too fast in enhancing relations with its northern neighbour. Interestingly, Nepali political leaders have been increasingly and more consistently supporting the change in Nepal-China relations.

It is widely understood in Nepal that though good relations with both China and India are essential but one is not a substitute for the other. India will continue to be a much wider partner in trade, culture, economy, transit and politics but China's importance in the development of infrastructures, trade and development can't be minimized. Nepal is sensitive to and desirous to protect both China and India's political and security concerns; including 'One China' policy and India's security concerns. Some radical leftist and opportunistic politicians may, however, create undue rift by spreading unwarranted anti-India sentiments periodically. In a similar vein, some media, politicians and officials in India unduly exaggerate Nepal's genuine desire and need to establish closer relations with China in matters of its national and development interests. India and Nepal both must be careful of such extremist and not be carried away in the best mutual interests of Indo-Nepal friendship.

Regardless, a balanced relation with India and China is considered critical for Nepal's security and development across political spectrum, intellectual mass and general public. Nevertheless, the overwhelming importance of Indo-Nepal relations given historical, cultural, political, trade and development ties with its southern neighbour is not to be undermined while balancing its relations with both neighbours. However, this does not mean that Nepal should not be part of RBI/OBOR. Nepal should devise projects and institutions to extract the maximum benefit, not be sucked in 'debt-trap' by accepting irrelevant infrastructures under BRI. And also further strengthen its relations with China in other areas of mutual interests; including transit arrangements to complement its arrangements with India. It would be both difficult and unwise for Nepal to fully ignore many legitimate concerns of India in economic, security and strategic areas. Consequently, it is in Nepal's best interest to have realistically balanced relations with both India and China, including matters related to trade, transit, investment, geo-politics and BRI.

It may be useful to stress here that historic and friendly Indo-Nepal relations are gradually warming up and returning to more normal situation. The new constitution was once revised and is being amended to address the legitimate concerns of indigenous, marginalized and Madheshi people. India has been gradually more sensitive to the sentiments of a broad mass of Nepali public and increasingly supporting Nepal's desire to handle its internal problems, including the ones related to the Constitution, by itself. In the sidelines of BIMSTEC meeting in Kathmandu in the second week of August 2017 Indian foreign minister Sushma Swaraj advised the belligerent Madheshi leaders belonging to newly cobbled up Rashtriya Janata Party (RJP) to participate in the third phase local election in Province 2 (which largely constitutes eight Madhesi majority districts) as other national parties and two important Madheshi parties are engaged in 1-3 phase elections already. The completion of local elections and seven provincial assembly elections followed by national legislature elections provided under the new Constitution 2015 by January 2018 helped Nepal to complete the much needed political transition and move towards stability and faster economic development.

As a continuing process of strengthening bilateral relations, Nepal's Prime Minister Sher Bahadur Deuba was a five-day state visit to India in August 2017. The key focus of the visit was to enhance friendly dialogue at the highest level, expediting implementation of already agreed projects of national importance (example Pancheswar multi-purpose water and power project that have been languishing for over two decades), geopolitics and effective implementation of a new Constitution. In addition, Nepal is likely impress further to the top Indian leadership it is in mutual interest to minimize micro-managing Nepali political affairs by using local Indian Embassy and intelligence apparatus and dealing them directly at the highest levels as needed.

DOKLAM INDIA-CHINA STANDOFF

The India-China Doklam standoff in Bhutan-India-China tri-junction started in June 2017. There are threatening messages to India from China to unilaterally withdraw its forces back to its territory in original position while India has been insisting on mutual withdrawal to original position both by India and China to maintain *status quo* existing before June. There is a fear of all out war between the two now for the first time after their 1962 confrontation; even though there is a wish and desire in the region and beyond that wisdom will prevail between the two Asian giants to resolve it diplomatically for their own economic and strategic interests as they have also been engaged in dialogue privately at different levels in spite of strong warnings and rhetoric from China. The problem started when China started to extend and expand roadway in Doklam, which is a contested border area between Bhutan and China, and unarmed Indian security people moved in and prevented the Chinese from building the road on Bhutan's behalf. The Indian action is allegedly based on the twin basis, that first, India is obliged to protect Bhutan and its territory under the mutual friendship agreement between the two countries. Second, any further increase of infrastructures and connectivity by China in this barren but strategic area will pose security threat to the narrow Siliguri corridor in West Bengal state of India known as 'Chicken Neck' that provides vital access to several north-eastern states of India, including Assam and Sikkim. However, China has been stressing that it is a matter between Bhutan and China to settle and India has no right to step in other nations' territory. There is a wider feeling that the Doklam Tri-Junction has largely cropped up and taking time to resolve due to nationalistic approach of both Chinese President Xi Jingpin and Indian Prime Minister Narendra Modi who are desirous to further consolidate their domestic power by presenting to their domestic constituencies that they will not budge against their competitors on matters of national sovereignty and territorial integrity. Given that Xi will be facing an all important 19th Communist Party Congress in October 2017 and Modi's eyes are fixed in 2019 Indian general parliamentary elections the two '19s' are critical for both to enhance their power further, which they may have assessed will be strengthened by Doklam-type standoff.

Also, India's non-participation in Beijing BRF in May 2017 and its unwillingness to support Xi's flagship project of century, BRI, is believed to be a key factor contributing to the declining trust between the two nations. In addition, joint naval exercise 'Malabar' in Bay of Bengal in July 2017 with focus on anti-submarines and anti-aircraft carrier focus conducted by India, Japan and US has not gone well with China as it was considered to be designed to limit its access to the Indo-Pacific area. The increasing Chinese war ships and submarine activities in the Indian Ocean and its recent establishment of a military base in Djibouti have displeased India as well as Japan and US. Consequently, a lot of complicated geopolitics is on the play in South Asia with big powers such as China, India, Japan, US and Russia being engaged with strong implications to peace, security and South Asian regionalism.

However, the worrisome aspects for SAARC, particularly for countries like Nepal, are how to deal such situations like Doklam standoff. First, there are pressures on Nepal to take sides by both when they are in conflict. Second, the Lipulek India-China-Nepal tri-junction was agreed to be India-China trade point by the two without consulting Nepal when they were in good terms. Consequently, Nepal periodically suffers when India and China are in both good terms and bad terms. Nepal has officially protested with India and China concerning their Lipulek agreement and asked them to recognize Nepal's right there. It has taken a neutral position on Doklam standoff advising India and China to resolve it diplomatically by mutual consultation. The position of Pakistan in the context would be different. Very likely, it would be pleased with the escalation and may support China's views in any eventuality given its tension with India and all weather friendship with China.

Also, Bhutan appears to be in a difficult predicament as it cannot deny India's involvement to protect its claimed territory in the shorter run but appears desirous to establish formal and closer ties with China; including by resolving border issues in Doklam and two other pockets, in the longer run. Any further complication between India and China on the Doklam standoff would also test the engagement of Japan and US as they are enhancing their strategic collaboration with India and that of Russia which has had strong relations with India but is also enhancing its geopolitical partnership with China and Pakistan.

CONCLUSION

SAARC governance on the whole is far from satisfactory even though there are big differences in governance pattern and effectiveness from one SAARC member state to another as they vary significantly in terms of size, economy, political set-up, conflict, media freedom, etc. However, all of them are characterized by high politico-bureaucratic corruption, unhealthy business-political nexus, engagement of criminals in politics and declining ideological-based politics.

India-Pakistan conflict continues to sap SAARC's energy and effectiveness. First, questions are abounding in the region and beyond asking whether it continues to be relevant and many consider it as almost dead. Some others believe it to be in a critical 'life support system'. However, there is still a range of professionals and enthusiasts, particularly in the smaller member states, who emphasize that it continues to be relevant for collective regional well-being even though it will need greater effort, particularly from India and Pakistan, to make it more functional and effective in the future.

Geopolitics in SAARC is rather complicated and makes its functioning tricky. Among others, China is already an important player in South Asia and will attempt to continue to expand its political, economic and strategic presence in the region. How India and China manage their geopolitical relations will clearly affect SAARC's functioning. In addition to its continuing trade and investment in the region, it seems committed and persistent to expand its influence in South Asia through its mega-project, OBOR or BRI. Pakistan is an enthusiastic participant in the China sponsored BRI; including through its CPEC. India opposes it largely based on its complaint that CPEC infringes on its sovereignty as it passes through Pakistan-held Kashmir and to a smaller extent it feels that India was not consulted adequately while launching the BRI.

Clearly, India is worried by the expanding Chinese presence and wants to contain China in South Asia, which has been traditionally its sphere of influence. With the help of Japan, it has initiated the AAGC with the aim of curtailing the fast expanding Chinese influence in Asia and Africa. The other five SAARC member states – Afghanistan, Bangladesh, Maldives, Nepal and Sri Lanka have formally joined in the BRI and hope to benefit from opportunity to get investment on much needed infrastructure, trade and development. Bhutan is the only SAARC member which has not joined, obviously due to the India factor.

Consequently, good governance and effectiveness of SAARC will largely depend on two key factors. First, how India and Pakistan resolve their conflict and pursue a more common vision for SAARC. Second, how geopolitics in South Asia will further shape; particularly how India-China rivalry will be managed. Also, good governance will depend on how corruption, unhealthy business-politics nexus, criminalization of politics, media freedom and decline in 'ideology-based politics' will be handled in months and years to come. In spite of poor performance of SAARC in the past 32 years, there still seem to be a strong critical mass of professionals, politicians and people in South Asia region, who feel SAARC is still a relevant mission to be pursued with better vision, commitment and coordination for the collective good of all the peoples of the region effectively utilizing resources and talent present and potential in the region.

NOTES

1. United Nations Economic Commission for Asia and Pacific (UNECAP), 'What is good governance', Bangkok, 10 July 2009.
2. International Monetary Fund (IMF), 'The IMF's Approach to Promoting Good Governance and Combating Corruption: A Guide', 20 June 2005.
3. N. Al-Rodhan, *Sustainable History and the Dignity of Man: A Philosophy of History and Civilisational Triumph*, London: Lit Verlag, 2009.
4. Som P. Pudasaini, 'Troubled Waters', *The Republica*, 8 June 2017.

5. Jatin Desai, 'Despite a Wily Pakistan, Modi must not Allow SAARC to Collapse', *Daily O*, 28 September 2016.
6. M.K. Narayan, 'Playing on Geopolitical Chessboard', *The Hindu*, 2 December 2016.
7. S.M. Naseem, 'SAARC's Make or Break Moment', *The Hindu*, 23 May 2016.
8. 'Pakistan Committed to SAARC Objectives for Prosperous Region: PM 'Nawaz', *Pakistan Today*, 8 December 2016.
9. 'PM Advocates for Continuation of SAARC', *The Daily Star*, 18 January 2017.
10. Ram Bhakta Thakur, 'SAARC Summit: A Challenge', *The Himalayan Times*, 4 October 2016.
11. Jayshree Sengupta, 'An Impasse in SAARC: Analysis', *Daily Mirror*, 2 February 2017.
12. Laxman Gunesekar, 'India-Pakistan Danger in a Nuclear Neighborhood', *Sunday Observer*, 11 June 2017.
13. Aditya Adhikari, *The Bullet and the Ballot Box*, New Delhi: Aleph Book Company, 2014.
14. T. Karki Hussain, 'China's Role in Indo-Nepal Relations', in Lok Raj Baral (ed.), *Looking to the Future: Indo-Nepal Relations in Perspective*, New Delhi: Anmol Publications, 1996.
15. Aamir Ilyas Rana, 'Belt and Road Forum: CPEC must not be Politicised, says Nawaz', *The Express Tribune*, 14 May 2017.
16. Brahma Chellaney, 'China-Pakistan water Pincer Against India: As Part of CPEC, Mega-dams are Planned in Gilgit-Baltistan', *The Times of India*, 16 May 2017.
17. Rana, no. 15.
18. Sachin Parashar, 'China an Economic Giant, Can't ignore OBOR: Nepal', *The Times of India*, 14 May 2017.
19. Avinash Nair, 'To Counter OBOR, India and Japan Propose Asia-Africa Sea Corridor', *Indian Express*, 31 May 2017.
20. *Ibid.*
21. *Ibid.*
22. Tom Phillips, 'EU Backs away from Trade Statement in Blow to China's "Modern Silk Road" Plan', *The Guardian*, 15 May 2017.
23. Shannon Tiezzi, 'What Did China Accomplish at the Belt and Road Forum?', *The Diplomat*, 16 May 2017.
24. Som P. Pudasaini, 'OBOR: Into the Unknown', *The Republica*, 13 May 2017

25. 'One Belt One Road Conference Concludes with 8-point Declaration', *The Kathmandu Post*, 19 January 2017.
26. Pudasaini, no. 24.
27. Tshering Chonzom Bhutia, 'Tibet and China's Belt and Road', *The Diplomat*, 30 August 2016.
28. *Ibid.*
29. Som P. Pudasaini, 'Milestone in Nepali-China Ties', *The Kathmandu Post*, 30 May 2017.

CHAPTER 15

The Impact of Political Instability in Governance in Nepal

Biswas Baral

INTRODUCTION

No government in Nepal has served out its full five-year term since the restoration of democracy in the country in 1990. In the 17 years since, there have been 15 governments changed. Good governance issues have been put on the backburner particularly after the 2006 People's Revolution which overthrew the autocratic monarchy. The whole focus of the political class since has been on writing a new Constitution, which, people were often given to believe, would solve all the country's pressing problems.

Nepal, finally, promulgated the much-awaited Constitution in 2015, but instead of helping solve problems, it only opened up new faults in Nepal along geographical and ethnic lines. So contested was the new charter that it was being amended, for the second time, in just a year and a half since its promulgation. But even these amendments are unlikely to satisfy all. So there is likely to be a high level of political instability in Nepal in the near future. Meanwhile, as governance was neglected, there has been a marked increase in corruption.[1]

The task of rebuilding the lives that were destroyed by the devastating 2015 earthquakes has been shelved.

Public-service delivery has deteriorated, as the country continues to witness rolling power-cuts and an acute shortage of drinking water (this in a country often billed as having the second largest hydroelectric potential in the world). Thankfully, the hours of power-cuts are drastically down since the start of 2017, partly due to electricity imports from India.

Law and order situation has also worsened as criminal groups have spread by taking advantage of the prolonged political transition. The police are corrupt and only serve the elite groups.

As a result of the supposed preoccupation with the Constitution, there was no election of the local level units in Nepal for two decades between 1997 and 2017. This resulted in rampant abuse of government funds going to districts and village development committees that were now run by corrupt bureaucrats. It was an open secret that local units of political parties took their 'cut' from these funds. There was little oversight over how these funds are spent. (Due to immense public pressure, the political parties were finally forced to declare local election on 14 May 2017.)

As the role of the state shrinks, there has been a marked increase in socio-economic disparities. All the good healthcare centers are clustered in Kathmandu; there are only a few good ones outside. Higher education is also heavily concentrated in Kathmandu. As they are deprived of even basic public services and as they have no gainful employment opportunities at home, most of the rural people have migrated to work in Gulf countries or to India.

It is, thus, extremely important to quickly settle any remaining constitutional disputes and retrain the focus on governance. So long as there is no viable constitutional settlement, political actors will continue to make excuses for their failure on governance.

There also needs to be a change in the political culture, whereby political parties stop meddling in vital state organs like the anti-corruption bodies and the police force. Currently, if one is not a card-carrying member of a major political party, one can't even be promoted in civil service.

Let us illustrate Nepal's governance failure with two cases: One relating to the CIAA, the constitutional anti-graft body and another to the failure to hold local level election. Many failings of the governance in Nepal will be evident in the study of these two cases.

CURIOUS CASE OF CIAA

The Commission for the Investigation of Abuse of Authority (CIAA) is the main anti-graft body in Nepal. It is a powerful constitutional body tasked with filing court cases against top-level civil servants who it believes have either abused their power or been involved in corruption. But ever since its establishment in 1990 following the advent of democracy, it has become a political hot potato.

This is because instead of working for the development of the country, as they had promised to do during their 1990 protests against the autocratic monarchy, all the major political players started scrambling for power. How to get to power and to remain there, through fair and foul means, became their sole preoccupation. In the new political space that had opened up for the political parties following the 1990 revolution, it was a free for all.

The political parties in power openly misused state resources to expand their party networks and to enrich themselves. The parties in the opposition also became preoccupied with how to topple the government and get to power so that they too could use state resources to expand their patronage networks.

It was natural for these political parties to try to appoint commissioners in the CIAA who would overlook their corrupt ways. Otherwise, they feared that they too could come into its dragnet. This was why appointments in the commission became controversial right from the start.

But even though the CIAA became a recruiting ground of ruling parties, once in a while it was lucky to get officials who, even though they were appointed along partisan lines, largely functioned above the fray of politics. Surya Nath Upadhayay was once such CIAA chief.[2]

During his tenure, Upadhyay was able to bring strong court cases against powerful politicians like Khum Bhadaur Khada and Chiranjiwi Wagle, which led to their successful prosecution and lengthy jail terms. This greatly spooked the big leaders of major political parties, who had heretofore believed that the CIAA, peopled by their hand-picked appointees, would not dare to go against them.

So when Upadhayay retired in 2006, the major parties conspired to deliberately keep the commission without its plenipotentiary commissioners. For the next eight years the CIAA was made virtually defunct, as it started bringing court cases only against 'small fish' while leaving the big ones off the hook.

Then, out of the blue, Lokman Singh Karki was appointed CIAA chief commissioner in 2013, even though Karki did not meet any of the constitutional requirements for the post. Karki, who was a government secretary during former King Gyanendra's direct rule, was someone implicated by a government commission in suppressing the popular revolt of 2006. He was also linked with various gold-smuggling rackets. And yet he was deemed fit to lead the country's main anti-corruption body, in what came as a rude shock to the whole country.

'External pressure' (namely India's) was said to have prompted the major parties to pick Karki.[3] India apparently wanted 'structural guarantee' to maintain its grip over Nepal. In this reading, Karki was appointed so that he could hound anyone seen as working against India's interest in Nepal with trumped up corruption charges.

But whether or not there was an external hand in his appointment, it did not behoove the democratic parties to try to deflect the blame on an external actor for what was also a clear sign of their own incompetence and self-serving nature. One reason someone with Karki's tainted past was appointed CIAA chief was that he was so corrupt himself – in sharp contrast to the squeaky-clean Surya Nath Upadhyay – that he would be in no place to prosecute anyone else for corruption!

The major parties realized their mistake only when Karki started to wantonly abuse his power and selectively target those who had criticized his appointment. His power grew to such an extent that people started to say that all the vital decisions in Nepal were made not in Singhadurbar (the seat of Nepali government) but in Tangaldurbar (the CIAA headquarters).

It would be three and a half years before the Supreme Court of Nepal annulled Karki's appointment, saying that he did not meet any of the criteria for the post. As of this writing, the Nepali parliament is considering a separate impeachment motion against Karki. But the risk is that in the name of taking out one rotten egg, the political parties might once again conspire to emasculate an important organization like CIAA.

This is not surprising. The Transparency International's Corruption Perception Index year after year flags Nepali political parties as among the most corrupt public entities in the country. Despite this, the major parties hesitate to appoint someone with both the moral clout and professional competence as CIAA chief, for they know that a truly independent commission would present them with an existential crisis.

Besides his personal failings, and there were a legion of them, one of the cardinal sins of Karki was that he got serious about investigating senior members of CPN-UML, the second biggest party in Nepali parliament. Also, Prime Minister Pushpa Kamal Dahal 'Prachanda' and his Maoist party were not happy that Karki was investigating the famous case of alleged misuse of money that was going for the upkeep of UN-monitored cantonments, where ex-Maoist fighters were kept after they first came above the ground in 2006. Among those being investigated were senior Maoist leaders, including Prachanda.

So even before the Supreme Court annulled his CIAA appointment, Karki was suspended as CIAA chief when 157 members of parliament (MP) registered an impeachment motion against him in parliament. Many believe the impeachment motion has been rendered moot following the court verdict to remove Karki.

But instead of being weakened, the anti-corruption body needs to be strengthened and given the necessary autonomy in order to prevent rampant abuse of power and illegal accumulation of wealth by public servants. For instance, in the fiscal year 2015-16, around 20,000 top civil servants did not submit their property details to the government, which is a mandatory provision. They clearly had something to hide.

According to National Vigilance Center,[4] another anti-corruption government body which is authorized only to investigate possible abuse of power – but, unlike the CIAA, not to bring court cases – these public officials include politicians holding state posts, officials of constitutional bodies, civil servants and senior army and police officials.

But instead of strengthening the CIAA by appointing a clean and competent Chief Commissioner, the political parties will look to delay the appointment for as long as they can get away with. Even before Karki's removal as CIAA chief, the major political parties had vastly reduced the CIAA's jurisdiction in the new Constitution they promulgated. The excuse was again that if they didn't do so, the CIAA could spawn another 'dictator' like Karki.

For instance, the CIAA's right to investigate 'improper conduct' of public officials was removed in the new Constitution promulgated in 2015. Nor can the commission now write to public office holders if it believes they are involved in improper conduct. By taking away its role of an ombudsman, the new Constitution limited the CIAA's remit to strictly investigating and pursuing corruption-related cases that are already filed with it.

Even though the CIAA currently does not have a permanent Chief Commissioner, it does have five commissioners. But fear among them runs high. They are in no mood to investigate suspected cases of abuse of power by top politicians lest they too be impeached like Karki. The commissioners are, thus, greatly demoralized.

This is a tragedy because at no point in the recent history of Nepal has a strong and independent anti-corruption body been needed more. For corruption is increasing not just in the public sector. The recently released Panama Papers have shown that many Nepali businessmen have stashed away their ill-gotten wealth in various tax havens. Likewise, even vital humanitarian organizations like the Nepal Red Cross Society, which has been involved in post-earthquake recovery and rebuilding works, have been found to misuse their funds, and very little is trickling down to actual quake victims. But there is currently no state mechanism to check these excesses of the business and NGO community. CIAA could be the perfect body for this. But instead of empowering the CIAA by appointing clean and efficient commissioners to run it and allowing them to investigate tax-evading businessmen and unruly NGOs, the political parties have reduced even its limited mandate.

WHITHER LOCAL ELECTION?

The lack of political commitment for clean and effective governance was also indicated by the fact that the elections for the local level units, people's first line of contact with elected government, had not taken place for two decades. (At the time of this writing, there were 744 local level units in Nepal.) The main reason there was no local election for such a long time was that the resulting power-vacuum served the major political players in Nepal just fine.

After the term of the last elected local units ran out in 2002, these elected bodies were replaced by (unelected) all-party mechanisms to oversee local development works. The local level politicians who controlled these mechanisms soon became notorious for gobbling up most of the development funds from the centre. As they were not elected and were not accountable to anyone, political parties simply started to divide the spoils among themselves. It was reported that as much as 90 per cent of such development funds ended up in the pockets of local politicians. As public pressure mounted at what was seen as open loot of state coffers, and on the advice of the CIAA, the government of Baburam Bhattarai finally dissolved these unelected bodies in 2012.

Since 2012, and as there was no local election, the all-party mechanisms were replaced by ad hoc committees overseen by local bureaucrats. The 2014 Carter Center report[5] on local governance in Nepal noted that these new committees were seen by the people as comparably much cleaner entities and they also had greater participation of marginalized groups and women. But the report also noted how political parties continued to 'influence the planning and implementation process at all levels' which in turn posed 'a significant challenge' to local development and governance.[6]

The other important finding of the Carter Center study was that the vast majority of those surveyed wanted to see local elections held at the earliest, which they felt was essential 'to improve performance and accountability of local bodies'.[7]

Interestingly, even card-carrying members of the political parties who were surveyed by the Carter Center were in favour of early local polls. But it is not hard to surmise that they were merely paying lip-service to what was a popular demand. In reality there was no urgency to act because they continued to have disproportionate say in how local bodies were run and how their funds were spent.

One excuse that major political actors repeatedly gave for their failure to hold local election was that they were busy fine-tuning the new Constitution. How could local election be held, they asked, when even the contours of future federal provinces remained blurry? The old dispute over federal demarcations – which includes the redrawing of the borders of local level units to be settled first. Moreover, with the Madhesh-based parties saying that they would boycott any polls without first amending the Constitution to their liking, holding local election would invite many more problems than it would have helped solve.

There was some merit to this argument. It was extremely important that the new constitution was made acceptable to a broad section of the society for its long-term survival. If the government forced local election before such a broadly acceptable constitutional settlement – in which case the Madheshi parties might have boycotted it – there would be a new risk of conflict. But then why could not local election be held before the drafting the new Constitution?

In fact, following the royal coup of 2001, when King Gyanendra assumed all executive powers, there was no environment for local elections. The king's direct rule (and constant meddling in national politics) came to an end only in 2006 following the second people's uprising. Then, the first Constituent Assembly elections were held in 2008, after which the focus of the political class rightly shifted to the urgent task of writing a new Constitution.

So there were some legitimate reasons for putting off local elections. Few people in Nepal believed that was the main reason for the long delay. The widespread belief was that no political party was unhappy with the political vacuum in local bodies, which the parties continued to milk to their advantage. This was the case both in the hilly regions as well as down in the plains.

Some of the issues that Madheshi parties have raised over the Constitution were genuine. But the abject failure of mainstream Madheshi parties to win over common Madheshis was evident in their poor showing in the second Constituent Assembly elections as well as the growing popularity of the more radical 'Free Madhesh' movement. The common perception, even among Madheshis, was that the mainstream Madheshi politicians were as corrupt as the Pahade counterparts they so reviled.

There was also room to question the intent of Madheshi parties because of their proposal that elections to local bodies should be held, if at all, only among 'non-political' actors. This effectively meant that whatever the outcomes of such elections, local level units would continue to be heavily influenced by political parties and they would continue to extract heavy rent from these bodies. This line of thinking was, thus, prevalent in major parties and smaller Madheshi outfits alike.

So the main reason there was no local election was not that the political parties had other more important priorities. It was that the existing system of division of spoils at the local level was rewarding them handsomely. The long delay in local polls also suggested that Nepali political parties are far from democratic. They will do whatever they feel is beneficial for them individually.

If they are people's representatives, the political parties must be in tune with popular sentiment. Besides the Carter Center study, another nationwide survey, this time undertaken by Search For Common Ground, noted that 'working of the government at the local and national levels appears not to be satisfactory and failing to fulfill people's expectations'.[8] This survey also found that an overwhelming majority of those surveyed were in favour of quick local election.

For the common folks, elections will bring changes to society and if there were elected local representatives, they could better 'facilitate development work, address local requirements and prevent corruption'.[9]

Political disagreements cannot be an excuse to deprive people of their first line of contact with elected government, on which they rely for most basic documents like birth and death certificates and which are directly responsible for canals to irrigate their agricultural land and for better roads to ease their mobility.

Denied of their right to choose their own representatives, and greatly dismayed at the lack of development in their communities, many Nepalis had started to question if there was any government at all in the country. The Nepalis who came of age during the two decades of the new millennium did not even know how local governance felt. The process of creation of new political leadership from the grassroots level also stopped. These developments had an insalubrious effect on the health of Nepali democracy.

CONCLUSION

The failure of the political parties to see beyond their petty interests has ravaged governance in Nepal. Three or four major parties are effectively running the country. The Nepali society has been so badly politicized that it has become impossible for anyone to rise to important public posts without becoming a card-carrying member of a powerful political party. So instead of strengthening democratic institutions, political parties have looked to pack them with their cronies.

No wonder common Nepalis expect so little from their government these days. However, this is not to suggest that it is all gloom and doom in Nepal. In fact, in recent times, there have been some welcome exceptions. Take the sweeping health reforms that Dr K.C. Govinda, a crusading orthopaedic surgeon, has been able to effect, almost single-handedly. Dr Govinda chose to campaign for these reforms through peaceful Gandhian protests. He has so far been in ten fast-unto-deaths, each time demanding urgent reforms in the way medicine is practiced in the country.

It is due to his tireless efforts that there will, in the future, be more doctors and hospitals in rural areas. More students from poor backgrounds will be able to pursue medical education. Medical colleges will not be able to extort their students that the country's public hospitals will be able to compete with the best private hospitals. The ultimate goal of Dr Govinda is to bring cheap and reliable health care to each and every Nepali.

The health minister, Gagan Thapa, seems as determined to enact the kind of reforms Dr Govinda wants. He has barred doctors in public hospitals from practising in private clinics during hospital hours, which was until recently a common practice. Likewise, he has been able to turn around the only state-run specialty cancer hospital by making its doctors more accountable for the health outcomes of their patients. The state of other public hospitals is gradually improving as well.

Then there is Kulman Ghising, the chief of Nepal Electricity Authority (NEA), the country's sole power utility, who has almost miraculously been able to remove the rolling power-cuts in Kathmandu, largely through better management of available electricity and through his clampdown on NEA staff who were illegally helping big industries reduce their electricity bills.

And there is Kanak Mani Dixit, the chief of Sajha Yatayat, who has been able to turn around a perennially loss-making public bus service into one of easiest, most efficient and cleanest means of public transport in Kathmandu.

But these are more personality-based success stories. They do not represent the kind of institutional change that will be required to improve governance in Nepal. For most of Nepal's public offices – from the 'lucrative' land revenue offices to the cash-cow of Nepal Oil Corporation, the country's sole importer and distributor of oil – are still notoriously corrupt. And this will continue to be the case so long as political actors do not show the maturity to appoint capable people to run them and so long as they do not stop needlessly meddling in their day-to-day functioning.

Some efforts at institutional changes have also been made. For instance, now every government office has to have a Citizen Charter that is clearly displayed out in the front. It details the rights of citizens and the duty of office-holders to serve them. But as the SFCG report notes, 'Citizen Charter is not very effective in raising the awareness of the general public, which is the primary purpose for which it was developed and distributed to government offices'.[10]

Initiatives like Citizen Charter, as such, have become cosmetic tools that the political class can conveniently point at to hide their own failure to institute good governance.

On a positive note, the parliament is currently considering a bill that would make election of local bodies mandatory two months before the expiry of the five year tenure of elected local units, so that there would never be vacuum at the local level. The bill also looks to bar people with criminal records from contesting local elections. Yet such efforts at institutional change are few and far between.

The political parties tried to justify all kinds of anomalies – including weakening the CIAA and not holding local election – on the pretext of the 'unique challenges' thrown up by transitional politics. But the state of political flux in Nepal will continue into the foreseeable future. This is why there needs to be a sustained pressure on Nepali political parties to immediately tackle important governance-related issues.

People have repeatedly told pollsters that their primary concern is everyday issues like drinking water, electricity, decent roads and a climate where they can work and earn well. This is not to ignore the demands for rights and greater representation of the heretofore marginalized groups. But rights, clean governance and development are not mutually exclusive domains.

Yet it will not be easy to get this delicate balance right. In poor and diverse societies, ethnicity continues to be a bigger political draw than routine promises of clean government development. This is why elections in Nepal are still fought (and won) largely along ethnic lines. Likewise, no high-level government appointment in Nepal these days is immune to accusation of ethnic favouritism.

So along with making government bodies clean and efficient, they also be need to be more inclusive so that people from every sector of the society feel adequately represented in governance, which in turn will increase their faith in the government.

In the end, the success of the likes of Kulman Ghising and Kanak Mani Dixit suggests that it is possible to vastly improve governance in Nepal if the political parties appoint the right people in the right place. Perhaps that is also the best way of starting the long process of building strong and durable democratic institutions. Also, if the local election could be held on time, there could be no bigger boost for the health of Nepali democracy.

NOTES

1. 'Nepal Slips 1 Position Down in Corruption Perceptions Index', *The Himalayan Times*, 25 January 2017.

2. 'Demoralized CIAA', Bhadra Sharma, *Republica*, 13 December 2016.
3. *Ibid.*
4. '19,213 officials didn't disclose property last year', *The Kathmandu Post*, 4 January 2017.
5. 'Local Governance in Nepal: Public Participation and Perception', *The Carter Center*, 28 February 2014.
6. *Ibid.*
7. *Ibid.*
8. 'Leadership and Governance in Nepal' (Findings from Baseline Survey 2014), *Search For Common Ground.*
9. 'Local Governance in Nepal: Public Participation and Perception', *The Carter Center*, 28 February 2014.
10. 'Leadership and Governance in Nepal', n. 8.

Index